TSQ Transgender Studies Quarterly

Volume 1 * Number 3 * August 2014

Decolonizing the Transgender Imaginary

Edited by Aren Z. Aizura, Trystan Cotten, Carsten Balzer/Carla LaGata, Marcia Ochoa, and Salvador Vidal-Ortiz

BOOK REVIEWS

ARTS & CULTURE

General Editors' Introduction

SUSAN STRYKER and PAISLEY CURRAH

A s we noted in the introduction to the inaugural issue of *TSQ*, and as the editors of this special issue, "Decolonizing the Transgender Imaginary," so forcefully reiterate, it seems especially important to mark the geopolitical home of this journal in anglophone scholarly networks in North America. That location and its relation to the accelerating (if still tenuous) institutionalization of transgender studies in the US academy foreground for the journal's project the inescapable framework of coloniality. The United States originated, after all, through processes of white settler colonialism, and since the nineteenth century it has undertaken ongoing neocolonial adventures of its own. The material conditions produced through this history necessarily inform all cultural production within their scope.

Making explicit a colonial/colonizing context that is routinely invisibilized in the United States feels doubly necessary given our journal's avowed hope of "changing gender" not just in the United States but elsewhere, in ways that allow for more expansive opportunities for life for anyone ill-served by existing gendering systems. We do so because we understand gender not just as a binary system of masculine/feminine codes or representations but also as a biopolitical apparatus that operates on all bodies to produce unequally distributed life chances; gender privileges not just men over women but also the legibly or functionally gendered over those who become inhuman waste through their incoherent, messy, resistant, or ambiguous relationship to biopolitical utility. How can one *not* resist such circumstances—and not just in relation to one's own situation but in solidarity with those whom one understands to be caught up in similar difficulties? But how can such an audacious undertaking avoid—or even undermine—the "colonial imaginary" that arguably subtends every gesture toward the global south and east that emanates from the global west and north? How, in particular, can the term *transgender*—grounded as it is in conceptual underpinnings that assume a sex/gender distinction as well as an analytic segregation of sexual orientation and gender identity/expression that are simply foreign to most places and times—possibly be imagined as a suitable framework for pursuing a proliferative, generative, and liberatory politics of embodied difference? These are questions that demand answers.

In titling this issue "Decolonizing the Transgender Imaginary," we pay obvious homage to Emma Pérez's (1999) influential formulation of a "decolonial imaginary" and, in doing so, implicitly ask what a "transgender imaginary" might be, how it is related to processes of colonization, and how—in theory as well as practice—it might be decolonized.

The "imaginary," a concept derived originally from psychoanalytic theory, is articulated most famously in Jacques Lacan's essay "The Mirror Stage" and describes a realm of psychical experience concerned with images, identification, and embodiment. In that essay, Lacan describes an infant, held tightly "by some support, human or artificial," who, upon perceiving itself in a mirror, "overcomes, in flutter of jubilant activity, the obstructions of his support" (Lacan 1977: 1). The psychical identification with a mirror image that maps the lived body's sensory and perceptual awareness of itself into a coherent picture that, in Lacan's account, is the foundational act of subjectivity is thus also, in his telling, a fantasy of mastery. It involves the aggressive subordination of other people and things to the secondary role of mere "support" that the emergent subject must "overcome" in a quest for autonomy. The mirror consolidates a "total form of the body . . . pregnant with the correspondences that unite the *I* . . . with the phantoms that dominate him, or with the automaton in which . . . the world of his own making tends to find completion" (2–3). The imaginary, in other words, is a scene of struggle and can itself be construed as a psychical colonization of an experienced world by a rapacious subject that, in Lacan's rendition, is unmarked as Eurocentric, bourgeois, masculinist, and white.

In Pérez's appropriation of the Lacanian imaginary for the purpose of "writing Chicanas into history," coloniality is ambient and omnipresent; it is that which fills the space between the embodied subject and the objectified image of the subject's body. Coloniality is identified with the material conditions that rupture and fragment the self, that shatter the representational mirror, and that must be overcome in order for Lacan's infantile Western subject to constitute itself as a mastered (and mastering) whole. Introducing the Other of coloniality simultaneously marks Lacan's putatively universal subject with its racial (and historical and cultural) specificities while opening a pathway through which the agencies of subjugated embodied subjects can become transformative of their worlds (Pérez 1999: 5). In opening that pathway, the imaginary comes to name the gap between acts of colonizing and a potential for postcoloniality; it becomes a virtual space for dreaming in the dark of how world, self, and other could be differently co-configured—or, in other words, decolonized.

A transgender imaginary, then, risks repeating the colonizing gesture of mistaking a mirrored surface's reflected images of the Same for the otherness of the Other. It can misrecognize different configurations of embodiment, identity, desire, and subjectivity for points on a map whose prime meridian runs through the United States, whose road signs are in English, whose background color is white, whose cardinal directions are man, woman, homosexual, and heterosexual, and upon which transgender is imagined as movement across the borders of this gridded space. It can orient a transgender subject toward travel in foreign lands, in search of ancestors and of kin, oblivious to material distinctions that render one a tourist and another a local, that enable mobility for some while constraining movement for others, that can put the lives of the many in service to the desires of the few.

At the same time, as Pérez points out, the imaginary is also a place where fragmented realities, fragmented bodies, and fragmented selves—whose fragmentations are themselves artifacts of colonizing operations that sunder what otherwise might be conjoined—can become legible and differentially articulated, and where the constitutive violences that have produced them (so often silenced) can be spoken out loud. In this sense, the imaginary can function as an interstitial, oppositional space—a fecund, choric "enspacement" that actively holds, and thereby enables, different possibilities for movements both individual and collective, any of which might manifest manifold decolonizing potentials, any of which might precipitate innovative and necessary actions. In this sense, a transgender imaginary that decolonizes can provide one vector toward a future more consonant with justice—a future in which varieties of bodies that trouble and contest the "total form" of the privileged Western body can each find, not the "completion" and "domination" foreclosed to them through their exclusion from a normative ideal but, rather, new strategies for ethical and political engagement with others and environs.

The works in this special issue offer a number of strategies for decolonizing the transgender imaginary. They speak in indigenous voices to break dominant epistemological frames, critique and deconstruct the colonialist logic within the social-scientific gaze, and confound the distinction between ethnographer and ethnographic subject. Autoethnographic trans-of-color writing opens a space of transformation between dominant discourse and lived experience. Poststructuralist refigurations of race, transgender, body, and technology dismantle the functional terms and categories through which colonialist biopolitics operate; they recast Lacan's "support, human or artificial" as a facilitative, co-presencing biotechnocultural milieu in which all bodies are characterized by an originary technicity and in which transsexual bodies are as un/natural as any other. The editors have also curated a provocative roundtable discussion among a transnational panel of activists, culture makers, and scholars of gender and sexuality who offer perspectives on decolonizing the transgender imaginary that range from the celebratory to the cynical.

And yet, despite the range of viewpoints expressed, the conversation on decolonization in transgender studies has scarcely begun. How, for example, might the field engage more explicitly with decolonial critical theory, such as that of Walter Mignolo on de/colonial aesthetics (Mignolo 2012; Mignolo and Escobar 2013), or work that explores sites of colonization that do not focus on the Euro-American nexus informing all of the work in this issue, such as Madina Tlostanova's feminist scholarship on resistant cultural production in post-Soviet central Asia (Tlostanova 2010)? How can engaged scholarship combine with inspirational pedagogies to inculcate decolonial perspectives or political activism among students doing transgender studies coursework, with consequences that extend well outside the classroom? How might decolonial strategies emanating from many sites of resistance and struggle throughout the world disseminate themselves through formal as well as informal education, academic as well as community-based research, and scholarship that draws on legitimated knowledges as well as subjugated ones? How could attention to decolonization in this moment of rapid institutionalization for transgender studies as an academic field leave an imprint that shapes institutional culture for a long time to come, or contribute to the redirection of institutional resources toward goals or groups that historically have been excluded from the university?

The issue editors' introduction to the works they have assembled here provides a more expansive contextualization of the pitfalls and promises of imagining the decolonization of "transgender" than we can sketch in these short prefatory observations; we want to highlight, before closing, their citation of decolonial feminist philosopher María Lugones. Lugones, the editors point out, understands resistance to coloniality as "a complex interaction of economic, racializing, and gendering systems in which every person at the colonial encounter can be found" (2012: 77). We share the perspective that *every* social encounter involves a "colonial encounter," given that coloniality is a global system in which we are all positioned regardless of whether we suffer or benefit from it, just as every social encounter is gendered, raced, and classed.

In recognition of the totalizing nature of colonialism, addressing the injustice of its racialized and spatialized maldistribution of the means of life is an ethical imperative, wherever and however one happens to have been positioned within the colonial system. As general editors of an academic journal of transgender studies, we are committed to answering that interpellative hailing in a manner peculiarly suited to the work we are undertaking here, however else we might (or might not) work on decolonization in other arenas. We hope that the discussions launched and the critiques advanced in the pages that follow can contribute something to the larger decolonial project raging far beyond this journal's reach and that they can also inform subsequent academic work in transgender studies, whether it is published in *TSQ* or elsewhere.

Susan Stryker is associate professor of gender and women's studies and director of the Institute for LGBT Studies at the University of Arizona and general coeditor of *TSQ: Transgender Studies Quarterly*. Her most recent publication is *The Transgender Studies Reader 2* (coedited with Aren Z. Aizura, 2013), winner of the 2013 Ruth Benedict Book Prize.

Paisley Currah is general co-editor of *TSQ: Transgender Studies Quarterly*; he teaches political science and gender studies at Brooklyn College and the Graduate Center of the City University of New York.

References

Lacan, Jacques. 1977. "The Mirror State as Formative of the Function of the *I*." In *Écrits: A Selection*, translated by Alan Sheridan, 1–7. New York: Norton.

Lugones, María. 2012. "Methodological Notes towards a Decolonial Feminism." In *Decolonizing Epistemologies: Latina/o Theology and Philosophy*, ed. Ada María Isasi-Díaz and Eduardo Mendieta, 68–86. New York: Fordham University Press.

Mignolo, Walter. 2012. *Local Histories/Global Designs: Coloniality, Subaltern Knowledges, and Border Thinking*. Princeton, NJ: Princeton University Press.

Mignolo, Walter, and Arturo Escobar. 2013. *Globalization and the Decolonial Option*. New York: Routledge.

Pérez, Emma. 1999. *The Decolonial Imaginary: Writing Chicanas into History*. Bloomington: Indiana University Press.

Tlostanova, Madina. 2010. *Gender Epistemologies and Eurasian Borderlands*. New York: Palgrave McMillan.

Introduction

AREN Z. AIZURA, TRYSTAN COTTEN, CARSTEN BALZER/CARLA LaGATA,
MARCIA OCHOA, and SALVADOR VIDAL-ORTIZ

A longside the emergence of research on gender-nonconforming and gender-variant practices and as a field over the last decade, transgender studies has been challenged to interrogate its whiteness (Roen 2006; Haritaworn and Snorton 2013). However, less work has appeared that would challenge transgender studies to look closely at its geographic and historical location as the product of a largely North American settler culture. Commenting on the intersections of queer studies and Native studies, Daniel Heath Justice, Mark Rifkin, and Bethany Schneider observe that despite queer studies' efforts to interrogate its "presumptive whiteness" and histories of racialization, these efforts still tend to efface the politics of indigeneity and settlement (2010: 6). European colonial expansion deployed gender and sexuality as technologies to categorize colonized bodies into distinct kinds (Stoler 1995: 7), while sexual and gender diversity in non-European contexts was used as a rationale to support the removal, "re-education," or wholesale genocide of colonized others (Miranda 2013). The traces of those histories of removal and dispossession remain, as do their imbrication in global sexual and gender politics. If transgender studies is now a field, it is time to highlight the necessary work of tracing histories of colonialism, gender, and sexuality that accompany the formation of that field and to undo them. How can we accomplish this when the term *transgender* itself does not begin to encompass the radically different relationships that gender nonconforming populations across the world have to health care, basic rights, safety from criminalization or stigmatization, and legal protection or regulation of bodies, identity, and space? Decolonial work is central to grasping transgender studies' own institutionalization as a field with a dedicated journal, *TSQ*. Despite the recent flourishing of transgender studies scholarship, much of this work either issues from or is based in North America or Europe. Early discussions within the *TSQ* editorial board touched on the importance of making clear *TSQ*'s status as a US/North America–based journal

TSQ: Transgender Studies Quarterly ★ Volume 1, Number 3 ★ August 2014
DOI 10.1215/23289252-2685606   © 2014 Duke University Press

and yet one that questioned assumptions about what that meant. This special issue is intended to bridge the gap between decolonial and critical ethnic studies work happening within North America and transnational work that highlights the multiple legacies of the European colonial project globally as they apply to gender-nonconforming knowledge and life. In a similar fashion to gender studies and queer studies (sometimes moving within or alongside those disciplines and sometimes radically separate from them), transgender scholarship must grapple with the racial and geopolitical economies and forms of governmentality that instill whiteness as the given of the transgender subject. It must also resist the assumption that European settler states initiate political models or progressive historical change, with other locations following. Most importantly, transgender studies needs to engage with *de*colonizing as an epistemological method and as a political movement. Hence the title of this special issue: Decolonizing the Transgender Imaginary.

The editors of *TSQ* asked five members of the editorial board to develop this issue, and we took on the task grounded in the work we've done across the diverse regions represented here. There are, of course, many obstacles to decolonizing English-language peer-reviewed academic writing. We offer these interventions as the beginning of a conversation intended to build decolonial approaches in transgender studies. Among the discussions the editorial group had, which confirmed our vision for this issue, was the challenge of rethinking academic writing and publishing outside the traditional, and sometimes colonial, enterprise. We hope that the articles included here reflect a form of resistance to these traditional ways of doing scholarship, particularly to social-scientific ways of knowing, even as some of the contributions engage with them. We thought it would be important to center our writing on the "I" (or the "eye"), to turn attention back toward the one writing or observing from a particular perspective, not in the manner of scientific authority (with its unvoiced I and unseen eye), not as social scientists who erase the other in the act of writing the Other, but rather to authorize knowledge of the marginalized and to promote the value of the I, and the eye, of those speaking from marginality (Clough 2000). We also considered the question of transnationality: how to solicit writing that engages with how gender-nonconforming and gender-variant subjectivities and practices are transforming across national and regional borders. However, at every moment in the production process, we had to remain aware that *TSQ* is a US-based journal. It is published in English and thus incorporates anglocentric elements from the beginning. It's our hope that as *TSQ* becomes a broader platform for transgender studies in multiple locations and through a diversity of written forms, we can pursue copublishing with other journals in the global South to provide greater access to and cross-pollination of trans inquiry. This work, published in such journals as *Iconos, Cadernas Pagu, Sexualidad, salud y sociedad, Nómadas, Revista de estudios sociales, Pambazuka News, Jindal Global Law Review, Indian Streams Research Journal, Working Papers in Gender/Sexuality Studies* (Taiwan), *Chinese Sex Rights Research,* and *CENTRO Journal,* can deeply inform the approaches developed in an anglophone context, which are often particularly insular due to the monolingualism of US academic training. Finally, we found it imperative to highlight writing that unsettled the hegemonic epistemological frames in which we find ourselves.

Decolonization in Context

We wish to frame this introduction by drawing from five decades of activism and scholarship in women of color feminisms and Native and Indigenous studies that instructs us in how to trouble the relationship between colonizing, academic work, and activism and in how we might understand decolonizing itself. In particular, we draw on a relatively recent wave of work with authors such as Chela Sandoval, María Lugones, and Emma Pérez. They help us to consider different models for knowing, forms of connecting, or being with, that may result in positive coalitional politics and that resist the gender and sexuality normativities of colonialism itself. For Pérez, the decolonial imaginary "embodies the buried desires of the unconscious, living and breathing in between that which is colonialist and that which is colonized" (1999: 110). Lugones refers to resistance to the coloniality of gender as "a complex interaction of economic, racializing, and gendering systems in which every person at the colonial encounter can be found" (2012: 77). Decolonization means something rather different in an Indigenous studies context, where the history and power relationships of settler colonialism— including the anthropological gaze—tend to render Indigenous populations' epistemological production of knowledge invisible. Drawing on Indigenous scholars Linda Tuhiwai Smith and Robert Allen Warrior, the editors of *Queer Indigenous Studies* understand decolonizing work as methodological both in the sense of a turn toward Indigenous knowledge making itself and in highlighting difference: "A methodological turn to Indigenous knowledges opens up accounts to the multiplicity, complexity, contestation, and change among knowledge claims by Indigenous people" (Driskill et al. 2011: 4). This includes discussions of the many differences in cultural and political understandings of gender and sexuality in Native and Indigenous contexts and the simultaneous undoing of the gendered and sexual violences of settler colonialism.

Finally, important work on Blackness, gender, and sexuality, such as that of M. Jacqui Alexander (2005), Sharon Holland (2000, 2012), Saidiya Hartman (1997) and Lindon Barrett (1999 and 2014), informs our understanding of colonization and enslavement as mutually constitutive processes of racialization, particularly in the Americas. To think the decolonial requires an understanding of the centrality of enslavement to the colonial project, though the time-depth of coloniality and its forms of administration vary significantly in different regions. The production of Blackness through colonization and enslavement entails processes of valuation, subjection, and subjectivity that mark not only our epistemologies but also our forms of social legibility and embodiment. M. Jacqui Alexander sees the "twin companions" of colonialism and slavery refracted in the encounter between Caribbean and African American scholars, calling us to attend to the "unfinished project" of decolonization and move away from racial polarizations endemic in these debates (Alexander 2005, 271). Sharon Holland's groundbreaking work on death and (Black) subjectivity, *Raising the Dead* shows contemporary manifestations of these processes, and argues for the formation of queerness and Blackness in the colonial "space of death" (2000, 70). In more recent work, Holland turns to the erotic, the space of desire, as a site for "the strange and often violent modes of racist practice" (2012, 9). Hartman's study of American selfmaking through slavery in the 19th century argues that the "engendering of race" happens through economic and legal processes that render the field of sexuality visible only within the constraints of subjecthood framed by these processes. The structural, physical, and juridical violence of slavery, then, frames how we understand the meanings and possibilities of all bodies within systems founded on it. The late Lindon Barrett also explored the valuation of racialized bodies in the literary and US national imaginary beginning with *Blackness and Value: Seeing Double* (1999). His last manuscript, recently released posthumously, engages the development of racialized Blackness in the context of modernity and the development of mercantile capitalism.

Decolonization never acts in the singular: it always already incorporates the language of the imperial gaze, or racial formation theorizing, or gendering practices. It also incorporates queries, assumptions, and impositions on the body and the sense of "realness" trans people are expected to accrue. In addition, Lugones's concept of the "coloniality of gender" shows us how gender and sexual diversity are filtered through a colonizing, binary gaze into naturalized ideas of "sex" and "gender" to begin with. If we challenge the epistemology of binary gender, we can begin to "unthink" this double bind, which produces the terms of recognition for trans subjects within medical governmentality and modern forms of self-making and citizenship. For at least five decades, trans experience has been subjugated under the reductive sign of surgical genital reconstruction ("the operation") or the exoticizing stereotype of the she-male; as Elijah Edelman (2012) notes in a transformative rereading of this history, trans figures are often articulated as sites of pleasure for others (as prostitute, spectacle, or comic absurdity) but rarely as a site of pleasure for oneself as trans. Decolonization of this oppression also requires displacing the temporalities of representation of trans experience, particularly trans women of color experience, as ending inevitably in violence or death due to trans people's own recalcitrant engagement in what are incriminatingly named "risky behavior" (sex work, drug use, walking while Black or brown). This "necropolitical" regime (Haritaworn and Snorton 2013) in which trans people of color are blamed for their own deaths must be countered with the ways in which trans and gender-nonconforming people survive, thrive, and fight multiple systems of oppression every day.

Decolonizing the Transgender Imaginary

If we are to decolonize the current imaginary of what it means to be trans, we will have to take the interventions of decolonial and critical race scholars as well as trans communities of color to heart. Here we are focused on the field of transgender studies. What does it mean to decolonize transgender studies? It means, first, to interrogate what transgender studies is and to understand it as having multiple nodes of emergence. The transgender studies canon (there is already a canon) is usually understood to mean writing by a number of anglophone trans theorists who challenged the use of transgender people as objects within medicine and psychiatry, law, and feminism, beginning in the early 1990s with Sandy Stone's "A Posttranssexual Manifesto" (1991). While this was and still is necessary work, it has been "course corrected" by commentary that interrogates the racial, colonial, and economic power structures that make some transgender lives more valuable and prone to gaining recognition and rights than others. This has resulted in something like a progress narrative for transgender studies, which some of us have subscribed to: that trans studies began with "the basics" and then evolved to incorporate an intersectional and critical lens. The insight we draw precisely from decolonial feminisms, Indigenous studies, and trans of color theory is to understand "theory" differently: not as knowledge that issues from within the academy or that aspires to academic recognition but that invents itself on the fly, in the midst of a campaign, in the telling of stories. Trans people have always done political and theoretical work that centers the dynamics of imperialism, colonialism, and the multiple histories of racialization (Retzloff 2007). This work has often been mistaken for first-person narrative, as if trans people are only qualified to "tell their stories" and require experts to interpret and theorize them.

In the United States, this theory-making project is currently taking place around the increased visibility of trans women of color in popular culture. Who could forget Laverne Cox's role as Sophia in the Netflix show *Orange Is the New Black*, the first time a trans woman actor has played a regularly-appearing transgender character in the history of US television? In her public appearances and in her own writing, Cox has refused to be cast as the transparent transsexual victim whose story must be interpreted by others and has adroitly brought a critical and intersectional trans politics to bear on her own unfolding celebrity. Cox's new project is a documentary about Cece McDonald, a trans woman of color who was imprisoned for defending herself against violent attackers in 2011. And in theorizing trans of color existence in writing on her website, Cox connects materialist feminist politics to the history of Black struggles for self-determination: "It's important for black people to reclaim our bodies, historically sold, raped, lynched, generally devalued as not beautiful and savage even. But as we reclaim our bodies it's important not to buy into the racialized mythology about them. My transsexual body often sought only as a site of sexual conquest and objectification is an interesting potential site for the subversion of that racist history" (2012).

In a similar way, in "Twin-Spirited Woman: Sts'iyóye smestíyexw slhá:li," Saylesh Wesley (Stó:lō) combines Indigenous studies methodology and storywork—considering personal experience in relation to elder knowledge—to relate the invention of new language to making a place for twin-spirit people within Stó:lō culture and tradition. Wesley's essay is engaged in the important project of recovering teachings and stories about twin-spirited or gender-variant people lost due to the epistemological and material violence of the Americas' colonization. Giancarlo Cornejo's essay "For a Queer Pedagogy of Friendship" recounts stories told to him by Italo, a Peruvian trans activist, about her childhood in Lima in the 1950s and 1960s. A sociologist, Cornejo attempts to disrupt the colonial ethnographer-informant divide by making visible the many ways in which solidarity and friendship are necessary for theory, politics, and survival. Cornejo's essay also highlights how violence toward trans and gender-nonconforming children not only issues from "strangers" but takes place most devastatingly in the spaces ostensibly intended to protect children: the school, the family, and law enforcement.

Decolonizing transgender is not a project that sits easily with transgender (or any category) as a stable or self-evident identity or with transgender theory as something based on the study of transgender subjects only. Rather than take transgender individuals as the subjects of research, there is currently a strong movement in trans studies to critique "transgender" itself as a biopolitical category that regulates and organizes bodies in a particular recognition framework or particular vectors of risk, value, and potentiality. Some of this work investigates objects (or relies on techniques) that are seemingly far removed from the work of decolonizing yet that nevertheless disrupt the operative logics of transgender biopolitics. Julian Gill-Peterson's work in this issue, for example, uses the animacy (Chen 2013) of the testosterone molecule both to follow the commodity chain and the ecology of synthetic hormones and to reimagine a technicity of transgender and the racialized body. Gill-Peterson aims to break down the biopolitical utility of the body figured as trans in a molar sense (a whole, integrated body with one identity), in the name of a molecular politics that has both analytical utility and resistant and transformative political potentials. This approach enables a constructive and productive rearticulation of race and trans in such a way that one is not derivative of or subordinated to the other; trans and race are each autonomous yet intra-active vectors of becoming.

Decolonizing transgender studies also needs to incorporate a transnational scope and methodology. By "transnational," we do not only mean work that focuses on regions outside Europe and North America but work that addresses the asymmetries of globalization (Grewal and Kaplan 2001: 664) and that interrogates the six-hundred-year history of European colonial expansion. This work must contend with how social understandings of gender and sexuality are very different outside a global North framework. Thus categories of gender-nonconforming practices or embodiments need to be understood in their geographic and cultural specificity and not simply as a local instance of a falsely universalized "transgender."

Tracing the transnational mobility of trans subjectivities and practices also means interrogating the logic of smooth circulation that mobility denotes in progress narratives of globalization. This issue's engagements with transnational trans theory highlight moments of mistranslation, cross purposes, collisions, and roadblocks in the global circulation of trans politics and culture more than they recount an enabling mobility. Aniruddha Dutta and Raina Roy, for example, look at the transnational expansion of the term *transgender* in the aid and development sector in India. Tracing the process of defining transgender in South Asian development discourse reveals a scalar hierarchy in which transgender stands in for the universal, the cosmopolitan, and the aspirational while terms like *kothi*, *hijra*, and *dhurani* are contrasted as mere local or vernacular terms. The consequences of doing so include the elision of the so-called local categories, away from development discourse in favor of transgender or MSM, thereby dividing communities who must identify their constituent populations *either* as men who have sex with men *or* as transgender. Dutta and Roy conclude not by advocating for a divestment from transgender but rather by critiquing the structural conditions within which transgender functions transnationally. In "*Toms* and *Zees*: Locating FTM Identity in Thailand," Jai Arun Ravine reflects on making the film *Tom/Trans/Thai* and on their broader project of attempting to locate female-to-male trans identity in Thailand, included within and sometimes entirely distinct from *tom*, the Thai term for a butch lesbian. In the film and in the essay that appears here, Ravine triangulates between the Thai understanding of *tom*, Western categories of transgender masculinity, and his own status as a mixed-race Thai American gender-nonconforming person. Ravine's essay highlights the role of desire for lineage and connection that attends diasporic queer and trans identity; it comments, too, on the failures of language to produce a desired recognition as well as on language's capacity to produce serendipitous connection across continents.

The legacy of European and American sexology's collection and categorization of "Native" sexual practices and gender embodiments grounds Seth Palmer's essay "Asexual Inverts and Sexual Perverts: Locating the *Sarimbavy* of Madagascar within Fin-de-Siècle Sexological Theories." Palmer reads perplexed French, British, and American interpretations of *sarimbavy* in part to make sense of the colonizing urge to understand and thereby manage the "diversity" of Madagascar's population but also to engage in criminological and sexological debates that support theories of inversion that have been directed at regulating gender-variant bodies everywhere. Palmer draws on queer historical methodologies that do not seek to recover or reclaim a queer or trans historical object but rather acknowledge the ways in which queer and trans historical objects haunt the colonial discourses we use to understand gender and sexual difference today.

Finally, the roundtable, "Decolonizing Transgender," brings together six scholars, activists, and culture makers (including some who are all three) who were asked in summer 2013 to participate in an email discussion about decolonizing work and transgender studies. The broader context of this conversation, as many of the responses point out, is a perceived link between the recent rapid rise in reported violence against trans people—usually trans women of color—and the simultaneous sudden increase of scholarship that concerns itself with transgender practices of life and the conditions of transgender health or well-being. How might these twin trends of increased visibility of, attention to, and seeming care for trans people be related? How might this increase serve those who are conferring the recognition better than those who are ostensibly being recognized? Our roundtable discussion reflects a prevailing wariness in many activist contexts that the institutionalization of transgender studies now underway can only result in the field's becoming divorced from the material conditions of trans existence. To voice the deepest criticism in the most direct terms: is not trans studies now taking up the topic of decolonization precisely so that those with the greatest access to institutional privilege profit, at the expense of the colonized, from the academic and political capital that this political issue confers? While not all of the roundtable participants agree with this prognosis, the discussion creates a useful space for interrogating the complicity of transgender studies in the very oppressions it claims to oppose and for asking at the same time how the field might better engage materially with dismantling white supremacy and colonization in all their forms.

As editors of this issue, we are conscious of the challenges this broader debate poses to *TSQ*'s own conditions of academic and cultural production as well as its institutional status. An instructive anecdote: in November 2013, at the joint annual meetings of the Association for Queer Anthropology (AQA) and the American Anthropological Association, Duke University Press first distributed promotional items as part of the "soft launch" of the TSQ marketing campaign. In addition to the journal's logo, these items bore a slogan that had been proposed by a fundraising consultant but that the general editors of the journal had rejected several months previously in favor of another slogan. Due to miscommunication between the general editors and the marketing department, the promotional items distributed at the AQA mistakenly said "Changing the way the world thinks about gender" instead of "We're changing gender." Whereas the latter is meant to convey an activist sensibility and to call attention to the intellectual and political labor involved in making gender systems more hospitable to gender-variant and gender-nonconforming lives, the former clearly (if inadvertently) reproduces the US and anglophone biases and colonizing frameworks that the journal avowedly seeks to resist. As the implied subject of the first slogan, TSQ is grammatically positioned as an agent that imagines itself as having the ability to transform the conditions of the object it acts upon; from context, with a US-speaking subject targeting the world, it is impossible for this slogan not to connote a colonial rather than decolonial imaginary. "Changing the way the world thinks" situates TSQ in an exceptionalist narrative in which the journal becomes a US flagship for exporting transgender studies to the "rest" of the world—a narrative that accommodates all too easily to a common, condescending attitude that more ignorant and less enlightened others elsewhere need whatever the United States is peddling. Given that the United States uses its questionable status as a bastion of LGBT freedom to shore up imperial projects and military intervention in the Middle East and elsewhere (Puar 2007; Mikdashi 2011), TSQ must resist the tendency to frame transgender politics in the United States as being the most highly evolved. The world knows plenty about transgender issues already. At its best, TSQ can help to illuminate that knowledge—and simultaneously, it can interrogate the economies of knowledge production that frame Euro-America as the center of official discourse about gender and sexual diversity.

Neither can we afford to ignore the conditions of the academic world into which this new journal emerges. TSQ is subscription based rather than open access at a time when, globally, academic publishers have increased subscription prices, meaning that libraries must reduce their journal holdings. The idea of the university itself has transformed from a putative "ivory tower" in which intellectuals could quietly write, protected from the demands of the market, toward a corporate neoliberal model in which value must be extracted from all research and teaching, with those projects that do not prove economically profitable being cut. In this new scholarly marketplace, diversity itself has been incorporated into the academy in order to manage and contain dissent (Ahmed 2012: 13) and to capitalize on racial and cultural difference. Transgender studies' new cachet must be understood as indicative of that tendency. Nonetheless, academic appointments designed for teaching and researching transgender topics remain scarce. Because of that scarcity, it is sometimes difficult to imagine that transgender studies has a secure future, particularly amid the disappearance of tenure-track jobs and the casualization of the academy. Meanwhile, the few positions dedicated to transgender studies that appear—mainly in the United States at this point—tend to initiate a huge response. It is clear that not enough jobs in transgender studies exist to employ all those who identify as transgender studies scholars.

Given this situation, it is worth pointing out that most of the contributors to this issue are junior scholars and, in some cases, independent scholars. This reflects the reality that even with the new institutional capitalization on diversity in all forms, the academy is both institutionally and informally structured to exclude people who are non–gender normative, and it is structured even more forcefully to exclude people of color and those for whom decolonial work is a primary concern. This is also a reflection of where much of the most exciting work is taking place: on the outskirts of academia and in the cracks between institutional structures. If trans studies can contribute to political change in any lasting way, it cannot merely become the preserve of white academics; it must ground itself in multiracial, transnational, grassroots organizing for political and economic transformation. However, we are also aware that for scholars and activists who are engaged in decolonizing and anti-imperialist work, "transgender studies" itself may not prove to be a capacious enough a moniker for doing that work—indeed, often the most useful political acts are those that are unrecognizable and uncategorizable. Thus we welcome future intellectual, affective, and political contributions to decolonial practice in whatever forms they take.

Aren Aizura is an assistant professor in gender, women, and sexuality studies at the University of Minnesota. He is the editor of *The Transgender Studies Reader 2* (2013). His work has appeared in *Medical Anthropology*, *Inter-Asia Cultural Studies*, and *Asian Studies Review* as well as in the books *Queer Bangkok*, *Transgender Migrations*, and *Trans Feminist Perspectives*.

Trystan Cotten is associate professor of gender studies at California State University, Stanislaus. His areas of research are transgender surgery and medicine and gender, sexuality, race, and migration in Africa and the African diaspora. His latest book is *Hung Jury: Testimonies of Genital Surgery by Transsexual Men* (2012).

Carsten Balzer/Carla LaGata is the senior researcher of Transgender Europe and lead researcher of the Transrespect versus Transphobia Worldwide project. S_he is coauthor of *Transrespect versus Transphobia Worldwide—A Comparative Review of the Human-Rights Situation of Gender-Variant/Trans People* (2012).

Marcia Ochoa is an associate professor of feminist studies at the University of California, Santa Cruz, and advises El/La Para Translatinas, an HIV prevention and human rights program for transgender Latinas in the Mission District of San Francisco. Her research focuses on transgender citizenship, modernity, and femininity in contemporary Venezuela and among Latin American immigrants to the United States. Her book, *Queen for a Day: Transformistas, Beauty Queens, and the Performance of Femininity in Venezuela* (2014), is a queer diasporic ethnography of media, gender, and modernity in Venezuela.

Salvador Vidal-Ortiz is an associate professor of sociology at American University in Washington, DC. He coedited *The Sexuality of Migration: Border Crossings and Mexican Immigrant Men* (2009).

References

Ahmed, Sara. 2012. *On Being Included: Racism and Diversity in Institutional Life.* Durham, NC: Duke University Press.

Alexander, M. Jacqui. 2005. *Pedagogies of Crossing: Meditations on Feminism, Sexual Politics, Memory, and the Sacred.* Durham, NC: Duke University Press.

Barrett, Lindon. 1999. *Blackness and Value: Seeing Double.* Cambridge: Cambridge University Press.

———. 2014. *Racial Blackness and the Discontinuity of Western Modernity.* Edited by Justin A. Joyce, Dwight A. McBride, and John Carlos Rowe. Urbana: University of Illinois Press.

Chen, Mel. 2013. *Animacies: Biopolitics, Racial Mattering, and Queer Affect.* Durham, NC: Duke University Press.

Clough, Patricia C. 2000. *Autoaffection: Unconscious Thought in the Age of Teletechnology.* Minneapolis: University of Minnesota Press.

Cox, Laverne. 2012. "Ain't I a Woman?" web.archive.org/web/20130906190908/http://lavernecox.com/gender-studies/aint-i-woman (accessed March 5, 2014).

Driskill, Qwo-Li, et al. 2011. Introduction to *Queer Indigenous Studies: Critical Interventions in Theory, Politics, and Literature*, ed. Qwo-Li Driskill et al., 1–28. Tucson: University of Arizona Press.

Edelman, Elijah Adiv. 2012. "Articulating Bodies in Tapestries of Space: Mapping Ethnographies of Trans Social and Political Coalitions in Washington, DC." PhD diss., American University.

Grewal, Inderpal, and Caren Kaplan. 2001. "Global Identities: Theorizing Transnational Studies of Sexuality." *GLQ* 6, no. 4: 663–79.

Haritaworn, Jin, and Riley Snorton. 2013. "Transsexual Necropolitics." In *The Transgender Studies Reader 2*, ed. Aren Z. Aizura and Susan Stryker, 66–76. New York: Routledge.

Hartman, Saidiya V. 1997. *Scenes of Subjection: Terror, Slavery, and Self-Making in Nineteenth-Century America.* New York: Oxford University Press.

Holland, Sharon. 2000. *Raising the Dead : Readings of Death and (Black) Subjectivity*. Durham, NC: Duke University Press.

———. 2012. *The Erotic Life of Racism*. Durham, NC: Duke University Press.

Justice, Daniel Heath, Mark Rifkin, and Bethany Schneider. 2010. "Introduction." *GLQ* 16, nos. 1–2: 5–39.

Lugones, Maria. 2012. "Methodological Notes towards a Decolonial Feminism." In *Decolonizing Epistemologies: Latina/o Theology and Philosophy*, ed. Ada María Isasi-Díaz and Eduardo Mendieta, 68–86. New York: Fordham University Press.

Mikdashi, Maya. 2011. "Gay Rights as Human Rights: Pinkwashing Homonationalism." *Jadaliyya* (ezine), December 16. www.jadaliyya.com/pages/index/3560/gay-rights-as-human-rights _pinkwashing-homonationa.

Miranda, Deborah. 2013. "Extermination of the Joyas: Gendercide in Spanish California." In *The Transgender Studies Reader 2*, ed. Susan Stryker and Aren Z. Aizura, 347–60. New York: Routledge.

Pérez, Emma. 1999. *The Decolonial Imaginary: Writing Chicanas into History*. Bloomington: Indiana University Press.

Puar, Jasbir. 2007. *Terrorist Assemblages: Homonationalism in Queer Times*. Durham, NC: Duke University Press.

Retzloff, Tim. 2007. "Eliding Trans Latina/o Queer Experience in U.S. LGBT History: José Sarria and Sylvia Rivera Reexamined." *Centro Journal* 19, no. 1: 140–61.

Roen, Katrina. 2006. "Transgender Theory and Embodiment: The Risk of Racial Marginalization." In *The Transgender Studies Reader*, ed. Susan Stryker and Stephen Whittle, 656–65. New York: Routledge.

Stoler, Ann Laura. 1995. *Race and the Education of Desire: Foucault's "History of Sexuality" and the Colonial Order of Things*. Durham, NC: Duke University Press.

Stone, Sandy. 1991. "The *Empire* Strikes Back: A Posttranssexual Manifesto." In *Body Guards: The Cultural Politics of Gender Ambiguity*, ed. Kristina Straub and Julia Epstein, 280–304. New York: Routledge.

Decolonizing Transgender in India
Some Reflections

ANIRUDDHA DUTTA and RAINA ROY

Abstract This essay is a set of reflections arising out of prolonged conversations in which we compared notes on our respective experiences as activist (Raina) and ethnographer (Aniruddha) working among, and to different extents belonging to, gender/sexually marginalized communities in eastern India. As we shall argue, the attempted universalization of transgender as a transnational "umbrella term" by the development (nongovernmental) sector, the state, and their funders tends to subsume South Asian discourses and practices of gender/sexual variance as merely "local" expressions of transgender identity, without interrogating the conceptual baggage (such as homo-trans and cis-trans binaries) associated with the transgender category. In the Indian context, this process bolsters the long-standing and continuing (post)colonial construction of hierarchies of scale between transnational, regional, and local levels of discourse and praxis, as evidenced in the relation between the hegemonic anglophone discourse of LGBTIQ identities recognized by the state and the development sector, on one hand, and forms of gender/sexual variance that are positioned as relatively regional or local on the other.
Keywords transgender; gender identity; India; South Asian studies; decolonization; LGBTQI

How does the transnational expansion of "transgender" as a rubric of identity and activism appear when we look at the phenomenon from the vantage point of communities and social movements of gender-variant persons in the global South, specifically South Asia? This essay is a set of reflections arising out of prolonged conversations in which we compared notes on our respective experiences as activist (Raina) and ethnographer (Aniruddha, henceforth Ani) working among, and to different extents belonging to, gender/sexually marginalized communities in eastern India. If "decolonization" implies the ability to freely question, critique, and, if necessary, reject globalizing discourses or practices, this essay considers the conditions of possibility for such critical engagement with the expanding category of transgender.

We do not intend to make a prescriptive argument regarding how to make *transgender* into a more cross-culturally inclusive term—indeed, as previous

TSQ: Transgender Studies Quarterly * Volume 1, Number 3 * August 2014
DOI 10.1215/23289252-2685615   © 2014 Duke University Press

critiques have pointed out, the imagination of transgender as an expansive category for all gender-variant practices and identities risks replicating colonial forms of knowledge production (Stryker and Aizura 2013: 8) or overriding other epistemologies of gender/sexual variance (Valentine 2007: 4). As we shall argue, the attempted universalization of transgender as a transnational umbrella term by the development (nongovernmental) sector, the state, and their funders tends to subsume South Asian discourses and practices of gender/sexual variance as merely "local" expressions of transgender identity, often without interrogating the conceptual baggage (such as homo-trans and cis-trans binaries) associated with the transgender category. In the Indian context, this process bolsters the long-standing and continuing (post)colonial construction of hierarchies of scale between transnational, regional, and local levels of discourse and praxis, as evidenced in the relation between the hegemonic anglophone discourse of LGBTIQ identities recognized by the state and the development sector, on one hand, and forms of gender/sexual variance that are positioned as relatively regional or local on the other. The increasing recognition of transgender identities as subjects of rights and citizenship is evident in a series of developmental, state, and legal policies, ranging from transgender-specific funding for HIV-AIDS prevention to recent directives in favor of transgender people's rights by the Supreme Court of India and the Indian Government's Ministry of Social Justice and Empowerment (UNDP 2008; SC 2014; MoSJE 2014). However, statist and developmentalist deployments of the transgender category may generalize linear narratives of transition and stable identification with the "opposite" gender as defining features of trans identities, and even when they recognize possibilities beyond the gender binary such as a "third gender," they tend to delimit and define such categories through a model of stable, consistent, and authentic identification that seeks to clearly distinguish transgender from cisgender and homosexual identities. But South Asian discourses of gender/sexual variance may blur cis-trans or homo-trans distinctions, and community formations may be based also on class/caste position rather than just the singular axis of gender identity. Emergent models of transgender identity certainly create new possibilities for social recognition and citizenship, but they may be colonizing precisely in the ways in which they may refuse or fail to comprehend many forms of gender variance relegated to the scale of the local, even though such discourses and practices may actually span multiple regions of South Asia.

However, such colonizing deployments do not necessarily exhaust or foreclose other evocations of the transgender category, particularly by people in the lower rungs of activism and the development sector. Such usages do not coalesce to a globalizing definition but may better translate or express the multifarious forms of gender/sexual variance found in India and South Asia. Thus there may be a decolonizing struggle over transgender itself, though the very emergence of transgender (rather than categories positioned as local) as a privileged site of such struggles is informed by its prior ascendance within the transnational development sector. We will not have space here to examine these hegemonic and counterhegemonic practices in all their nuances; rather, we will attempt to delineate some of the systemic conditions under which hegemonic usages of transgender emerge or counterhegemonic practices might become possible, particularly from the purview of working-class and/or *dalit* (lower or oppressed caste) communities who cannot freely access or modify statist and developmentalist usages of the transgender rubric.

Some clarifications before we begin. We realize that our collaboration and this essay itself are also implicated in the aforementioned scalar hierarchies. We are unequally positioned within transnational economies of knowledge production; Raina's location as an activist working with small community-based organizations in India restricts her access to academic and cultural capital, whereas Ani's position in US academia entails a privileged role in structuring and translating our concerns to a Northern audience. Yet we hope that our collaboration may also indicate variant circuits of dialogue and exchange that interrupt the unidirectional transmission of high-end knowledge from the "West" to the "rest," as exemplified by the dissemination of transgender itself.

Further, our analytic purview is largely limited to feminine-identified gender-variant persons assigned male at birth, particularly the *kothi* and *hijra* communities of West Bengal in eastern India, rather than masculine-identified trans or gender-variant people. *Hijra* is a well-known term connoting a structured community of feminine-identified persons who pursue distinct professions such as ritualized blessing during weddings and childbirth; *hijras* typically dress in women's clothes and may undergo penectomy and castration (orchiectomy) but also commonly designate themselves as distinct from men and women (Reddy 2005: 134; Nanda 1990). *Kothi* is one of several South Asian terms for feminine male-assigned persons who may or may not present or identify as (trans) women; while *kothis* do not form separate clans like *hijras*, some *kothis* may also join *hijra* clans or professions (Dutta 2013: 494–95). In the following sections, we consider the interface between these largely working-class, oppressed-caste communities and subcultures and transgender as an emergent category of identity and representation.

* * *

One potential risk of our critique, which we wish to guard against at the outset, is the implication of cultural dualisms between the West and the non-West. Transgender, in itself, need not be perceived as exogenous or foreign by Indians or

South Asians who identify as such. Online forums such as the Facebook group Transgender India, activist groups like the Association of Transgender/Hijra in Bengal, and films on "male-to-female transgender people" like *Rupantar* (*Transformation*, dir. Amitava Sarkar, 2009) are evidence that there are already many adoptions, translations, and hybridizations of transgender as a rubric of identity. Like other seemingly foreign terms such as *lesbian* or *gay*, *transgender* has been found by many to be a suitable word for expressing who they are, and many may use the term (or its translated counterparts) in itself or in conjunction with terms like *hijra* or *kothi*. Given the hybrid postcoloniality that foundationally marks many articulations of "Indian culture" today, none of these subject positions can be seen as inauthentic vis-à-vis their sociocultural context—which would mimic right-wing religious and political viewpoints that have denounced the emergence of LGBT activism and identities as a form of corruptive Westernization.

However, while there are certainly ways in which transgender has emerged as a South Asian category of identity and community formation, the same ease of adoption, translation, and negotiation vis-à-vis the transnational circulation of "transgender" and "transsexual" categories may not be available to everyone. As Gayatri Chakravorty Spivak argues, one cannot simply endorse postcoloniality or hybridity without recognizing how agency and mobility within transnational circuits of exchange is often shaped and restricted by class/caste location and one's position within the international division of labor (Spivak 1999: 361). Only a relatively small proportion of people in India can access the Internet or have fluency in English as the hegemonic transnational medium through which categories like transgender disseminate. Moreover, as we demonstrate below, for many working-class and *dalit* gender/sexually variant communities, transgender (or TG) has arrived as a constrained rubric of representation for gaining funds and recognition, without much freedom to negotiate or alter its usages at higher levels of activism or funding. As an emergent hegemonic category, transgender may offer representation and upward mobility for people who fit official definitions, but it may elide or delegitimize working-class and *dalit* discourses and epistemologies of gender/sexual variance that are not entirely legible in terms of hegemonic usages of transgender—even as these groups, particularly *kothi-hijra* communities, must increasingly represent themselves as TG to be intelligible to high-level networks of large nongovernmental organizations (NGOs), transnational funders, and the state. Thus while "transgender" is not indubitably foreign or colonizing, its hegemonic position in discourses of activism and funding reflects inequalities within the hierarchical political economy of social movements and the nonprofit sector, even as the category may be appropriated or translated in ways that subvert these hierarchies.

An emerging body of scholarship within South Asian sexuality studies has critiqued the elitist or colonizing potentials of gay/lesbian identity politics in India, which can serve as a point of departure for critiquing the hegemonic emergence of transgender, but which we also seek to question or go beyond. In keeping with historiographical work on South Asia that has argued that colonial administration calcified ambiguous social boundaries into rigidly bound identities (Dirks 2001), this body of scholarship has claimed that the consolidation of homosexual personhood and identity during the period of globalization is largely propelled by urban activists, the law, and the state and potentially erases tropes or idioms of (particularly male) same-sex desire that are not based on personhood or interiorized identity (Khanna 2009; Katyal 2010; Boyce and Khanna 2011). Akhil Katyal argues that the interiorized conception of sexual identity, which classifies people based on their inner essence of homo- or heterosexuality, may elide behavioral and habit-based idioms of desire prevalent in South Asia that do not connect same-sex practices with distinct forms of personhood (2010: 24). Paul Boyce and Akshay Khanna argue that the creation of a minoritized homosexual subject, separate from mainstream heteronormative society, by "principally urban" activists and communities is largely unsuited to the Indian context, as it erases how same-sex practices are diffusely scattered within "putatively heteronormative social formations" among actors who largely do not distinguish themselves as homosexual (2011: 90–97).

While we share concerns about the imposition of identitarian divides, we seek to go beyond this mode of critique through the gendered analytic lens offered by transgender studies. The aforementioned critique, while questioning the homo-hetero divide, takes the male-female binary for granted and assumes the unmarked gender normativity of sexually variant males/men without considering how putative participants in "same-sex" behavior may be socially marked or unmarked on the basis of gender. Often, same-sex-desiring men who do not claim a distinct identity may gain their anonymity by virtue of their masculine gendering, which permits a degree of sexual license, whereas feminized male-assigned persons (whether they desire men or not) have less access to such unmarked flexibility, being subject to stigmatizing labels like *gandu* or *chhakka* (roughly: fag, sissy), common to many South Asian languages. As Katyal notes in passing but does not analyze, *gandu* (feminized, anally-penetrated person) is a much more pejorative label than *laundebaaz*, the man who plays around with boys (2010: 24). This suggests that "same-sex" practices in South Asia are not just diffusely spread among "men" but are fundamentally constituted vis-à-vis gender normativity or variance and that gender variance, often perceived as being connected to same-sex desire, serves as a significant axis of social demarcation. Thus while sexuality may not have been a distinct axis of personhood in India prior to the emergence of the modern homosexual, the gendering of sexual behavior and the (homo)sexualization of gender variance (as in *gandu* or *chhakka*) seems to have a longer legacy, which may inform both patterns of discrimination and resistant formations of community and identity (Reddy 2005; Hall 2005). As we shall argue, people inhabiting the intersections of gender/sexual variance have not only formed communities prior to contemporary identity politics but have also been amenable to interpellation within newer rubrics such as MSM (men who have sex with men) and TG, which are thus not *only* urban or elite in origin but draw from these community formations and interact with them in potentially both liberatory and oppressive ways.

Raina's experiences as an activist and long-time participant within *kothi-hijra* communities and Ani's experiences as an ethnographer who was gradually included as a community member suggest the range and span of these communities. As a child, Raina dressed up secretly in clothes meant for (cis) women, discovered her attraction for men, and faced repeated abuse as an effeminate boy (*meyeli chhele*) in school. As an adolescent in the late 1990s, she discovered an old cruising area around Rabindra Sarovar, a chain of lakes in south Kolkata. There, she was introduced to a local community of feminine male-assigned persons, mostly poor or lower middle class, who formed a loose sisterhood among themselves and spoke a generationally inherited subcultural argot that was broadly similar to the language used by *hijra* clans (see Hall 2005). They used the terms *kothi* and *dhurani* to designate themselves, words that are unknown in standard Bengali. While they primarily cruised or undertook sex work with men outside their immediate circle, there were also less visibly articulated forms of desire (e.g., *kothis* who desired women or other *kothis*). The community included both those who wore standard male attire (*kodi kothis)* and feminine-attired *kothis* (variously called *bhelki, bheli,* or *bhorokti kothis*). *Kothis* could also switch or transition between *kodi* and *bhelki* states. Raina herself alternated between androgynous and feminine attire before mostly adopting the latter. While some of them joined *hijra* clans and professions, underwent castration-penectomy and adopted consistent feminine attire, others, like Raina, did not join *hijra* clans formally, even if they wore female-assigned clothes. Moreover, some would temporarily join *hijra* clans and professions while remaining *kodi* at other times. These varied practices do not signal an unfettered fluidity, as there were also intracommunity tensions around gender and respectability. When Raina took to feminine clothes, she was distanced by some *kodi* friends who regarded public cross-dressing and *hijras* as being disreputable. Meanwhile, some *hijras* and *bhelki kothis* regarded *kodi kothis* with suspicion for their duplicitous overlap with social masculinity and privilege. Yet friendships and sisterhood within the community also crossed these divides; some of Raina's closest friends are *kothis* who are mostly *kodi* or who cross-dress sporadically, given that they share many commonalities in terms of geographic and class location even though their precise gender identities or expressions may differ. Subsequently, as Raina moved to other cities for professional reasons, she made contacts with broadly similar communities with different names depending on cultural and linguistic context. In north Bengal and the neighboring country of Nepal, a similar spectrum of people called each other *meti*. In Delhi, *kothi* was commonly used within the community, but *hijra* clans would also call them *zenana* or *zenani* (Urdu words for effeminate/feminine persons). Through a very different trajectory as an ethnographer, Ani discovered similar communities with mutually intelligible subcultural languages in various districts of West Bengal in the late 2000s, including terms such as *kothi*, *dhunuri*, and *dhurani*. As zie transitioned from a relatively *kodi* youth to a more *bhelki* visibility, Ani was gradually interpellated into these communities as a friend and sister.

Taken together, our experiences indicate translocal and transregional networks that enabled us to find shelter within a range of overlapping languages and communities. As most book-length studies of gender variance in India have focused on organized *hijra gharanas* or clans (Nanda 1990; Reddy 2005), these diverse communities, and particularly their transregional connections, have been only partially and fragmentarily documented in the literature (Cohen 1995; Hall 2005; Reddy 2005; Dutta 2012). Given the existence of these communities, a conceptual polarity between gender/sexual identities and more fluid practices is not adequate, since gendered differences seem to have prompted the emergence of community formations *prior* to the contemporary moment of "global queering." Rather, we may need to explore the bridges and gaps between these community formations and emergent forms of identity politics.

∗ ∗ ∗

Transgender has emerged as a prominent category in the Indian LGBTIQ movement and development sector relatively recently, roughly around the late 2000s. While the term has been used since at least the late 1990s by upper-tier activists and within acronyms like "LGBT," its increasing adoption by relatively low-rung community-based organizations (CBOs) may be linked to shifts in the pattern of funding available to such groups. Since 2007, the Indian state and transnational funders have increasingly recognized "transgender" people, particularly male-to-female trans people, as a "high risk" group for HIV infection (NACO 2007: 13). This shift in funding has been charted elsewhere in more detail (Dutta 2013), so we will only provide a brief contour here. The second phase of India's National AIDS Control Program (NACP-II, 1997–2007) recognized MSM as a high-risk group (NACO 2006). In this period, "transgender" was used sporadically by particular activists such as Tista Das, one of the first trans women in

West Bengal to undergo modern "sex change" or gender-affirmation surgery, as distinct from *hijra* castration-penectomy (Das 2009). However, the government did not define transgender as a target group for developmental aid or HIV intervention, though it did use the colonial category "eunuch" to designate *hijras* (NACO 2006: 43). This period saw the establishment of many CBOs in eastern India that received funds under the MSM rubric, such as MANAS Bangla, a CBO network in which Raina worked for several years. These CBOs typically drew membership from *kothi-dhurani* communities rather than focus on gender-normative MSM. Raina recalls going around with other fieldworkers in various cruising sites and finding potential community members whom they would interpellate as *kothi*, which gained popularity as a more common usage relative to similar terms like *dhurani*. Lawrence Cohen has argued that the *kothi* became an "emergent reality" during the expansion of HIV-AIDS intervention projects as fieldworkers interpellated more and more people into the category (2005: 285). However, Raina's experiences suggest that the *kothi*, rather than marking a new social emergence, marked a further consolidation and expansion of the networks in which she had participated in her youth (see Dutta 2013: 501).

The third phase of the NACP (2007–12) classified *kothi* as a high-risk subgroup of feminine MSM (NACO 2007: 13). Simultaneously, "transgender" entered the NACP lexicon, but NACP guidelines took transgender to largely mean *hijra*, replacing their earlier designation as eunuchs (13). Subsequently, in 2008, the United Nations Development Programme (UNDP), a multilateral organization that assists the Indian state with its AIDS program, organized consultations to assess gaps in HIV-AIDS infrastructure, where upper-tier activists demanded greater, more specific provisions for transgender people—including and beyond *hijras*—but also conceded that it was an ambiguously defined category (UNDP 2008). This prompted UNDP to fund regional consultations organized by large metropolitan NGOs in 2009, which aimed to arrive at a common transregional definition of TG in consultation with community representatives. Transgender was defined as an umbrella term, including both *hijra* and *kothi*:

> Transgender is a gender identity. Transgender persons usually live or prefer to live in the gender role opposite to the one in which they are born. In other words, one who is biologically male but loves to feel and see herself as a female could be considered as a male to female transgender person. It is an umbrella term which includes transsexuals, cross dressers, intersexed persons, gender variant persons and many more. In eastern India there are various local names and identities, such as Kothi, Dhurani, Boudi, 50/50, Gandu, Chakka, Koena. . . . Among these, the most common identity is Kothi. A few transgender persons also believe in a traditional culture known as Hijra . . . with its own hierarchical social system. (SAATHII 2009: 17)

Besides obvious problems like the total exclusion of trans masculine identities, this articulation of transgender as an umbrella term resulted in the scalar subsumption of "local names" under transgender as a common (trans)national, cross-cultural signifier. As a universalizing rubric, *transgender* subsumes terms that are now posited as merely local variants, even if they actually span multiple regions of South Asia and thus belie their containment to the scale of the local. The scalar hierarchy between transnational/universal/cosmopolitan and local/particular/vernacular discourses or categories thus *emerges* during this definitional process rather than preexisting it. As transnational feminists have argued, the hierarchy between global/local cannot be taken for granted, and scale is continually in the making (Mountz and Hyndman 2006). Through such ongoing constructions of scale, the understandings of gender/sex associated with transgender become the governing rubric under which regional subordinates must be organized rather than a resource that varied idioms of gender/sexuality can negotiate in their own terms, through their own spatial or temporal scales.

Moreover, this process does not merely subsume, it also potentially elides and erases. As seen in the above document, transgender is imagined as an encompassing umbrella term that is almost infinitely extensible across various cultural contexts. Yet it is restrictively defined in biologically essentialist terms as identification with the gender "opposite" to one's "biological" sex through linear (male-to-female) transition, with only a token acknowledgment of gender variant and intersex persons who may not fit the binary. Thus while it seeks to encompass varied idioms of gender, it also carries assumptions that may contravene the discourses of gender/sexual variance that it claims to include. Following the emerging definition of transgender as a "gender identity" understood primarily through a binary transitional model, the state has tended to categorically separate funding for transgender groups from the (homo)sexual category of "men who have sex with men," belying the overlap between sexual and gender variance evidenced in the previous classification of *kothi* as MSM (WBSAPCS 2011). Thus while transgender is defined as an open-ended umbrella term, it also potentially imposes homo-trans and cis-trans borders over complex spectral communities such as Raina's friend circle in south Kolkata, with their shifting *kodi-bhelki* and *kothi-hijra* boundaries, and class/caste-based overlaps between male-attired *kothis* and those who wear feminine clothes and/or join the *hijras*. The scalar ascendance of transgender as a trans/national umbrella term tends to establish the cis/trans and homo/trans binaries (and thus the male/female, man/woman divides) as putatively cross-cultural and ontologically stable rubrics, such that local discourses or practices of gender/sexual variance are simply assumed to be intelligible and classifiable in terms of the aforementioned binaries.

Following the initial articulations of transgender as an umbrella term in the HIV-AIDS sector, recent policy directives such as a report by the Ministry of Social Justice and Empowerment (MoSJE) and a judgment by the Supreme Court of India (SC) have also defined transgender as an umbrella category, extending its use beyond HIV-AIDS prevention (MoSJE 2014: 7; SC 2014: 10). Significantly, these institutional declarations explicitly include both binary (male-to-female or female-to-male) and "third gender" identities as subjects of rights and empowerment. However, they also recommend procedures for the certification of gender either by state-appointed committees (MoSJE) or through psychological tests (SC) to legally validate someone's preferred option as male, female, or transgender/third gender, which may further entrench the state-sanctioned adjudication of the boundaries between different gender categories and between cis and trans identities (MoSJE 2014: 34; SC 2014: 84). As an umbrella term, "transgender" is therefore marked by a foundational contradiction between its supposed indefinite extensibility across different sociocultural forms of gender variance and its imposition of new categorical assumptions and identitarian boundaries. As a result, ongoing attempts to define the scope of transgender as a category for funding and representation have prompted bitter border wars and activist conflicts regarding whom to include or not. *Hijras* have been included with relatively little controversy given their old status as eunuchs or a "third gender"; indeed, in some official usages, "transgender" may primarily serve to designate *hijras* (NACO 2007: 13). However, *kothi* and similar terms become particularly controversial due to their spectral nature and previous classification as MSM. The MSM-TG border wars and attendant debates over classification have been described by one of us in detail elsewhere (Dutta 2013). For our purposes here, we will focus on the role of these conflicts in the aforementioned elision of local categories. The controversy regarding the status of *kothi* peaked during consultations in 2010 preceding the launch of Project Pehchan, a new HIV-AIDS intervention program funded by the Global Fund to Fight against AIDS, Tuberculosis and Malaria. Raina was present at one of these consultations in Kolkata, where one set of activists accused other activists, who had previously identified as *kothi* and MSM, of being men who were masquerading as TG to gain funds. This may be seen as an intensification of the existing tensions between differently gendered subject positions in *kothi-hijra* communities, as described above. On the other hand, one of Raina's *hijra* friends willfully added to the confusion by stating that she was *hijra* by profession, TG by gender identity, and MSM by sexual behavior, much to Raina's delight. Despite such attempts to confuse the boundaries, eventually, the controversy resulted in *kothi* dropping out as a term of representation within the development sector. Since 2010, most CBOs in West Bengal have officially identified their constituencies as either TG or MSM, and *kothi* has fallen out of official activist usage.

This shift has also fueled a division between public representation and intracommunity usages. Even after the ascendance of transgender, *kothi* as a term of identification has remained close to our hearts. As Raina puts it, when a *kothi* sees another community member on the streets of Kolkata, they do not usually call out to each other as "hey, you transgender!"—rather, they feel more comfortable hailing each other as *kothi*. Yet when speaking to funders or state officials, CBO leaders typically represent their constituency as transgender without referencing local terms. This disjunction between subcultural terms and official usages of transgender signals a split between the affective register of community building and the language of political representation. Even when Raina and her friends do use "transgender" among themselves, their usage is often different from official discourse and may flexibly include people who would be identified as feminine gay men or MSM by funders (e.g., Ani in hir more *kodi* days). While this suggests that intracommunity usages resist hegemonic definitions and demonstrate alternative appropriations of transgender, the split between these distinct registers also serves as a constraint that limits upward mobility in terms of linguistic facility in English and the ability to employ the politically correct discourse du jour. While both of us can negotiate between subcultural intracommunity usages and organizational discourse, most *kothis* have not had the training or privilege to be able to do so, which restricts their mobility within activism and the development sector.

∗ ∗ ∗

Moving on from the level of official representation, the increasing circulation of transgender as a category associated with certain ideas of gender may also bolster social hierarchies and forms of stigma around gender identity and presentation. In many emergent articulations of transgender identity, "transgender" and "transsexual" are loosely conflated, and the Bengali translation, *rupantarkami* (someone who desires transformation in *roop*, or form), can signify both senses (Das 2009). In many usages, "transgender" connotes an MTF (male-to-female) or FTM (female-to-male) model of identity and the affirmation of one's womanhood or manhood through some form of transition from one sex/gender to another (Das 2009; SAATHII 2009). However, in contexts where contemporary methods of transitioning have largely not been available, people within the *kothi-hijra* spectrum have devised trajectories of sartorial, bodily, or behavioral feminization that need not imply identification with social or ontological womanhood per se but, rather, may be expressed as a separately gendered subject position. For instance, several *kothis* of our acquaintance assert than while they are *like* women or have a womanly or feminine psyche (*mone nari*), they are not women as such (also see Reddy 2005: 134). Raina herself generally presents as a (trans) woman but does not identify as either gender (Ani, having come to hir subject position via the academy and queer theory before hir introduction to these communities, is another case altogether). Further, as Gayatri Reddy argues in her ethnography of *hijras* in South India, *hijras* may elect castration-penectomy and other methods of feminization such as hormonal treatments and yet not wish to socially "pass" as women, even if they are pleased when such passing does occur (Reddy 2005: 134–36). Indeed, *hijra* livelihoods like blessing people for money *depend* on their perception as distinct from both men and women. In this context, the advent of a new discourse of trans womanhood, whether accompanied by gender affirmation surgery or not, creates new possibilities of personal and social identification, which may have life-affirming implications for some people. We do not seek to rehearse the facile critique of transsexuality as conformist and reproducing binary gender, as if nontranssexuals do not do so all the time (Valentine 2012). At the same time, both of us have encountered gendered and classed hierarchies between emergent models of trans womanhood and older forms of feminization and gender liminality. Given that *hijra* communities and *kothi* forms of public visibility (such as flamboyance, sex work, and cruising) are often socially disreputable and stigmatized, some CBO leaders actively advocate that community members fashion themselves as women rather than *hijra/kothi*—to quote one such person, "the way that you people behave in public, does any woman behave like that? No wonder you have no respect in society." Indeed, as observed by Raina, the imputation of *hijra*-like behavior may even become a form of shaming and insult within some *kothi*/trans communities, in contrast to the proud avowal of *hijra* identity by *hijra* clans. This intensification of social stigma against gender liminality by holding up (middle class, upper caste) womanhood as a more desirable and respectable ideal of self-fashioning may be paralleled by a hierarchy between castration-penectomy (called *chhibrano* in the subcultural language) and the achievement of what trans women like Tista have termed their "complete" (*sampurna*) womanhood through "sex change" surgery (Das 2013). Over the last few years, both of us have encountered *kothis* who identify as (trans) women and deride *chhibrano*, saying they would never settle for anything "less" than "full" SRS (sex reassignment surgery). Such equations between transition, womanhood, and completeness (*sampurnata*) perpetuate the stigmatization of *hijras* and nontranssexual *kothis* as less than human and heighten the challenges faced by those who cannot afford, or do not want, "complete" womanhood or "full" transition.

Further, while the aforementioned hierarchies may be seen as related to restrictive articulations of transgender identity that exclude or deride nonbinary possibilities, even inclusive definitions of the category often imply a singular or consistent model of gender identity that may elide or delegitimize various unruly and inconsistent forms of identification practiced by *kothis* and *hijras*. Even pluralistic definitions of transgender often assume a stable model of gender based on primary, consistent, and singular identities, wherein trans people may have a variety of identities, but each identity is assumed to be singular, consistent, and mutually exclusive with the others, thus reflecting the social imperative of authentic identification, as also required by modern citizenship and biopolitical power. ("Identity" in its very semantics implies singularity or, at best, the combination of singular-consistent identities). This is not to criticize people for desiring stable or officially recognized identities—many of us may need one to survive in contemporary societies—but to critique the *structural* imperative of authentic and consistent identification, which is particularly evident in defensive assertions that trans and queer people are "born this way." In our perception, this imperative is reflected in the proliferation of attempts to build stable cartographies of trans identities, such as those reflected in several popular introductory guides to gender identity and trans issues produced in the United States, which are also gaining circulation in Indian online trans spaces (Hill and Mays 2013; Kasulke 2013; Bauer 2010). Typically, these guides feature a list of trans identities led by trans men and women and followed by genderqueer people, cross-dressers, drag queens and kings, and so on (the latter categories progressively coming closer to gender instability and the cis-trans border and thus unevenly included). A trans woman, to be respected as such, has to be seen as really and only a woman: to suggest that she may potentially be *also* genderqueer, third gender—or worse, a feminine male—can only be seen as offensive misgendering. This is probably partly prompted by hostile tropes of the deceptive-pathetic transsexual in the West, wherein trans women are seen as deceptive "men" or pathetic failures at femininity (Serano 2013). To counter the forcible assignment of "real" or "birth" genders and assert the validity of trans identities, there is a systemic compulsion to exert a strong mono-gendered claim to trans womanhood (or manhood)—one fallout of which is the neat separation of binary and nonbinary identities, recreating a majority-minority dynamic wherein (trans) men and women are followed by a trail of genderqueer/bigender/agender "others." As one "Trans 101" rather despairingly states, "Just as nobody knows why there are so many cis people, nobody knows why there are so many binary identified folks" (Bauer 2010). However, this may be less an empirical constant and more the result of a system that makes it imperative to assign or claim a primary gender and confers legitimacy based on such identification, belying the shifting nonbinary positionalities occupied by many trans men and women, which must be downplayed relative to their *primary* identification. This process parallels the longstanding but never entirely successful attempt to dissociate gender variance from gay identity, wherein effeminacy/gender variance becomes downplayed within mainstream gay identities and the primary gender of gay people becomes defined in terms of masculinity (Valentine 2007). Various practices of gayness that belie stable definitions of "manhood" must be deemphasized for "gay" to retain its stable (cis) gendering and attendant privileges. Once categories such as "trans women" or "gay men" are seen as *necessarily* mono-gendered and evacuated of their historical association with gender liminality, "binary" people tend to be naturalized as majorities, leaving a trailing bunch of explicitly, exclusively nonbinary people. Such a schema would fail to understand how social or legal binary identities and nonbinary practices or subject positions may be negotiated and lived simultaneously, creating unstable assemblages rather than essentialized identities.

In contrast to the structural imperative of stable gender recognition, *hijras* and *kothis* may deploy various unruly, changeable practices of identification and citizenship arising from complex strategies of survival and self-assertion in societies that have not provided them with stable options rather than from any abstract radical politics. *Hijras* who have undergone castration-penectomy may procure and use official female identification documents and yet purposely contravene female identification in other contexts—for instance, by dramatizing physical discordance from femaleness by thickening the voice or by employing characteristic gestures such as the *thikri*, a loud clap, which immediately marks one as *hijra*. One of our *hijra* friends recently obtained a female voter card which she proudly flaunts, but she objects if otherwise perceived as a woman: in her words, "I went to a house where they mistook me for a woman: I just gave three claps!" Thus there may be *simultaneous* identifications and disidentifications with femaleness that cannot be comprehended by the aforementioned trans cartographies (or, at best, may be relegated to a "bi-gender" minority categorically separate from trans women, denying how *hijras* may be *both* women and not-women). Further, some *hijras* and *kothis* may have a combination of identity documents under "male," "female," and more recently, "other"/"transgender" categories, due to the varying circumstances in which they procured the documents. We have known *hijras* and *kothis* with multiple identity cards who have had problems accessing healthcare services due to the expectation of a stable, singular identity. Moreover, since the entry of "other" and "transgender" as official gender categories recognized by the Indian government, there have been ongoing debates about whether *hijras* and other transgender people should be classified as female or other/transgender, often with the assumption that there could be a generalized answer to this question (see Kushala 2011). Obviously, lumping trans people into either "female" or "other" categories, each exclusive of the other, presents two problematic options. The recent MoSJE and SC directives recognize both binary-gendered trans people and a third or nonbinary category and seek to enable individual choice over identification rather than impose any one category on all trans people; however, they still operate on the assumption of a fixed and consistent identity that must be legally validated through expert committees, psychological tests, or surgery (MoSJE 2014: 34; SC 2014: 84, 108). While enabling individual access to and choice over official identification is crucial, at the same time, it may be necessary to destabilize the polarity between binary and nonbinary (or "third gender") identities—and more broadly, to question the requirement of singular, consistent identification in order to access rights and citizenship. Otherwise, emergent transgender epistemologies that attempt to classify mutually exclusive, primary gender identities over and above the binary-defying practices of many queer, trans (and even cis) lives may fail to comprehend multiple or noncoherent gendered identifications or practices enacted by a single body and may elide or erase temporally unstable or non-unidirectional trajectories of gendered transition. In such epistemologies, the subject positions and practices of *hijras* and *kothis* can only linger on as an exotic, precarious species of gender variance, as remnants of archaic forms of gender liminality, or as after-thoughts tagged on as an et cetera to trans cartographies—rather than as people who powerfully instantiate the gendered instabilities that foundationally mark many LGBTIQ subject positions and indeed, sex/gender itself.

∗   ∗   ∗

The emergence of transgender is an ongoing and unpredictable process, and we can draw only a provisional conclusion to our reflections here. Given that transgender may serve as a useful and even life-saving rubric for service provision, politics, and funding, we do not advocate a disengagement with the category but a critique of the structural conditions and assumptions within which it functions. Rather than use transgender as an umbrella term encompassing all possible gender variant identities, it is perhaps better deployed as an analytic rubric for variant and liminal gendered *positions*, such that to access the benefits or services provided through the category (e.g., HIV prevention, gender-affirmative care, antiviolence work, crisis support), one does not have to *identify* with any pre-given understanding of transgender. This process of deontologizing transgender (dissociating it from ontological identification) has to be coupled with the critique and gradual dismantling of the scalar hierarchy between "transnational" and "local" or "regional" discourses, so as to enable more equitable conversations and engagements with other epistemologies of gender/sexual variance or marginality. Evidently, the definition of transgender as a universal(izing) term does not truly value the diverse understandings of gender/sexual variance in different regions, and even pluralistic definitions of transgender tend to recreate a majoritarian dynamic in which everyone has to have a (consistent) identity, and some identities must trail behind others. Variant imaginations of scale are crucial to challenge these colonizing implications of the transgender category, such that local or regional discourses are not compelled to be legible in terms of globalizing understandings of gender, and the latter also become accountable to the former. Beyond discursive realignments, this necessitates material transformations. The way in which each region or community may build distinctive movements and approaches, network with each other, and forge counterhegemonic translations with the transgender category is restricted through a centralized structure of activism, funding, and scholarship wherein they become just subregions within a preconstituted trans/national domain. More egalitarian exchanges necessitate a gradual dismantling of the centralized and tiered structure of social movements, with funders, NGOs, activists, and scholars based in Western or postcolonial metropolises at the top and small CBOs near the bottom. The decolonization of transgender is not likely to be achieved in isolation from the transformation of the political economy of social movements, the dismantling of scalar geographies of development, and the class/caste/racial hierarchies within which they are embedded. Therefore, in the end, we wish to stress that decolonizing transgender is not just a project to include external forms of cultural difference into existing structures and epistemologies but is internal to the deconstruction and democratization of LGBTIQ activism both inside and outside the "West."

Aniruddha Dutta is an assistant professor in gender, women's, and sexuality studies and Asian and Slavic languages and literatures at the University of Iowa and also works as a volunteer with community-based organizations in West Bengal, India. Hir book project, tentatively titled "Globalizing through the Vernacular: The Making of Sexual and Gender Minorities in Eastern India," is in progress.

Raina Roy, who also goes by Rana, the male version of her name, is an activist working with trans and gender-variant communities in West Bengal and Delhi. Her professional affiliations have included staff positions with Pratyay Gender Trust, Kolkata, MANAS Bangla, and the Society for Human Alliances and Needs, Delhi.

References

Bauer, Asher. 2010. "Not Your Mom's Trans 101." *Tranarchism*, November 26. tranarchism.com/2010/11/26/not-your-moms-trans-101/.

Boyce, Paul, and Akshay Khanna. 2011. "Rights and Representations: Querying the Male-to-Male Sexual Subject in India." *Culture, Health, and Sexuality* 13, no. 1: 89–100.

Cohen, Lawrence. 1995. "The Pleasures of Castration: The Postoperative Status of Hijras, Jankhas, and Academics." In *Sexual Nature, Sexual Culture*, ed. Paul R. Abramson and Steven D. Pinkerton, 276–304. Chicago: University of Chicago Press.

———. 2005. "The Kothi Wars: AIDS Cosmopolitanism and the Morality of Classification." In *Sex in Development: Science, Sexuality, and Morality in Global Perspective*, ed. Vivienne Adams and Stacy L. Piggs, 269–303. Durham, NC: Duke University Press.

Das, Tista. 2009. "Bibhatsa-bibar" ("Monstrous"). *Swikriti Patrika*, no. 6: 9–15.

———. 2013. "Ami kichhutei tomar chhele hote chai na ma" ("I Do Not Want to Be Your Son, Ma"). *News Bangla*, June 21.

Dirks, Nicholas B. 2001. *Castes of Mind: Colonialism and the Making of Modern India*. Princeton, NJ: Princeton University Press.

Dutta, Aniruddha. 2012. "An Epistemology of Collusion: *Hijras, Kothis*, and the Historical (Dis)continuity of Gender/Sexual Identities in Eastern India." *Gender and History* 24, no. 3: 825–49.

———. 2013. "Legible Identities and Legitimate Citizens: The Globalization of Transgender and Subjects of HIV-AIDS Prevention in Eastern India." *International Feminist Journal of Politics* 15, no. 4: 494–514.

Hall, Kira. 2005. "Intertextual Sexuality: Parodies of Class, Identity, and Desire in Liminal Delhi." *Journal of Linguistic Anthropology* 15, no. 1: 125–44.

Hill, Mell Reiff, and Jay Mays. 2013. *The Gender Book*. www.thegenderbook.com/the-book /4553374748 (accessed January 14, 2014).

Kasulke, Sarah. 2013. "Everything You Always Wanted to Know about Transgender People but Were Afraid to Ask." *Buzzfeed*, July 22. www.buzzfeed.com/sbkasulke/everything-you -always-wanted-to-know-about-transgender-peopl.

Katyal, Akhil. 2010. "No 'Sexuality' for All—Some Notes from India." *Polyvocia* 2: 21–29.

Khanna, Akshay. 2009. "Taming of the Shrewd Meyeli Chhele: A Political Economy of Development's Sexual Subject." *Development* 52, no. 1: 43–51.

Kushala, S. 2011. "The Majority of Transsexuals Like to Be Women." *Bangalore Mirror*, March 21.

MoSJE (Ministry of Social Justice and Empowerment). 2014. "Report of the Expert Committee on the Issues relating to Transgender Persons." socialjustice.nic.in/transgenderpersons.php (accessed April 16, 2014).

Mountz, Alison, and Jennifer Hyndman. 2006. "Feminist Approaches to the Global Intimate." *Women's Studies Quarterly* 34, no. 1–2: 446–63.

NACO (National AIDS Control Organization). 2006. *Annual HIV Sentinel Surveillance Report 2006*. New Delhi: Ministry of Health and Family Welfare, Government of India.

———. 2007. *Targeted Interventions under NACP III: Core High Risk Groups*. New Delhi: Ministry of Health and Family Welfare, Government of India.

Nanda, Serena. 1990. *Neither Man nor Woman: The Hijras of India*. Belmont, CA: Wadsworth.

Reddy, Gayatri. 2005. *With Respect to Sex: Negotiating Hijra Identity in South India*. Chicago: University of Chicago Press.

SAATHII (Solidarity and Action against the HIV Infection in India). 2009. "Report of the Regional TG/Hijra Consultation in Eastern India." www.saathii.org/orissapages/tg_hijra _issues_consultation%20.html (accessed January 14, 2014).

SC (The Supreme Court of India). 2014. "National Legal Services Authority versus Union of India and Others." judis.nic.in/supremecourt/imgs1.aspx?filename=41411 (accessed April 16, 2014).

Serano, Julia. 2013. "Skirt Chasers: Why the Media Depicts the Trans Revolution in Lipstick and Heels." In *The Transgender Studies Reader 2*, ed. Susan Stryker and Aren Aizura, 226–33. New York: Routledge.

Spivak, Gayatri Chakravorty. 1999. *A Critique of Postcolonial Reason: Toward a History of the Vanishing Present*. Cambridge, MA: Harvard University Press.

Stryker, Susan, and Aren Aizura, eds. 2013. *The Transgender Studies Reader 2*. New York: Routledge.

UNDP (United Nations Development Programme). 2008. "Missing Pieces: HIV Related Needs of Sexual Minorities in India." http://www.ph.undp.org/content/dam/india/docs/msm_publications.pdf (accessed April 15, 2014).

Valentine, David. 2007. *Imagining Transgender: An Ethnography of a Category*. Durham, NC: Duke University Press.

———. 2012. "Sue E. Generous: Toward a Theory of Non-Transexuality." *Feminist Studies* 38, no. 1: 1–19.

WBSAPCS (West Bengal State AIDS Prevention and Control Society). 2011. "Advertisement for Inviting Applications from CBOs for Empanelment." Kolkata: Ministry of Health and Family Welfare, Government of West Bengal.

Twin-Spirited Woman

Sts'iyóye smestíyexw slhá:li

SAYLESH WESLEY

Abstract Coast Salish people, particularly the Stó:lō of the lower Fraser Valley, have lost much of their language, histories, and teachings as a result of colonization. One such important identity that has been forgotten or erased is the two-spirited role. The author wishes to revitalize the cultural roles of transgendered/two-spirit people within the Coast Salish territory and ways in which they historically contributed to their societies prior to colonization. Traditionally, the Stó:lō are matriarchal and matrilineal, and only grandmothers can create any new laws for their descendants. Thus given the vital role played by the author's grandmother in her process, this essay is a long-overdue proposal to all living grandmothers not only to stand by and accept their two-spirited grandchildren but to call for a celebration of their coming out. This visionary work serves to inspire future generations of Stó:lō to fully embrace *all* members of their community, especially two-spirits. The first *Sts'iyóye Smestíyexw Slhá:li*, or *Twin-Spirited Woman,* as this essay is about, offers an example to this sacred work.
Keywords two-spirit; transgender; gender; restoration; reconciliation; indigenous; twin-spirited woman; storytelling; queer; LGBTQ

> To decolonize our sexualities and move towards a Sovereign Erotic, we must unmask the specters of conquistadors, priests, and politicians that have invaded our spirits and psyches, insist they vacate, and begin tending the open wounds colonization leaves in our flesh. . . . A Sovereign Erotic is a return to and/or continuance of the complex realities of gender and sexuality that are ever-present in both the human and more-than-human world, but erased and hidden by colonial cultures.
> —Qwo-li Driskill, "Stolen from Our Bodies: First Nations Two-Spirits/Queers and the Journey to a Sovereign Erotic"

The Stó:lō people of British Columbia's lower Fraser Valley have ancient stories, or *Sxwōxwiyám*, to turn to when seeking traditional knowledge or teachings; however, the vast majority of these stories have been forgotten due to the colonial effects of assimilation. As an mtf transgendered Stó:lō citizen and PhD student in

TSQ: Transgender Studies Quarterly ∗ Volume 1, Number 3 ∗ August 2014
DOI 10.1215/23289252-2685624 © 2014 Duke University Press

gender, sexuality, and women's studies, I have made every effort to locate any precontact stories of the Stó:lō two-spirits, but to no avail so far. In this essay, I endeavor to re-member the past differently, marshal new traditions and language together in ways that create a new vision of the future. For the Coast Salish territory, I wish to illustrate how we historically contributed to our society prior to colonization. My grandmother has overcome the colonized homophobia imposed upon her enough to coin a title for me from our Halq'eméylem language. Given it has been her acceptance I wanted most of all, I would like to propose to all living Stó:lō grandmothers, the *Sisele*, that as the traditional makers of all laws on our matriarchal lands, they support this long-overdue initiative to reclaim lost identities erased through Western gen[der]ocidal action. The restoration of lost identities back to the Stó:lō nation would further reestablish the identities deleted by Western gen[der]ocidal actions. This essay is a movement toward personal healing and internal reconciliation for the Stó:lō as a whole. I feel that what my grandmother has done for me is a perfect example for this.

As Canada currently seeks to reconcile[1] with its indigenous people against whom it practiced genocide, in my case, as an mtf person who has lost access to traditional knowledge about people like me, I feel the need for this country to atone for its gendercide. While this reconciliation is important, it is more crucial that indigenous people reconcile among themselves first.

Therefore, this essay is intended not only to regenerate the lost teachings and stories of all Stó:lō two-spirits but also to offer a new beginning toward a new realization and acceptance for all indigenous people. As a member of the Stó:lō nation, I have inquired with elders and consulted all published works for a Halq'eméylem translation, and I have found that *two-spirit* is not yet a part of the Halq'eméylem language, nor can it be found in the English-to-Halq'eméylem dictionary (First Voices 2013a). Upon my request, my grandmother has been the first to conjure a Halq'eméylem term for my transgendered identity. In the recounting of my grandmother's work, I follow the "story-work" methodology of Stó:lō scholar Jo-ann Archibald, articulated in her *Indigenous Storywork* (2008), whereby personal experience is considered in relation to stories of the elders, to craft an analysis that takes indigenous knowledge seriously. This is my story and analysis woven together.

First, I share some of my history in order to clarify how I carry both Stó:lō and Tsimshian bloodlines. Approximately three years before I was born, my maternal grandmother moved from the Fraser Valley, her traditional Stó:lō territory situated in Southwest British Columbia, Canada.[2] During this time, she was still married to my late biological maternal grandfather, who was also Coast Salish from the Musqueam nation located in Vancouver's Point Grey area. Their marriage had dwindled at this point, and they agreed to separate and divorce. She was federally contracted at the time to travel around the province to promote and help preserve all traditional fine arts that many nations were quickly losing. On one of these excursions, she landed in Terrace, a small north coast town of British Columbia. This is when she met and eventually married my late step-grandfather who was a resident of Terrace and a member of the Tsimshian nation. The Tsimshian territory spreads vastly across the Pacific Northwest Coast and geographically includes Terrace and Prince Rupert, British Columbia, as well as southern parts of Alaska. Her plan was to send for her children from her previous marriage once she was settled, and my mother, a teen at the time, was one of them. Before my grandmother had anticipated, my mother showed up on the Greyhound bus from Chilliwack, because she missed her mother too much to wait any longer. It was not long before she met my father, who was not only Tsimshian but also my step-grandfather's maternal nephew. Thus this new grandfather of mine was also my great-uncle by blood.

My parents eventually married and I was born on October 28, 1972, at the Terrace Mills Memorial Hospital. The time of my birth was 10:30 p.m. My mother almost bled to death after an extremely difficult three-hour labor, and she remained as a patient for another week to recover from a life-saving postdelivery surgery. As I was jaundiced and three weeks premature, I had to be incubated in hospital for another two weeks. This birth resulted in two quite profoundly different stories, one from my maternal (Stó:lō) grandmother and one from my father. He tells that the night I was born, the northern lights danced across the clear night sky more brightly than he had ever witnessed, and they apparently lasted throughout the night. To him, this was a spiritual sign. What is more significant is that he was not a spiritual man. He took the northern lights as an omen that his first-born son was going to be special—which I feel I have proved true. In those days, and in a town like Terrace, a son had great expectations placed on him to become a "man of men." Terrace was, and still is, a very redneck little city; "Indians" must overcompensate for anything and everything they do. The racist attitudes toward the indigenous populations in this rural community have changed little over the years that I have visited, so I understand the double work any "Indian" has to do to fit in. I cannot imagine what my father envisioned for me as his potential "hero" of a son, but he responded to the northern lights with hope that I would do him proud and with a belief that something divine acknowledged his vision for my future. Though these hopes for me weren't necessarily achieved as he imagined they would be, I must share that he is now absolutely proud of who I have become.

My grandmother's story is different. She first told it to me when I was about thirteen years old. She shared that my mother had almost bled to death as a result of my delivery. She also explained that such a difficult birth foretells a difficult life for such a child (according to her elders). As both the Stó:lō and

Tsimshian are matrilineal, it goes without saying that I am to identify as Stó:lō even though my blood is a blend of the two, and to this day, she maintains political jurisdiction over me. Perhaps this is why she felt she had the right to share what she did, as hurtful as it might seem. Throughout the remainder of my teenage years, it seemed that what she had foretold in regard to how tumultuous my life would become had come true. I was nearing the end of puberty. I knew that I was not the *man* that I was expected to be. Every night I prayed that a supernatural force would transform me into a "normal boy." Over the course of my lifetime and despite my family's dismay over my apparent lack of masculinity, my grandmother did love me and played a critical role in bringing me up. I spent many weekends throughout my childhood under her loving care, and there are no sad stories I can tell, except for the time she told her version of my birth. I never again felt her angst toward me until I came out as transgender. In fact, when I was a child, she would allow me to play with dolls and dress up like a bride, and she would have tea parties with me when no one else would. It hurt her to see how my family would shame me to the soul for indicating in any way that I was not supposed to be a boy. Ultimately, I loved my grandmother from the day of my memories and still do today.

I was also close to my maternal auntie, almost ten years my senior and my grandmother's youngest child. She was genderqueer like me, except the polar opposite. She, in her own crass words, "was supposed to have a pecker." By the time I was courageous enough to come out, my aunt had yet to do so. My entire family knew that she was, as everyone thought, a "lesbian," even though she later confessed to also being "trans" like me. Her story is even more painful than mine, and I will not delve into it here. When I was twenty-three, I came out to her and to the rest of my family. I started off identifying as gay, since it seemed less scary than to say I was actually a woman; however, I announced my true trans identity over the phone to my aunt. She was incarcerated at the time for dealing drugs and prostitution. She warned me: "Don't tell anyone! I don't want you to go through what I did!" She was the first in our extended family to break the ground for homophobia internally, as one might well imagine, and she faced far worse consequences for being gay than I would. Against her plea, I went ahead with revealing the truth about my identity. I was willing to be cast out from my family, but I hoped for at least some acceptance. Otherwise, I would have had to find a way to end my life for the mistake that I felt I was. Over the next little while, my aunt was released from prison, and we became even closer. My seemingly smoother journey of coming out compared to hers years earlier gave her the courage to do the same.

All this time, my grandmother had remained as diplomatically mute as possible, I think for the sake of my aunt and me. In 1997, about three years after I told our family I was gay, I phoned her: to tell her that I was transgendered and ask if she would host a "coming out" feast for us. She said she could not fathom how I came to be this deviant, and how I thought I should be blessed with such a celebration. Perhaps in her mind, I should have grown out of my feminine phase. Needless to say, the conversation ended with her hanging up the phone and me in tears. In 1999, my aunt passed away from a heroin overdose. As keen as she was to continue negotiating her queer identity, she did not survive her own demons. For my grandmother, this was a loss from which she never fully recovered. I have since prayed these words to her countless times:

> I invite you Grandmother, to shape-shift your own thought process and open your mind a bit more and see that I am still, essentially, the grandchild with whom you shared a reciprocal loving relationship. I am not asking you to change who you are in principle, but rather, that you attempt to enhance your ability to be more at peace with diversity given your late daughter's fate. Perhaps I can take this opportunity to point out metaphorically that you too are akin to being two-spirited. In your stories of your cultural immersion combined with your experience as a converted Catholic, and how you now dwell (to some degree) in both faiths, you too share your own duality. Albeit, it isn't about your gender or sexuality, but in your own words "To Thine Own Self Be True" you justify your bi-culturalism and I beg that you accept my two-spirit identity all the same. I am, after all, a descendant of your rich bloodline, so there must be something worthy I can offer. The creative juices within you that produce your baskets flow through me too. I am taking what you taught me and now weave my own stories. My baskets are not literal, but they are certainly coming out to be "masterpieces" that would be finished perfectly with your loving pride.

My grandmother is a world-renowned basket weaver who not only continues to pass on her mastery of Stó:lō styles of weaving but single-handedly revived the lost Tsimshian cedar bark and spruce root weaving and taught it back to them. I have since rooted in Chilliwack because my parents also divorced after fifteen years of marriage. My mother took my sister and me back to her home-town, and here I stay. In April 2012, my grandmother's second husband tragically passed away. This event prompted her to return to Chilliwack, since it is where the bulk of her children and their families live. This was a difficult transition for her, given that she is at this point in her 80s and that she has lived in Terrace for nearly forty years. In the last two years since she returned, my relationship with her has been entirely reshaped. As well, I am now her primary caregiver. Our closeness has given me the opportunity to become her weaving apprentice. I have learned to gather and prepare strips of cedar and roots for weaving; sitting with her, I have learned basic techniques for making baskets and shawls. And as she shares with me her most cherished indigenous knowledge, I also share with her my insights about being two-spirited and how I have learned about this concept in university. Though this is uncharted territory for her, her receptiveness has clearly developed. She places absolute priority on higher education for her children and grandchildren. She feels as though if she had had the opportunity to get a postsecondary education that she would have become a scientist. Instead, she only received a grade six education in an Indian residential school. Though she still wrestles with the idea that I am now a woman, she respects my academic achievements and my natural flare for weaving. Given that I have revealed the emotionally awkward aspects of our relationship here, I want to emphasize that it is the progress we have made, not the pitfalls, that I wish to spotlight. My grandmother's instinctual *trans*phobia is not her doing. This is the "good work" of the Catholic Church and the rest of the colonial project; but as mentioned, our budding friendship also works to reprogram her worldview.

While my grandmother speaks English, learned at residential school, her first language is Halq'eméylem (First Voices 2013b). And recently I asked if she could meditate and conjure a title for me as a male-to-female in our traditional language. As previously mentioned, no such thing exists in recorded history. I had already shared with her what I have learned in university about two-spirited identities and so she took some time to think about it. Eventually, she came up with a Stó:lō two-spirited identity for me in our mother tongue—an exchange that remains surreal and miraculous. She coined the term *Sts'iyóye smestíyexw slhá:li*. When she handed the piece of paper to me with this title on it, she included the English translation, "Twin-Spirited Woman," and explained that I could interpret it as "two-spirited woman," or "twin-soul woman," or "same spirit as a woman." Ultimately, she left it open for me to decide how I would like to interpret it, given that our language is much more fluid than English. As a fluent speaker of Halq'eméylem, she has taught me that our words were able to wield various contexts and concepts depending on the discussion. Therefore, she gave me permission to decipher for myself how *Sts'iyóye smestíyexw* translates. This was truly a "HALLELUJAH!" moment. I then asked her if it would have made sense to introduce my late aunt as *Sts'iyóye Smestíyexw Swí:qe*, or "Twin-Spirited Man," and her response was something to the effect of "I guess if she would have wanted to."

As I state in the opening paragraphs of this essay, the Stó:lō have lost much of their Halq'eméylem language, histories, and teachings to colonization. As a result, any such focus on gender transition challenges many perspectives, particularly for gender-normative kin who must adjust their worldview once a family member discloses that she or he will change gender. I share this because I have observed how those who loved me were tremendously bewildered by my dramatic transition and how, fifteen years later, this shift is not yet finished for everyone. For the most part, my family and community members have come a long way. Many did not know how to perceive me in a literal sense; some still do not. I remain troubling and/or invisible in their presence. Most have come to a frame of mind where *I am* who *I am*. Or, "That's just the way she is," with no agenda or bias, just matter-of-fact acceptance. In other words, they have achieved true contentment with my identity and in some cases have found even more love and respect for me as a result of my transformation, given how they have witnessed my life-and-death struggle with it.

This leads to the complexities of the term *two-spirit* and how perplexing it is for everyone's psyche to negotiate. For instance, any given cisgender Stó:lō person who identifies as a contemporary two-spirit may not feel like a "twin-spirited woman" (i.e., my aforementioned late aunt might have adopted "twin-spirited man"). It only makes sense for them to choose how they wish to identify in Halq'eméylem as I have. In the introduction to the anthology *Queer Indigenous Studies* (Driskill et al. 2011), the authors suggest that the continued use of the prototype *two-spirit* is problematic: like *lesbian*, *gay*, *transgender*, and other terms, *two-spirit* "inevitably fails to represent the complexities of Indigenous constructions of sexual and gender diversity, both historically and as they are used in the present" (3). However, they also contend that two-spirit is a starting point toward the decolonization of queer indigenous identity in general. This admittedly implies that all cisgender queer people have both male and female spirits; it seems important to keep two-spirit open for such individuals to self-identify as to whether or not they understand themselves to have "two" spirits (3). Moreover, I tell my story in order to isolate my specific "queer" Stó:lō identity that makes space for other transfolk of my nation and subsequently for all queer indigenous people who remain unidentified and/or displaced from their home territory(s). In other words, I happily share the newly conceived *Sts'iyóye smestíyexw* status with any who feel it fits, though it is only an invitation. As each nonindigenous person who fits under the evolving LGBTQ spectrum has the right to self-determine where they fit and/or how they identify, it makes sense that the same goes for the Stó:lō "LGBTQ." Should any of those who do not identify as transgender wish to quest for a customized Halq'eméylem title as I have, then all the power to them.

Qwo-Li Driskill and colleagues also tell me to "talk back" to Western scholarship and compile and publish my own story: to claim first-voice authority as a contribution to the academic mainstream. Their message encourages me to bring what remains still in the proverbial closet—the lost and stolen history(s) that, until recently, remained the work of white scholars to excavate (10). However, I am grateful to some of these scholars who have engaged in this work, especially for any recent work that attempts to capture accurate and articulate accounts with clear integrity (Morgensen 2011; Rifkin 2012). However, I am fortunate to be able to bring a firsthand, lived experience to enrich this budding field. In this sense, I make every attempt to "link arms together" with other two-spirited theorists and philosophers to continue imagining what our scholarship should look like (Rifkin 2012: 18).

As previously mentioned, the term *two-spirit* is not in the English-to-Halq'eméylem dictionary. Thus it is necessary to work to reestablish the best or most appropriate "fit" to name this term and determine how it may serve as an addition to the Stó:lō gender binary.[3] Coast Salish nations traditionally hold ceremonial gatherings to "stand-up" ones who are receiving such names or honors,[4] and as our systems of passing knowledge and title down are matrilineal, only the eldest woman can legitimize this sort of work. I would thus require my grandmother to endorse this vision and support the endeavor to gift these roles back to the Stó:lō. I have truly become not only her granddaughter, but also her friend and teacher who helps to reshape her worldview, which includes my queer identity. She now understands that the "grandson" I once was remains very much alive through my female eyes. For a woman of her age and stature, this is no small feat.[5] The Catholic Church and the Canadian Indian Residential School system (which only closed in 1996[6]) have thoroughly accomplished their assimilationist goals in her. Coincidentally, it was the grandmother who raised the children prior to colonization. So, in effect, my grandmother and I have fallen back to ancestral ways of child rearing. I realize I am not a child, according to Western ideology, but I place myself in this stage given that I am "first-born" as *Sts'iyóye smestíyexw slhá:li*, and my legacy for the Stó:lō has begun.

As a philosopher and dreamer, I have come to know that fantasies of how the past could have been different are senseless, but I *do* know that there are miracles yet to unfold and that there is a possibility that my writing of this essay may very well become one. With Archibald's notion of "storywork," which gives academic freedom to scholars to cite indigenous elders and the stories they share as legitimate sources, I am secure in the fact that my grandmother has full authority to contribute to my work as she has in this essay. Storywork also has "the power to educate and heal the heart, mind, body and spirit," which is the absolute goal I have attempted to harness since the onset of my transition through the writing of this essay (Archibald 2008: back cover). Also, my work aims not only to "share back" what I have come to know but to support the change of the Coast Salish cultural landscape toward a setting that continues to honor and fulfill whatever remains necessary to please our Ancestors and to include *Sts'iyóye smestíyexw slhá:li*—while continuing to cultivate what "culture" is, how it will continue to evolve and adapt to our ever-changing world, and to "gift back" (143) fully our traditional matriarchal systems of governance and title. In order to reestablish such two-spirit roles, it is crucial that matriarchal systems replace the current Indian Act elected-chief system of governance,[7] given the grandmothers' role of making any new "laws" and/or "declarations" that hypothetically include the reclamation of *Sts'iyóye smestíyexw slhá:li*. I am certain the Ancestors have been wondering where we, as two-spirits, have been on "This Side."[8]

Current indigenous scholars such as Archibald and Driskill have contributed the use of indigenous words, names, and concepts. Many of these warriors may not have many more than my forty years, and though not all of these warriors are Stó:lõ, I instinctively follow my teachings as a *xwélmexw te Semá:th* (Sumas Nation member) and regard them as elders, meaning that I am respectful of their knowledge and courage to speak what is in their hearts. In one of my conversations with my grandmother, she mentioned how she still notices my former "male" self peeking through my female identity. In a way, it is as though I have developed two personalities: the beloved [but vulnerable] male child who finds refuge in the arms of the protective and much more competent big sister. My grandmother explained to me in that conversation she misses her grandson but that she has come to really respect the woman I have become. It does, however, make her happy that "he" comes out and will say something funny and/ or endearing in a way that only he could. As "he," I was much more emotional and extreme, with melodramatic outbursts and passion. I was not able to function well in the world, but my effect on a crowd was undoubtedly appreciated, given my alleged sweet nature. As "she," I am much more focused, serious, and even ambitious. I am well aware that it is "she" who has taken "us" this far with regard to education: I am now in a PhD program. While he remains very much a child, she has become a fully functioning adult.

I am fully committed to meeting the need to "stand-up" all roles (restorer, empowerer, healer) for future and ongoing battles toward the seemingly infinite uphill climbs toward liberation, self-determination, entitlement, title, restoration, privilege, empowerment, and decolonization. As I currently live and work on my own traditional Coast Salish territory, then perhaps the Halq'eméylem terms *xéyt* (transform it) or *méa:ylexw* (revive; come back to life) would serve more appropriately and inclusively to the aforementioned ideologies. As such, the articulation process for this essay feels intrinsically off, as if I am attempting to fight fire with fire—though this may prove to be ironically effective in other instances. Speaking in my own Halq'eméylem language would make for as close to perfect a way as possible to honor any who have been invisibilized (i.e., Stó:lõ women and *Sts'iyóye smestíyexw slhá:li*). It would then seem as though I would be more effectively fighting fire with water.

In the beginning of August 2012, a number of years after the phone call story with which I introduced this essay, I had the opportunity to work with my grandmother on a cedar bark shawl project I had wanted to do for a long time. As I mentioned above, she is a world-renowned Stó:lō weaver known for her skills and genius as the person who also revitalized the lost Tsimshian basketry techniques. I asked her to teach me to weave my garment. In my mind, I envisioned myself dancing around a gathering floor cloaked by my proud *Syewá:l* (Ancestors), particularly those who have been waiting for *Sts'iyóye smestíyexw meá:ylexw* (twin-spirits to come back to life). This was not an easy task for either of us, as this became a dual mission for me: to learn to weave such a garment as well as to request a specific identity for me that comes from our Stó:lō language and her Stó:lō consciousness. If I can borrow Driskill's words, from "Doubleweaving Two-Spirit Critiques, Building Alliances between Native and Queer Studies": "By pulling together splints from both disciplines [native studies and queer studies], we can doubleweave Two-spirit critiques that challenge and sharpen our scholarship and activism" (2010: 79). Driskill's words help me understand this weaving project and its dual purpose. As such, my grandmother and I embarked on serious work: this work not only taught me the skills to craft such a piece but also worked to *re*story the two-spirit beings who have long disappeared from her elders' memories and give them back to her. As my mind has transformed from child to inquisitive adult, I have come to know that to ask her (or any other elder) questions regarding culture and history must be done very carefully and that I must accept a nonresponse when they do not wish to answer at the time. To question and/or comment intermittently while an elder speaks often hinders what they are sharing and can abruptly stop the story or teaching. Usually, learning happens when they simply start talking about the *old days* and the *old ways* and lose themselves in these inner dialogues. I just listen, pay very close attention, and do the best I can to carefully take follow-up field notes. Serendipitously, I had just completed a research methods course the day before my weaving education began, and I had acquired new ethnographic tools; thus I went in with brand new "participant observation/observant participation" lenses. Also, I quickly realized that when I signed myself up for my grandmother's "course," attendance and punctuality were key—even though she provided no syllabus indicating these parameters. I had to tread carefully, every day and every moment of my learning. I waited for an opportunity to present itself to propose again what I had attempted to do since that painful phone call nearly fifteen years earlier. As much time, space, and worldviews as had passed for everyone, and for those who I was and had remained connected to since I came out as transgendered, I knew shifts in perspectives had to take place. My grandmother was not excused from this critical shift. I knew she would have moments where she would be softer with me given that I pleased her with my weaving progress, or at the very least, I hoped for that. So far, she has accommodated this crucial endeavor of mine, and I could not be more relieved. At this point, I can only offer limited, albeit significant, findings from my quest to determine what *Sts'iyóye smestíyexw slhá:li* truly means. I do know that it is nothing short of a miracle. It is a miracle that she coined this title for me specifically, even though it went painfully against her colonized "homophobic" way of thinking after her eighty-plus years of living.

In the summer of 2011 I was approached by a prominent Tsleil-Waututh (Burrard First Nation) family and received a very esteemed invitation to "open the floor" for the memorial gathering of their late two-spirited son. This role involves attendance as an honored guest: to witness how a family honors their belated, and also to dance ceremonially to honor the one who has passed. In a Coast Salish Memorial gathering such as this, the teachings say that as four years have passed since the loss, the family will gather and rejoice one last time, and from there on in, they will cry for them no more. As I am a "Dancer,"[9] and a two-spirited one at that, I was asked especially because the young man who passed was also two-spirited. For this reason, I knew I wanted to make a special cedar bark cape to do justice to his beautiful memory. I knew him personally and remember well his sweet and feminine nature, and so I wanted to do justice to the beauty with which he carried himself. This occasion was a milestone not yet achieved before this moment, given there had never been a "two-spirited theme" for any event of this nature in recorded history, so I had never felt so compelled as when I was asked to undertake this important project. It was unprecedented that the family would bring his two-spiritedness to the forefront of this gathering and felt surreal for them to ask me to perform in such an important role. I needed to dance for more than just this memorial—for five hundred–plus years of two-spirited ancestors and their deleted identities. Ceremonial dances of this kind require some physical exertion. The rigorous style of dance must keep in time to a steady drumbeat. My cape is very heavy; I knew I would have to dance with added weight. Added to this was my age: I was already forty. I was concerned that I would not be able to complete my dance around the floor: as the date of the gathering drew near, I jogged daily to get my wind up. While I ran to shape up, I prayed that I would have the strength to make it around the floor and finish strong. When the time finally came, I unveiled my garment, fastened it around my neck, and could only hope that my spirit and body would not fail me. I do not recall anything beyond that point. I do not remember feeling the weight of my cape, but I do know I was flying. Before long it was over and I was back at my seat. Though the cape was heavy, it turned out that I had made myself wings. I made it around and, according to others present at the event, my feet did not touch the ground. It was a momentous occasion, and I still feel butterflies when I think about it today. I wove the cape you see me wearing in figure 1 in the summer of 2012 under my grandmother's mentorship. It took approximately two months to prepare the bark and only a few days to weave.

Although the Canadian government made a very successful attempt to erase *Sts'iyóye smestíyexw*, some of us live on to tell new stories and to re-generate an entire gender and sexuality category that has been put away for so long. I invite other self-identified *Sts'iyóye smestíyexw* to pray together, laugh together, and weave our stories into a new *their*story. This invitation, of course, includes all that represent the spectrum of difference as the acronym *LGBTQ* intends, given that not all will identify as a "twin-spirit-to-a-woman" as I do. There are many *Sts'iyóye smestíyexw* who have passed and who never experienced the emancipation of a true coming-out as those of us who are left behind now have the privilege to do.

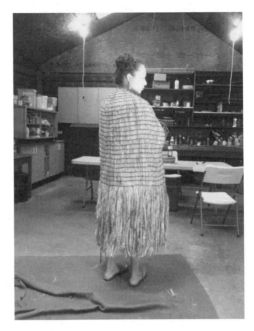

Figure 1.   The author wearing a cedar cape she wove in the summer of 2012. Photograph by Charlotte Point

My grandmother and I have come a long way since 1997. I have had to heal and spiritually strengthen myself for independence because, at that point in time, she was not able to accept my transgendered identity within her political gaze. I can now say that this has changed. *Xexa:ls* (four children of *Xa:ls*, the Creator/Transformer) have had pity on me.[10] They helped her to shape-shift her mind to one that demonstrates that transformative thinking and learning stop at no age. Now this new chapter begins, and the Coast Salish people as a whole can continue flourishing in their feasts with this new story.

Saylesh Wesley (Stó:lō/Ts'msyan) is completing her PhD in Simon Fraser University's Gender, Sexuality and Women's Studies Department. Her research aims to re-story the deleted queer and two-spirit identities of the Stó:lō people as well more broadly for all Coast Salish.

Acknowledgments

Angela Pietrobon must be acknowledged for her much-appreciated edits to this paper as well as my wonderful PhD committee supervisors Deanna Reder and Dolores van der Wey.

Notes

1. See Truth and Reconciliation Commission of Canada 2014. This website details how the federal government aims to make amends and rebuild relationships with the surviving students, whose attendance in residential schools was mandatory nationwide, as well as acknowledge the travesties to which it subjected all First Nations peoples in this legislated attempt.
2. See the working map showing the First Nations peoples of British Columbia and their territories (British Columbia Ministry of Education 2014).
3. As an example, see Wesley Thomas's (2010) categorization of Navajo gender systems.
4. Coast Salish people have adopted the idea of "standing-up" individuals to receive names, honors, or blessings at traditional longhouse gatherings.
5. She is an eighty-six-year-old hereditary "Big Woman" of the *Semá:th* (Sumas) Territory, located in the Fraser Valley along the Canadian/United States border. In other words, if we went back in time five hundred years, she would be the sovereign ruler and owner of the Fraser Valley, not unlike a queen.
6. See CBC News 2008 for more information on the history of residential schools in Canada.
7. See Aboriginal Affairs 2012 for more on elections under the Indian Act and Indian Band Election Regulations.
8. I refer to "This Side," or *third* dimension: those of us who are living in the flesh, as opposed to "The Other Side," or the Spirit world, where late Ancestors dwell, according to the Stó:lō.
9. For more information about spirit dancing and its importance, see Bergen and Kelly 2013.
10. For more information about the Stó:lō Transformer figure, sometimes referred to as "Creator," and his Divine Children (*Xa:ls* and *Xexa:ls*), see Hanson 2014.

References

Aboriginal Affairs and Northern Development Canada. 2012. "Backgrounder: Indian Act Elections." September 5. www.aadnc-aandc.gc.ca/eng/1100100016233/1100100016234.

Archibald, Jo-ann / Q'um Q'um Xiiem. 2008. *Indigenous Storywork: Educating the Heart, Mind, Body, and Spirit*. Vancouver: University of British Columbia Press.

Bergen, Rachel, and Stephanie Kelly. 2013. "Spirit Dancing: How Two UBC Students Gained Access to Report on This Secretive Aboriginal Tradition." Canadian Journalism Project, May 1. j-source.ca/article/spirit-dancing-how-two-ubc-students-gained-access-report-secretive-aboriginal-tradition.

British Columbia Ministry of Education. 2014. "First Nations Peoples of British Columbia." www.bced.gov.bc.ca/abed/map.htm (accessed March 6, 2014).

CBC News. 2008. "A History of Residential Schools in Canada: FAQs on Residential Schools and Compensation." May 16. www.cbc.ca/news/canada/a-history-of-residential-schools-in-canada-1.702280.

Driskill, Qwo-li. 2010. "Doubleweaving Two-Spirit Critiques: Building Alliances between Native and Queer Studies." In "Sexuality, Nationality, Indigeneity," ed. Daniel Heath Justice, Mark Rifkin, and Bethany Schneider. Special issue, *GLQ* 16, no. 1–2: 60–92.

Driskill, Qwo-Li, et al. 2011. Introduction to *Queer Indigenous Studies: Critical Interventions in Theory, Politics, and Literature*, ed. Qwo-Li Driskill et al., 1–28. Tucson: University of Arizona Press.

First Voices. 2013a. "About the People." Halq'eméylem Community Portal. www.firstvoices.com /en/Halqemeylem (accessed March 6, 2014).

——, 2013b. "Halq'eméylem Words." www.firstvoices.com/en/Halqemeylem/word /8315275ef45b39c6/Halqomelem (accessed March 6, 2014).

Hanson, Erin. 2014. "Oral Traditions." Indigenous Foundations, University of British Columbia. indigenousfoundations.arts.ubc.ca/home/culture/oral-traditions.html (accessed March 6, 2014).

Morgensen, Scott Lauria. 2011. *Spaces between Us: Queer Settler Colonialism and Indigenous Decolonization*. Minneapolis: University of Minnesota Press.

Rifkin, Mark. 2012. *The Erotics of Sovereignty: Queer Native Writing in the Era of Self-Determination*. Minneapolis: University of Minnesota Press.

Thomas, Wesley. 2010. "Navaho Cultural Constructions of Gender and Sexuality." Trans Bodies across the Globe, Department of Gender Studies, Indiana University Bloomington. December 17. transgenderglobe.wordpress.com/2010/12/17/navajo-cultural-constructions -of-gender-and-sexuality/.

Truth and Reconciliation Commission of Canada. 2014. "Reconciliation . . . towards a New Rela-tionship." www.trc.ca/websites/reconciliation/index.php?p=312 (accessed March 6, 2014).

For a Queer Pedagogy of Friendship

GIANCARLO CORNEJO

Abstract This hybrid essay/narrative attempts to give an account of the survival of a "queer" subject, specifically a trans child living in Lima, Peru, in the 1950s and 1960s. My theoretical claims may be simple, but the survival of this trans child was anything but simple. The essay argues that in the survival of this child, friendship played a vital role.
Keywords transgender; queer; friendship; Peru

This hybrid essay/narrative has quite modest theoretical objectives. I attempt here to give an account of the survival of a "queer" subject, specifically a trans child living in Lima, Peru, in the 1950s and 1960s. My theoretical claims may be simple, but the survival of this trans child was anything but simple. I argue that in the survival of this child, friendship played a vital role. I am interested in the capacity of friendship "to jam *whatever* looks like the inevitable" (Freeman 2010: 173).

Her name is Italo. I met her in the summer of 2007 in Lima. This narrative focuses on certain episodes of Italo's childhood. Of course, Italo's life is far richer and more complex than my short narrative. Although there has been a lot of pain in her life, it has also been filled with pleasure, love, and rebellion. Nowadays Italo combines LGBT activism and militancy, advocating for communities of people living with HIV/AIDS, with her professional life as a hair stylist and, more recently, a nursing assistant in a hospital. On more than one occasion, heteronormative norms and agents have tried to kill her, but they have failed utterly to do so. I deeply hope to give homage to this survivor.

From the beginning I was impressed by Italo's identitarian "polygamy" and her resistance to the normative expectation of gender coherency: Italo proudly proclaims to be "gay with gays, and *travesti* with *travestis*." She also describes herself as an "androgynous gay" or as an "intermediate trans." She says that she is not quite trans because she does not use makeup or dress "like a woman" and not quite gay because she has long hair and a generous bosom. She claims to be like a salamander that can camouflage in and habituate to any

TSQ: Transgender Studies Quarterly ∗ Volume 1, Number 3 ∗ August 2014
DOI 10.1215/23289252-2685633 © 2014 Duke University Press

context. At least once I have heard her characterize herself as a woman trapped in a male body. Italo is now around sixty years old. She lives with her parents and three of her siblings in a large but humble house in a working-class district of Lima.[1]

This hybrid essay/narrative is based on two interviews I conducted with Italo during 2007, both of which took place in Italo's house. Each interview lasted more than two hours. All were accompanied by a lot of laughter but also tears and silences (most of which were never silent), by my (sometimes impertinent) questions, and by her (generous) answers. My methodological options tend to place me in the position of the (scientific) ethnographer, but I have attempted just like Italo to disrupt some disciplinary categorizations. These disruptions imply contradictions I cannot disavow. On the one hand, I have avoided ultratheorizing this narrative. I did my best to counter the competitive urge to make my theories always prevail over those of Italo. Thus I have avoided quoting Italo directly as a way of making visible my intervention in this narrative. This option makes explicit that I am theorizing Italo's experiences (or some of them) against my desires not to.

Naming is a very complex political matter, and naming through gender is no exception. In this essay, I use a feminine pronoun to refer to Italo, and this to me is quite surprising, because in Spanish I refer to her using feminine and male pronouns seemingly indifferently—as most of her friends do and she herself does. This essay tends to stabilize her own practices of naming that are far more queer. But I wanted to keep the "contrast" between her first name, her bodily materiality, and her gendered position. I think that my option is especially problematic when talking about Italo's early childhood, because at that time she did not use female pronouns to refer to herself. But I nonetheless found value in this choice; it stresses Italo's transness and my belief that there is no past that lasts forever. Another difficulty related to naming is to recognize that the attempts to define Italo's identity are destined to fail. Nevertheless, I use here several names to refer to her: *travesti*, trans, homosexual, *maricón*, and queer. While the first four labels are used by Italo to talk about herself, the latter is not. My choice of the term *queer*, itself very problematic, is based on my sense that the term offers a promise of imagining different times (pasts, nows, and futures) for our bodily materialities and identities in which they can coexist together. I acknowledge that this is a risky move, because it could erase several of the other identities Italo uses, especially trans and travesti identities.

Italo herself is familiar with the complexities of naming. She chose for herself a name that is not socially considered feminine. This is important: Italo does not necessarily seek a rigid gender coherency between bodily, linguistic, and social markers. Thus to say that Italo chose her name does not do justice to the fact that her name allegorizes a space of encounter of diverse affects and memories. At birth, her parents assigned her the name Gustavo. Because Italo was very thin as a child, his extended family started to call him *Tallo* (stem). When Italo started to create bonds with gay and trans communities, she accepted from them the name Italo. Some queer people call her Itala sometimes, but Italo seems to prefer to keep this history of displacements of her own name. Maybe Italo knows that a name never condemns one to an unavoidable destiny, that names have histories that can be quite tangled, and that all history can be rewritten. The history of Italo's name holds an intimate relationship with the history of her body. It is for this reason, and because Italo has authorized me to do so, that I do not use a pseudonym to refer to her. Before continuing, I have to admit that Italo's (hi)story queerly touches me, and I have to ask you to allow yourself to be queerly touched by this (hi)story.[2]

* * *

The first years of Italo's life were full of joy. She lovingly remembers that from about three, she was a boy living with her mom and one of her brothers at the home of her godparents, a straight married couple with a luxurious house in an upper-class district in Lima. The godparents had two daughters of Italo's age with whom she played. Italo worshiped them. They would dance ballet, go swimming, and play with pretty dolls. By age five, Italo remembers that she first desired a man, a man around fifty years old, an intimate friend of her godparents, whom she saw naked in one of the bathrooms of the house. *But nothing lasts forever, especially if you are queer*, and her happiness was interrupted. This family moved to Honduras, and after their departure, Italo was forced to return to the house of her biological family in a Lima working-class district. This transition was quite painful and traumatic not only because she lost people she loved but also because how she was seen, and consequently the ways in which she saw herself, would change radically. While her brothers spoke "bad words," Italo never said bad words, and she was very effeminate. But the greatest difference was in the gaze of the people around her. Her effeminacy in this new context occupied a centrality for which she was not prepared. When she spoke with me, she recalled the pain caused by her family and their neighbors when they would tell her, oftentimes shouting: "Don't behave like that!" "Put your hands normally! Don't break your hands!" "You are not a girl!" "Walk like a man!"

Italo speaks of an affective and economic opulence that she enjoyed through her bonds with the upper-class family via the establishment of non-biological kinship relationships. Although Italo did not explicitly say so, I thought that perhaps her mother was a domestic worker in that house. While this supposition could be true, it might easily be false. By interpreting her story this way, I make sense of a bond that I (like Italo) read as exceptional in a city like Lima, in which colonial and neocolonial forms of relationships among different races and classes continue to persist. Taking this into account, perhaps the exceptionality with which Italo experienced this period can be complexified. Her godparents were loving but severe. However, in Italo's narrative it seems that their home did not hold a marked heteronormative burden. It may be that Italo was free of such heterosexist enslavement because of her young age. Or maybe it was not important (to these godparents) to impose a hegemonic masculinity to the "son" of a domestic worker, something that perhaps would not have been the case with (and for) a hypothetical biological son and heir. And there is always the possibility (a possibility that I unfairly dismissed too early) that indeed this bourgeois family valued, respected, and recognized Italo's femininity.[3]

Italo's survival demanded a lot of her imagination. Italo did her best to disidentify herself from prescribed norms over her body. For example, Italo never played soccer or with toy cars; instead, she loved playing secretly with the dolls of her sisters. Italo adored the daughters of her godparents, because with them she could explore possibilities otherwise denied her for her gender and class origin. But Italo's disidentifications had serious consequences for her: in her "new" environment she was constantly and violently punished for believing that she was not a man, that she was not *chola*, and that she was not poor.[4]

In Italo's narrative, she moves from a space of love inhabited by a small community that cared about her to a state of self-enforced solitude. In her new home, she was denied familial affection by her brother, who was an "example" of male heterosexuality and who treated her with hostility, and by her sisters, who were allowed to do the things that Italo wanted but that she could not do without punishment.

Italo was now just eight years old. One night after playing with her brothers, she was assigned the task of returning the ball they had just played with to one of her friends, a boy of her age whom everybody called *maricón* (faggot.) Italo recalls that at that time she did not know what that word meant. Her friend lived at the end of a long and modest street. On the way, Italo was approached by Jaime, a young man in his early twenties, who told her, "I want to talk to you." Italo recognized that he was drunk. She refused to talk with him because she had been forbidden by her parents to talk with drunk people; besides, his persistence frightened her. She ran to her friend's house and gave him the ball. Italo was terrified; she knew she was being observed by the man and so asked her friend to walk her home. Along the way, both children were intercepted by Jaime, who was now accompanied by a group of young men. Having no other alternative, Italo pushed her friend toward her persecutors and tried desperately to run. For a second, Italo believed she had escaped, but Jaime and his accomplices caught her. They twisted her arm and held her by the neck. Italo screamed and cried desperately, but no one responded. Though the men violently tried to force her to remain silent, before they were able to carry Italo into a dark room, another child from the neighborhood saw her, and Italo screamed with all her might, "Tell my brother!" The kid then asked these men, "What are you doing to this boy?" They pulled a knife and threatened him, and the boy, fearing for his own life, ran away. In the room, as Italo resisted and screamed, the men cut her chest with the knife, ripped off her clothes, and raped her one after another. They then succeeded in silencing her by threatening to kill her parents and siblings if she told anyone.

When I was listening to Italo, I was trying not to cry, but this ultimately was impossible. Soon Italo was crying, and it was not long before I was doing the same. Tears can be contagious! At the same time, what came to my mind was a saying in Peru that goes something like "the man who is raped is turned into a *maricón*." This assertion of "common sense" is heteronormative. But it also potentially conceals disruptive contents in order to suit hegemonic heterosexual desires. It seems that (not only) "someone" becomes a *maricón* after being raped but that that someone is raped in the first place because he is already read as a *maricón*. And this *mariconería* (faggotry) is associated with a lack of masculinity. For that reason, this heteronormative belief affects not only the victim of rape but potentially many other subjects/objects. We need only to remember that there are other children in this scene who are also violated (in different ways). There is the other kid who was called *maricón*, and we can easily suppose that most of the times it was in very violent ways. As soon as Jaime approaches Italo, she senses the unavoidable approach of danger. So she asks the other *mariconcito* if she can walk with him, and then those men persecute both. Had this other *mariconcito* been persecuted before? Did he intimately know and share Italo's fears? There is also the other kid who was menaced and who may have thought that he was in danger of a similar fate to Italo's. His question ("what are you doing to this boy?") is answered with a threat backed by a knife. Perhaps his body and his positions were not too different from those of Italo. Perhaps Italo recognized this, and that is why the fact that this kid did not try to help her hurts her even more.

This is a bloody exercise of performativity by which heterosexual masculinity is constructed as an origin and which produces sexually marked bodies, some bodies being deemed as "other" and as legitimate to violate. These offenders need to create a *maricón*, Italo, to erect and legitimize their identitarian affiliations with masculinity and to justify their (heterosexual) male homosocial desire. They need to produce abnormal subjects to "give birth" to the male normal subject unpolluted by any stain. According to Mary Douglas (1966), the limits of the body are fragile and unstable and threatened by various forms of pollution. Judith

Butler (1990) rereads Douglas's arguments to assert that the limits of the body are the limits of the socially hegemonic. Butler also argues, around Julia Kristeva's *Powers of Horror* (1982), that the boundary between the internal and the external is ambiguous especially within and through the excremental ducts. To Kristeva shit stands (as abject) for a threatening external menace, one which is also an internal menace. The successive anal penetrations of Italo that day serve to stabilize the boundaries of the bodies of her attackers. In this way Italo is literally reduced to shit.

If the rape of Italo has the effect of producing a *maricón*, it is also because it produces straight men. This production of straight men can be thought of as a declaration of identity. One that proclaims "I am a straight man" and for that demands a blood sacrifice. In this scene, only the child is a *maricón*, not the aggressors, despite the fact that the desiring subjects in question are these twenty-something-year-old men who assault her. These men showcase a complex and anxious desire for bodily pleasure, for bodily limits, and for a fixed identity as "straight." This is a mechanism of power/knowledge that pathologizes sexualities and gender performances alternative to an imagined heterosexuality, but at the same time it denies and attempts to vacate its own inalienable queerness. These male rapists represented themselves as a collective male body (one body made of the mesh of many men and their intimacies) that violates an abject(ed) body. They succeeded in establishing murderous boundaries between heterosexuality and queerness but only momentarily. Boundaries, especially if they are sexual or gendered, are always precarious. And perhaps because they are precarious, these demands for pure and clear-cut identities often end with violent—paranoid, homo-transphobic,[5] and heteronormative—outbursts.

After having been violated, stabbed, and abandoned by the men, Italo arrived at her house, climbing through a window so no one could see her. She went directly to the bathroom, and in the mirror she saw her body covered in blood. Sobbing and moaning silently she took off her torn and bloodied clothes as quickly as possible and threw them away. That night she tried desperately to sleep, but she could not. On the following nights she had harrowing dreams of her rapists overrunning her bedroom, returning to rape her again and again. She said nothing to her parents, and they did not act as if they had noticed anything. Italo could not tell her parents of this horrible aggression. The threats of which she was a victim could not be countered. Yet to reduce Italo to a condition of radical subordination even in that moment of extreme violence fails to do justice to her. After being so violently made shit, she needed to take off her bloodstained clothes and dispose of them. What might have Italo intended by this? Rocío Silva Santisteban, writing in the context of political violence in Peru in the decades of the 1980s and 1990s about the successive rapes by male soldiers against Giorgina Gamboa, calls our attention to the fact that the first thing Giorgina did after the brutal occupation of her body was to leave behind her bloody clothes. Of this Silva Santisteban says: "The only way to survive this deadly wound is conceiving of a possibility for symbolic resurrection, of being able to join life in a 'fair' and 'healthy' manner" (2008: 85). Although Italo's rape was a deadly psychic wound, the act of throwing out her bloodstained clothes could be read as a silent cry of life, of not allowing herself to be obliterated by violence. To take off her blood-stained clothes is to struggle for life even when one has been radically expelled from the notion of "human life."

Some time later, Italo told two of her school friends what had happened. This turned out to be a big mistake: they spread the news throughout their school and never spoke to her again. The violence committed against Italo was not perceived as such. Ultimately, what had happened not only made her supposed impurity more visible but also threatened to contaminate those around her.

But there was also someone who was not afraid of her. Soon thereafter the *mariconcito* who owned the ball entered her class. Italo immediately realized that despite being the same biological age, her friend was much more mature. Italo told him everything. Her friend looked at her straight in the eyes and said with conviction: "Don't worry because if they touch or grab you again just tell them that they have raped you, and that you are going to talk with the police, and that the police will go after them to kill them." Italo memorized those words and she repeated them when one of her assailants intercepted her with the intention of raping her again. This strategy worked; the rapists never attempted to touch her again. Her aggressors may have thought that identity declarations and their dominion over Italo would last forever. *But nothing lasts forever, especially if you are a mariconcito.*

Italo learned a hard lesson and an enabling one: shit is sticky. She learned this from her queer friend. Her friend already possessed a vivid knowledge about homo-transphobic violence from his own experience and about ways of negotiating and dealing with it. He taught Italo some of this knowledge; this would open previously unimaginable possibilities for her. And importantly, Italo later taught some of those lessons to many other subjects and communities. Another important lesson that Italo learned from this queer kid was the meaning of *maricón*. In fact, Italo learned and participated in the collective creation of new meanings of *maricón*, as we will see.

Some lessons are very difficult to learn (and to teach), and others are not. While Italo was very open to the lessons of her queer friend, her aggressors were not. Although they did not rape Italo again, they did harass her. These young men where friends of her older brother, and they constantly warned him that Italo was a *maricón*. As a result, her brother became her worst enemy. He never missed an opportunity to beat and torture her. He inflicted even more violence on her body every time he found her with her queer friend. And every time Italo complained about the daily abuse to her parents, they would say, "If I have a *maricón* son I'll kill him." What becomes of a person whose death is considered a necessity for social harmony? The worst part is that her life was threatened by people she deeply loved. So when Italo characterizes that moment of her life as a living hell, she does not exaggerate. At this point in her narrative, it was very difficult for me to ask questions, because I was very afraid of hurting Italo or, even worse, of being complicit in any way with her aggressors. I remember thinking that it felt impossible to ask her if she did not suspect that the success of the threats of her parents, expressed in their implicit approval of her silence, were not based on at least a partial knowledge of her queerness. And I found this thought so disturbing, because it implies that the threats of death launched by her own parents were not that different from those of her rapists.

Italo usually remained silent when she was hit. *But nothing lasts forever, especially if you are a little travesti.* And one day when her brother hit her as usual for secretly maintaining her friendship with her queer friend, Italo could not take it any more and started throwing dishes at him, wanting to hurt him. The sound of the dishes crashing on the floor and against the walls was accompanied by her enraged screams. Her screams repeated just one sentence: "Yes, I am a *maricón*! Yes, I am a *maricón*! Yes, I am a *maricón*!" Her brother called her *maricón*, as did her neighbors, her classmates, her rapists, and her parents. *Maricón* to Italo (like to many other queer subjects) sounded like a chorus, because, as Butler (1990) argues, this insult bases its power in its violent historicity. When someone interpellated her as *maricón*, he or she did it for all the people that have yelled *maricón* at her before, and for all those who will do it after. Italo desperately repeated the word *maricón*, accepting that label: "Yes, I am a *maricón*!" Not only did her repetitions attempt to respond to each and every one of the homo-transphobic interpellations that she had received, but her repetitions are an invocation for other realities, possibilities, and futures.

Although Italo hated living in her working-class district, she changed her mind when she met a colorful group of queer and trans kids and teenagers on its streets. Most of them were between ten and thirteen years old. They called themselves "*Las trece conchitas*," which literally translates to "the thirteen little shells." "Concha" also refers to what is commonly understood as female genitalia. The *conchitas* used that name despite the fact that there were more than thirteen of them. Italo remembers that they would be pursued by men in their cars. Some of the men were probably motivated by homo-transphobia, but others by lust. And in many cases, *las conchitas* shared this lust too. What Italo most enjoyed of her friendship with *las conchitas* was their daily sharing of stories and experiences. These friendships opened previously unavailable social, affective, and sexual possibilities to her. *Las conchitas* gave her the gift of enduring the hell that her life had become after the rape. For her, these queer friendships were the difference between dying and clinging to life.

Michel Foucault (1996) attributes to queer friendships a radical creativity that does not condemn them to a simple parodic repetition of social norms. For Foucault, queer friendships can create new ways of life.[6] When I think of *las trece conchitas* I cannot avoid thinking about the conjunctions of pleasures and bodies that Foucault calls for at the end of the first volume of *The History of Sexuality* (1978). Although it is not clear to me whether Italo had sex with any of *las conchitas*, their friendships produced important changes in her own sex life. After the rape, Italo had thought for a time that sex and misery go always together. With her queer friends, she (re)discovered that sex, pain, and violence were not always linked. In Italo's narrative, only after meeting *las conchitas* was she able to explore eroticism with men of varying ages—some were children like her, others were adults several decades older. Here friendship has a reparative role: friendship can create affective spaces that heal wounds inflicted by social norms. If for Italo her body was a site of social abjection, after meeting *las conchitas* it also became a space that defied biological frontiers and allowed her to dream about, and begin acting on, desires for embodiment and life that were socially categorized as unrealistic or impossible. *Las conchitas* taught her how to roll her t-shirts and to put them in her chest to simulate breasts. Indeed, these queer friendships created pleasures and bodies for which heterosexual norms did not have scripts, or at least not good scripts.

To emphasize the reparative effects of friendship here does not preclude the existence of disputes and quarrels within these communities. It was not uncommon for *las conchitas* to fight over a guy or about the degrees of visibility of their sexual difference. Moreover, *las trece conchitas* could get Italo into trouble. In one of her physical education classes, three *conchitas* approached her in front of her teacher, loudly calling her "Fanni!" Italo tried ignoring them, but her teacher understood the situation and could not stop laughing. Italo started laughing, too. The laughter did not prevent Italo from seeking out these particular *conchitas* that night and hitting them so that they would never "out" her without her permission. Italo had become one of *las conchitas*; in this way she earned the right to fight with her friends.

Neither did the *conchitas'* friendship stop the homo-transphobia that confronted Italo daily in her school. What the friendship did was to put an end to her tolerance of homophobic violence. When Italo was in seventh grade, there was a boy who always yelled at her, *maricón*! and once spiked a pen in her arm. In response, Italo raised her fist and broke his nose. As a form of punishment, she was sent to the principal's office. In eighth grade, another boy shouted *maricón*! at

Italo, and when she confronted him, he slapped her in the face. One more time Italo raised her fist and broke his nose. Italo was again sent to the principal's office. Since Italo had now acquired a reputation for breaking straight boys' noses, on the first day of school the following year the principal warned her: "One more nose and I will expel you from the school." A few days later, during a class break, some *conchitas* came to visit her. They had also came to admire the bodies of the most handsome and athletic of the guys of Italo's class, hoping to see them playing soccer. One of the boys noticed the presence of *las conchitas* and asked Italo, "Are you a *maricón*?" Italo proudly answered "Yes. Is there a problem?" The boy said "yes" and slapped her face. Her friends rushed to constrain Italo, who may have wanted to break another straight nose. They reminded her that she was threatened with expulsion, but this led her to stop going to classes and to hide that from her parents.

The queer friendships of *las conchitas* meant that Italo no longer experienced pain in solitude. During the period when she did not attend school, she met a policewoman who seemed very kind. Perhaps the kindness of this woman resides in the fact that unlike other adults, she actually listened to Italo. Convinced by her demeanor, Italo told her all that had happened. At that moment Italo felt that a huge weight had been removed from her, but some days later she would realize that she had made a mistake. The police officer told everything she had heard to the principal of her school. Italo had thought that she would bear the pain of her secrets alone or with the friendly support of her queer friends. *But nothing lasts forever, especially if you are a conchita*. When her mother heard the rumor that her son was skipping classes, she checked Italo's notebooks and found that nothing had been written in them in the last few weeks. Early the next day they went together to the school, Italo to her classes and her mother to the principal's office. Within a few minutes, some girls warned Italo that her mother had fainted. Italo ran desperately to the office. When she arrived, she saw her mother crying and everyone else staring at her. Her mother then looked at her and asked her how it had all happened. At that moment Italo wanted nothing more than to escape, but the principal would not allow that, instead calling in all of Italo's teachers. They supported her and testified as to her good behavior and outstanding academic performance. And although Italo asked the principal to not do so, she expelled the boy who had kept his nose intact after having bullied Italo.

After this, quite frightened, Italo went to her house, and to her surprise found no one there. She grabbed a backpack and she put everything she could into it, including her and her sister's clothes, her birth certificate, and some savings. She hid everything on the roof. Her plan was, the next time that her parents hit her, "I grab my stuff and go." All the broken noses perhaps presaged things to come. Her silence would be broken. Yet the disclosure also (re)opened some of her psychic wounds and threatened her body with extermination. As she retells it, at that moment the only possibility she could imagine after being outed in that way was being kicked out of her home. The sexual assault had confirmed her subordinate position in front of her family and did not allow them (or her) ambivalence or hesitation. Her parents would assume, she thought, following heteronormative common sense, that after being raped she was now a *maricón*, someone to be despised by them. In this way the constant threats that she suffered as a child would come true. Her terror from this was more than justified, yet her planning to escape showed that she continued to cling to life and that her persistent desire to live became possible only after meeting her small community of gay and trans kids. Italo could imagine taking flight from her house and community because she had already been embraced by *las conchitas*. They had taught her other possibilities of living.

When Italo's parents returned that afternoon, they did not give her the beating she had imagined. Instead, they asked her to accompany them to the police station. There, the policemen listened to the parents denouncing the rape of their son. But these officers were more interested in gazing at Italo's body than in listening to her parents. She wanted to die out of shame. Some police officers took her alone to a back room to supposedly continue with the questioning. But what they did instead was to show her their genitals and then masturbate. They said things like, "Look at my penis. Do you like it? Why don't you suck it?" After ejaculating, they took Italo back to her parents, advising them to take Italo for medical examinations to corroborate the rape. To be examined made no sense, since her rape had been four years earlier and she had had sex with many other men since. Italo asked (almost begged) her parents to drop the matter and to return to their house.

This scene in which the young Italo is confronted by the police alludes to her unreality. Italo was not intelligible, her life was not conceivable as a possibility of being. The police took Italo for questioning, but from the beginning they did not expect any response from her other than sucking their cocks. They compulsively repeated the homophobic fantasy that believes all *maricones* want and deserve to be raped. Although inevitably Italo had to live this (state) sexual violence as a reenactment of the rape she had suffered at the age of eight, and even if her silence was also reactualized, her aggressors were unable to inflict the same damage on her. This is an important difference: Italo now had a community of friends, and with them she had changed. With *las conchitas* she created a "now" that was very different from the time of her rape.

When the three returned to their house, her father tearfully told Italo something that she would have never imagined. "Son, I wish you were a man, but if you've decided to be what you want to be, I support you. I am very sorry that you haven't told me what happened to you, but from now on no matter what I'll be by your side. And none of your brothers or any motherfucker is going to lay a finger on you." These words marked an important event in her life. For the first time ever, her father recognized the queer life of his son as a possibility, and he had promised to help her to live that possibility. He did so, at least in their home. For the first time, her father saw her not simply as the projections of his heterosexist desires. Although this parental statement of support and recognition is very important, so is Italo's community of gay and trans kids. It is very common to hear (especially, but not exclusively, in the most reactionary sectors) that LGBTQI communities can only copy (previously and unproblematically defined) heterosexual kinship models. My interest lies in showing that if someone copies or imitates in this story, it is the (presumably) heterosexual father of Italo. Italo's father learned from *las trece conchitas* to imagine the life of his child in ways other than those prescribed by hegemonic norms. He learned from them the beauty of friendship. This straight-identified man began to value life with forms, textures, colors, and flavors other than those of a dichotomous heteronormativity. The *trece conchitas* taught him that he needed to distance himself from a culture that was trying to kill his son.

After this episode, Italo's parents became closer to Italo and to her gay and trans friends. They welcomed some of the *conchitas*, letting them live in their house after their parents had thrown them out on the street. They talked with the families of these queer children and encouraged them to question their own homophobia. Italo cannot contain her pride in revealing that after these conversations, several of her queer friends were welcomed back into their own homes. Here we can see an act of reciprocity from Italo and her parents to these queer children. If Italo at various times was sustained by them, she also helped to sustain them. Italo learned from *las conchitas* that friendship is tested precisely in the hardest times. Italo's parents had learned from *las conchitas* how to be friends of their queer son. And now they wanted other families to learn how to be friends of their queer children. The queer pedagogy of friendship working here has only one certainty: *nothing lasts forever, especially if you love queers.*

* * *

Italo taught me that friendship is something one needs to learn. Here I would like to translate this reflection into the ethnographic encounter. As the families of these queer children have learned the value of friendship from them, perhaps ethnographers can also learn the same lesson. Perhaps thinking about the encounter between the ethnographer and the informant in terms of friendship can counter the urge to make the ethnographer's theories always prevail over those of the informant—an urge intimately bound to an unacknowledged desire of the ethnographer to make his or her theories look far more intelligent than the informant(s).[7] This kind of paranoid thinking is of no help when we talk about friendship.

Of course, to think of this relationship as friendship also carries many risks. As Don Kulick (2006) asserts, an unproblematic ethnographer's identification with the dispossessed can make invisible his or her masochistic investment in enjoying the privileges of power structures and can erase the subjectivities of many marginalized communities. Perhaps we should return to Foucault in thinking about friendship as a project, as an unfinished project that always takes effort. Following Foucault, we should remember that friendship cannot transcend power relationships. One of the most obvious asymmetries in the ethnographic encounter has to do with the power of narrating. In this piece, we read my version of Italo's childhood, not her version of her childhood or her version of my childhood.

I admit that I would like to think of Italo as a friend, but I cannot make that statement, mainly because she is a person I do not see often and because of the many privileges that I enjoy that separate us. What is certain is that Italo offered me that which is basic in any friendship: vulnerability. Italo did not offer me her vulnerability as a spectacle but as an invitation to reciprocate. As Ruth Behar (1996) argues, ethnographies are often a business of making other people vulnerable. But queer friendships require the recognition of mutual vulnerability. In my case, I had previously attempted the impossible task of reciprocating Italo's generosity in writing about my own vulnerability, that of my own queer childhood (Cornejo 2011). And this is an impossible task because, like Kath Weston, I must acknowledge that "reflexivity is not, in itself, an equalizing act" (1998: 201). Recently, I met Italo to share that autoethnographic essay with her and also to show her a draft of the essay that you are now reading. She generously gave me some comments and suggestions. She shared with me the lyrics of a song (a sort of hymn) that the *conchitas* sang to themselves:

Somos somos unas putas   (We are we are whores)

unas prostitutas del   (prostitutes of)

mismo burdel burdel burdel.   (the same brothel brothel brothel.)

At this moment I do not want to interpret the lyrics of this song, I just want to stress that Italo always has more stories to tell—but also some complaints. She was very insistent, after reading the piece, on the fact that she did not blame her parents for her rape or what happened after. In some ways I think she reads my narrative as judging her parents in an unfair way. And she might be right. It also became obvious that we were now in different places than we had been a few years ago. Italo did not allow me to freeze her in the role of a (or my?) "queer heroine." While I do not know if Italo thinks of me as a friend, she told me that we both have something in common: the desire to resist. Perhaps Italo and I are not yet friends, but we always can become friends.

Giancarlo Cornejo is a PhD candidate in the Department of Rhetoric at the University of California, Berkeley. He is very interested in the question of queer survival, in exploring what makes a queer- or trans-habitable life. He tends to work with a style of writing very invested in narrative or storytelling. His essays have appeared in international journals such as *Cadernos Pagu*, *Estudos feministas*, *Íconos*, and *Nómadas*.

Acknowledgments

I want to thank and to dedicate this paper to Italo. In it, I tried my best to reciprocate her generosity. The first incarnation of this project was as a chapter of my BA dissertation in sociology at the Pontifical Catholic University of Peru in 2008. Gonzalo Portocarrero has been a brilliant interlocutor since then. During those days, Patricia Ruiz Bravo and Juan Carlos Callirgos also made invaluable contributions to this project. More recently and in the United States, I deeply thank Juana María Rodríguez, Salvador Vidal-Ortiz, Mark McHarry, and Michelle Potts for their committed and generous readings.

Notes

1. Throughout the years, Lima has changed a lot. In the 1950s and 1960s, the decades in which the events that this narrative recalls took place, Peru and its capital city, Lima, were experiencing the consequences of some important changes. In 1956, women (well, nonindigenous Spanish-speaking women, to be more accurate) voted for the first time. These decades also witnessed intense migration, migration mainly from the Peruvian highlands to Lima. During these years it became clear that the "face" of Lima and of its inhabitants was experiencing a metamorphosis. These dynamics reflected but also enabled important political work of racial and sexual decolonization. But these movements also awakened many racial and sexual panics. These panics were partially responsible for the exclusion of many people in Peru. It was in 1968 that these political reconfigurations reached the *Palacio de gobierno* with the left-wing general Juan Velasco as president of Peru. It is a paradox of Peruvian history that the most progressive Peruvian president of the twentieth century was a military officer who ascended to power through a coup d'état. Velasco, with the advice of many left-wing militants and professionals, attempted an agrarian reform that was a direct critique of the continuity of colonialism in the Peruvian republic and of the expropriation of the most basic rights of *indios* and indigenous communities. But of course changes do not come in a single direction. In 1975, the Peruvian oligarchy supported a right-wing military officer, Francisco Morales Bermúdez, to lead a counterrevolution. Peruvian oligarchy since then has created many narratives that construct Velasco's government as a monstrous

dictatorship and as the biggest enemy of democracy. These elites fought with other narratives that reclaimed or reappropriated the most radical aspects of those years. Actually, the Peruvian right wing has not only produced narratives to counter more progressive ones but had attempted, and attempts, to eradicate and erase even the fact that these promises for a more just and democratic country did exist once in Peru and still exist today. I think that this is similar to the memories of many queer childhoods. It is as if (some) heteronormative norms not only work to repress any queerness in childhood but also act systematically as if queerness never existed in the first place. The 1980s and 1990s were marked by a civil war in Peru between two political parties—*Sendero Luminoso* and *Movimiento Revolucionario Túpac Amaru*—and the Peruvian state. This war used the bodies of indigenous peasants as a battlefield. In 2003, the *Comisión de la Verdad y Reconciliación* published its conclusions. It estimated that the number of deaths caused by this war was 69,280. Most of the victims were male indigenous peasants. That commission recollected most of its information though oral testimonies. Some of these testimonies were screened through TV. Because of this, I wonder if Italo's narrative of her queer childhood, a narrative that she shared with me in 2007, is related to the telling of all these narratives about previously unspeakable violences.

2. Carolyn Dinshaw (1999) conceptualizes historical encounters as queer touches. This turn to a painful past or history has an important place in queer studies. See Love 2007.

3. Whatever the case, we cannot make an ahistorical generalization about the upper classes of Lima from Italo's experiences with this particular upper-class family. Likewise, we cannot think of upper classes in Lima as intrinsically less homophobic than their middle- and working-class counterparts. For instance, Patricia Ruiz Bravo (2001) argues that homophobia plays a key role in the constitution of contemporary upper-class masculinities in Lima. In the same way, and for similar reasons, we cannot make a generalization about the working classes in Lima. What I do hope is to contribute to demystify the exoticist perception that depicts "Latin American working classes" as intrinsically more permissive or even tolerant of sexual and gender dissidents, especially trans people. Those kinds of statements, unfortunately common even in Peruvian LGBTQ activism and scholarship, tend to deny the structural difficulties and challenges that Peruvian queer working-class subjects, and especially trans working-class people, face on a daily basis.

4. *Cholo* (the masculine noun) and *chola* (the feminine one) are complex racial markers in the Peruvian political and cultural landscape. They tend to stress an ambivalent tension about and a desire for miscegenation between white colonizers and indigenous native populations. And just like "queer," it is also a name intimately associated with pain and shame, but like "queer," it has been reclaimed and reappropriated.

5. *Homo-transphobia* is a term that I use to reference the kind of queerphobia targeting mainly trans people. I use it to stress the continuities that do not exclude tensions between homophobia and transphobia and consequently between homosexual and trans identities (see Cornejo 2013).

6. It is not a secret that Foucault's insights on friendships are based mainly on adult gay males in the West. What is surprising is that the most intelligent and recent readings of these Foucauldian views are still centered on white first-world gay male subjectivities and communities. A notable exception is Jafari Allen (2011).

7. Viviane Namaste (2000) rightly criticizes the functional and hierarchical relationships between queer theorists and their idealized trans subjects/objects. She also argues the importance of exploring the conditions of survival and erasure of trans people.

References

Allen, Jafari. 2011. *¡Venceremos? The Erotics of Black Self-Making in Cuba*. Durham, NC: Duke University Press.

Behar, Ruth. 1996. *The Vulnerable Observer: Anthropology That Breaks Your Heart*. Boston: Beacon.

Butler, Judith. 1990. *Gender Trouble: Feminism and the Subversion of Identity*. New York: Routledge.

Cornejo, Giancarlo. 2011. "La guerra declarada contra el niño afeminado: Una autoetnografía queer." *Íconos: Revista de ciencias sociales*, no. 39: 79–95.

———. 2013. "Fronteras que matan: Autoritarismos y homo-transfobias." In *Sombras coloniales y globalización en el Perú de hoy*, ed. Gonzalo Portocarrero, 227–37. Lima: Red para el Desarrollo de las Ciencias Sociales en el Perú.

Dinshaw, Carolyn. 1999. *Getting Medieval: Sexualities and Communities, Pre- and Postmodern*. Durham, NC: Duke University Press.

Douglas, Mary. 1966. *Purity and Danger: An Analysis of Concepts of Pollution and Taboo*. London: Routledge and Kegan Paul.

Foucault, Michel. 1978. *An Introduction*. Vol. 1 of *The History of Sexuality*. Translated by Robert Hurley. New York: Vintage.

———. 1996. "Friendship as a Way of Life." In *Foucault Live: Collected interviews, 1961–1984*, ed. Sylvère Lotringer, 308–12. New York: Semiotext(e).

Freeman, Elizabeth. 2010. *Time Binds: Queer Temporalities, Queer Histories*. Durham, NC: Duke University Press.

Kristeva, Julia. 1982. *Powers of Horror: An Essay on Abjection*. New York: Columbia University Press.

Kulick, Don. 2006. "Theory in Furs: Masochist Anthropology." *Current Anthropology* 47, no. 6: 933–52.

Love, Heather. 2007. *Feeling Backward: Loss and the Politics of Queer History*. Cambridge, MA: Harvard University Press.

Namaste, Viviane. 2000. *Invisible Lives: The Erasure of Transsexual and Transgendered People*. Chicago: University of Chicago Press.

Ruiz Bravo, Patricia. 2001. *Sub-versiones masculinas: Imágenes del varón en la narrativa joven*. Lima: Centro de la Mujer Peruana Flora Tristan.

Silva Santisteban, Rocío. 2008. *El factor asco: Basurización simbólica y discursos autoritarios en el Perú contemporáneo*. Lima: Red para el Desarrollo de las Ciencias Sociales en el Perú.

Weston, Kath. 1998. *Long Slow Burn: Sexuality and Social Science*. New York: Routledge.

Asexual Inverts and Sexual Perverts

Locating the Sarimbavy *of Madagascar within Fin-de-Siècle Sexological Theories*

SETH PALMER

Abstract At the turn of the twentieth century, a series of troublesome encounters unfolded between several French colonial medical doctors and gender-variant, male-bodied persons (*sarimbavy* in Malagasy). Medico-ethnographic texts were published in academic journals in the French metropole based upon these doctor-*sarimbavy* interactions. This article reveals how *sarimbavy* were situated within the biopolitics of colonial penal, labor, and medical infrastructures in Madagascar. Additionally, by following the bibliographic trail of the *sarimbavy* figure in documents published in England and the United States, this article exposes how initial encounters in the colony were entextualized and deployed as evidence for sexological arguments in Europe and North America. Throughout, *sarimbavy* were read variously as asexual and sexual, as externally perverted and internally inverted, as artistic, degenerate, and ill. The ways in which the spectral figure of the *sarimbavy* moved across multiple empires highlights the colonial impulse at the heart of the Euro-American endeavor to further sexological theory.

Keywords transgender; sarimbavy; madagascar; colonialism; medicine; sexology

> What are, in reality, these Malagasy *sharimbavy*? Pederasts, prostitutes, or sexual
> inverts? I believe that they are neither one nor the other.
> —Émile Laurent, "Les Sharimbavy de Madagascar"

D r. Émile Laurent's attempt to categorize the *sharimbavy* who appeared before him in 1911 was ultimately a futile one. Laurent, a French colonial doctor stationed on the island of Madagascar, acknowledged that any single classification within preexisting European sexological frameworks—including pederasts, prostitutes, and sexual inverts—was unable to encompass *sharimbavy* identity. This was, as Ann Laura Stoler (2009) has argued, reflective of the epistemological anxiety existent in the colonial construction of ontological categories. Throughout Madagascar, *sarimbavy* proved to be perplexing native specimens for

French explorers and colonial medical doctors, whose urge to make sense of their difference was but one manifestation of the broader imperial urge to order the biodiversity of the colony within the context of emerging evolutionary thought. Concomitant with these encounters in the Indian Ocean was the rapid urbanization of Western Europe and North America, which led to a growing preoccupation with societal well-being and the development of new criminological approaches to governing deviant behavior. Thus, ultimately, Laurent's inquiry about *sarimbavy* was not relegated to Madagascar; colonial doctors used *sarimbavy* to engage in sexological and criminological debates flourishing in the French metropole as well.[1] Through the publication of articles in medical and criminological journals in Paris, these medico-ethnographic narratives were reinterpreted by European medical experts and deployed as citational evidence in sexological theories of "inversion" during the fin-de-siècle. By following *sarimbavy* "along the grain" (Stoler 2009) of global sexological discourses at the turn of the twentieth century, I take up the call by Ann Laura Stoler and Frederick Cooper to engage in historical research that examines how colonial discourses traveled along and across empires (1997: 13). Surely, it was through these sorts of border crossings that the discipline of sexology was forged. As I will show, the desire to control *sarimbavy* in sexological and criminological texts mirrored the desired control of the colony, the colonial subject, and the sexual invert everywhere. The study of *sarimbavy*-ism, whether humanistic or scientific, criminological, anthropological, sexological, or eugenic, became a conceptual tool from which to develop theory and promote governmental regulation (or deregulation) of gendered/sexualized difference in the Indian Ocean, Europe, and North America. By invoking the figure of the *sarimbavy*, as Lisa Lowe has done with the "Chinese coolie" (2006) and Roderick A. Ferguson with the "black drag-queen prostitute" (2004), I illustrate how its spectral quality has traveled transnationally and been used by a variety of actors to further their own ideological positions. The ephemeral images of *sarimbavy* in two French colonial medical articles resonate with much of the scholarship within queer historiography concerning the theoretical potentiality of a haunted archive.[2] This literature often conjures, however, a troublingly universalized notion of the "ghost" (Eng 2010: 166–98; Freccero 2006; Muñoz 2009: 33–48). Working from a queer, postcolonial perspective, Anjali Arondekar (2005, 2009) challenges, in Naisargi N. Dave's words, "the feminist and queer scholarly belief that sexuality must be 'recovered' from its states of loss and deliberate obfuscation" (2011: 15). Other queer archival projects, such as Heather Love's *Feeling Backwards* (2007), have analogously perturbed the desire of historical researchers to superficially uncover, discover, and ultimately claim the very object of their anachronistic admiration. This essay draws from this rigorous scholarship by reflexively acknowledging the troubling, affective responses of a haunted researcher. Simultaneously, by reading the *sarimbavy* character "along the grain" of global sexological discourses at the turn of the twentieth century, this essay illustrates how colonial infrastructures in Madagascar were centrally organized by race, sex, gender, and sexuality.

Literally translated, *sarimbavy* is the "image of a woman," although it refers to a distinct Malagasy sexed/gendered/sexualized category of personhood. From a Western, anthropological perspective, it could be translated to gender-variant and/or same-sex-desiring male-bodied persons. The orthographic diversity represented in the words *sarimbavy*, *sharimbavy*, *sekatses*, *sekatra*, *saikatra*, and *tsecats* illustrates the ongoing colonial project of alphabetizing Malagasy into Latin script.[3] References to gender-variant, male-bodied persons appeared as early as the seventeenth century in Etienne de Flacourt's *Histoire de la Grande Isle Madagascar*. According to Flacourt, *tsecats* stated that they had always lived as women and that they "serve God by living as such. They hate women and do not want to frequent [*hanter*] them" ([1661] 1995: 172). Interestingly, while the French word *hanter* in this context best translates to the verb "to frequent," it can also mean "to haunt."

Several French colonial doctors depicted *sarimbavy* in articles published in academic journals between 1899 and 1911. In these accounts, *sarimbavy* were situated within, and called into question, fin-de-siècle sexological theories by medical doctors who felt compelled to determine the etiology of *sarimbavy* difference. Their articles clearly portray the ways in which late nineteenth-century sexological theory, and the very notion of "homosexuality" itself, developed in tandem with the project of global imperialism (Aldrich 2001; Bleys 1995). As Rudi C. Bleys argues, at this time "the discursive exchange between ethnological description and sexological theory intensified alongside the increasing impact of science upon the regulation of sexuality both within Europe and in its colonies overseas" (1995: 146). As these medico-ethnographic texts were increasingly entextualized—removed from their original ethnographic context—they were used to both validate *and* invalidate theories surrounding "inverts," "perverts," "degenerates," "Uranists," "homosexuals," and "intermediate types." Writings by Dr. Antoine Lasnet (1899), Dr. Rencurel (1900), Dr. Edmond Jourdan (1903), and Dr. Laurent (1911) cemented the *sarimbavy*'s place within the Euro-American imagination.[4] A photograph is included in two of these accounts, one in the article by Jourdan (1903: 811) and the other in Laurent's (1911: 243). Laurent's photograph represents a group of five *sarimbavy* wrapped in white *lamba* (fabric) standing in front of a brick wall. The anthropometric photograph included in Jourdan's article exhibits a *sarimbavy* named Rabary from both a frontal and side perspective. Rabary stands erect in a white, tailored dress. These photographs, which are not included in this article, represent both the semiotic and literal, embodied violence that Euro-American sexology often enacted upon gender-variant persons. However, as Love (2007: 1) argues, it can be productive to embrace, and not simply turn away from, such "painful" texts and images. Love invites us to "risk the turn backward, even if it means opening ourselves to social and psychic realities we would rather forget" (29). In so doing, we may find that the violence of the past provides insight into "the damage that we live with in the present" (29). Additionally, to assume to know precisely what the affective impacts such photographs had on the lived experiences of these or contemporary *sarimbavy* is to fall prey to the kind of anachronistic methodology that I explicitly critique.

And yet, the impulsive desire to read from one's cultural and temporal position is perhaps inevitable. I could not help but find the white fabric in both images, while typical of the historical time period, to be eerily reminiscent of my own Eurocentric, present-day notion of a ghost. Tellingly, the images of these *sarimbavy* have haunted me throughout this research project and have led to my own epistemological *mal d'archive* of sorts (Derrida 1998). By following the entextualized spirits of *sarimbavy* along the grain of transnational sexological discourse, I too have become obsessed, possessed even, by their haunting gazes; they stare back at the camera, thus compelling the viewer to recognize their own complicity in the disturbing process of objectification.

Population and Productivity in the Pronatalist Colony

The section that follows charts the ways in which the desires of colonial apparatuses in Madagascar intersected in the lives of gender-variant and sexually nonconforming Malagasy persons.

As Janice Boddy has succinctly remarked, at its most fundamental level, human colonization "was and is an inherently corporeal enterprise" (2011: 119). Indeed, the need for a local labor force was explicitly corporeal. Early on, the French colonial administration instituted a corvée system to realize the construction of public works, drawing from the precolonial Merina kingdom's concept of *fanompoana* (Campbell 1988; Cole and Middleton 2001: 29–30). This system, forged through a decree issued on October, 21, 1896, by Governor-General Joseph Gallieni, ordered every Malagasy man between sixteen and sixty years of age to work for at least fifty days annually (Gallieni 1908: 63–64). Labor was, as in all colonial political economies, a key concern for the French administration. Scholarship on colonial labor history in Madagascar (Campbell 2003; Feeley-Harnik 1991; Sodikoff 2005) has since elaborated upon Virginia Thompson and Richard Adloff's (1965: 449) assertion that "before World War II, Madagascar was one of the French colonies having the largest number of labor laws." This legislation was directly tied to a concern for "underpopulation," a common source of anxiety within the French and British Empires more generally (Cooper 1996: 410) but especially in Madagascar (Campbell 2003: 86–90). Léonce Jacquier (cited in Feeley-Harnik 1984: 5) wrote a thesis on Malagasy colonial labor law in 1904. In it, he argued that Madagascar was one of several "colonies of exploitation," which was too harsh to develop as an intensive settler colony, thus requiring a large, native labor pool (Jacquier 1904: 6). As Jacquier explained, the population of Madagascar was estimated at four and a half million in 1896. By 1900 the estimate had dropped to three million, and by 1904 it was reestimated to be only two and a half million (28). These demographic findings must have been devastating to the colonial regime, one that was founded upon exploitative labor.

Interactions between French colonial doctors and *sarimbavy* were thus inevitably colored by such concerns, but they were also influenced by the pronatalist movement in mainland France. The goals of the movement collided with the practice of medicine and the expansion of colonialism: "Pronatalists attributed depopulation to the disappearance of 'natural' distinctions between the sexes, asserted that society was becoming increasingly feminized, and questioned the virility of French men" (Cook Andersen 2010: 418). Fear of gender transgression was linked, of course, to the changing societal expectations of French women (Roberts 2002). But as Cook Andersen illustrates, these concerns could be applied to male-bodied persons as well: "Pronatalists criticized the célibataire [single man], as well as men who seemed to lack essential masculine qualities. This latter category included men who aspired to little more than the sedentary life of a bureaucrat, were homosexual, or were in poor physical condition" (2010: 424). The French Empire in Madagascar relied upon male labor (and, implicitly, female domestic and reproductive labor) to develop the colony (Sharp 2003). As has been described by other scholars, some men were excluded from having to participate in the corvée, including men "who were infirm or who already worked on private plantations, for the military, or elsewhere in the colonial service" (Sharp 2002: 197). However, researchers have largely ignored the compulsory hetero-reproductive practices that were affirmed through these policies. A mandate issued by Gallieni in 1898 implemented several new protocols, including the regulation and enforcement of (heterosexual) marriage and the exemption of fathers from serving in the military. Fathers with five or more children were absolved from paying taxes, and the development of the *Fête des enfants* and medical system, both explained below, were also instituted (Lasnet 1911).

The *Fête des enfants*, organized by Gallieni, was an event that valorized the reproductive success of Malagasy families, but particularly Merina ones.[5] The celebration was first instituted in Indochina, where Gallieni thought it proved successful (Au 2011; Rajaonah 1999). The most reproductively successful mothers were provided monetary awards, and "the latest statistics detailing the rapid growth of the population" were shared at this public event (Cook Andersen 2010: 437–38).

In his words, Gallieni hoped "to associate in the mind of the Malagasy people the *natural* taste for popular celebration with the idea that one must honor plentiful families" (1908: 209, emphasis added). In parades, some children even dressed as forced laborers, with spades and shovels in hand (Rajaonah 1999: 121–22). The governor-general's wife, Marthe Gallieni, worked to collect clothes to give to children during the celebration—children that would, she wrote, "become our best assistants [*auxiliaires*] in the future" (1903). In hoping to decrease the infant mortality rate (and increase the longevity of Malagasy workers), a colonial pamphlet ends with an imperative directed at Malagasy mothers: "You will not fail in your task, you will not abandon your children and you will teach them to become vigorous and strong men. . . . Do not forget, Malagasy mothers, that your country needs to have many children and that the government promises to give aid and assistance to abundant families. Honor mothers who have many children!!!!!" (Rapport sur le fonctionnement de l'assistance médicale 1903: 57). Left unstated was the fact that the need for able-bodied, disease-free, reproductive Malagasy persons was primarily an economic one (Cole and Middleton 2001). The discourse employed by the report reflects the kind of hetero-patriarchal structures often bolstered by colonial institutions. Despite Jasbir Puar's (2007) assertion that late twentieth- and early twenty-first-century colonization has begun to embrace queer bodies, identities, and practices, previously imperialism was founded almost exclusively upon "the establishment of heterosexual relations of rule" (Alexander 2005: 198).

On December 11, 1896, a new medical school was added as an attachment to the hospital in Antananarivo, along with an adjacent *l'hôpital indigène* for natives, under a colonial decree by Gallieni. The medical school trained native Malagasy doctors primarily to administer vaccinations against smallpox throughout the island (Merlin, Mafart, and Triaud 2003: 17–18). Other scholars have shown how colonial medicine in the Malagasy context was not simply a paternalistic gesture of goodwill but an instrumental one in which medical practices were heavily implicated in the development of "science" and its accompanying penal, fiscal, and labor structures (Esoavelomandroso 1981; Jennings 2009; Koerner 1994). While the development of medical schools aided the island's colonial economy, it was simultaneously integrated into *la mission civilisatrice*. An article from 1903, which described the new school, bemoaned the inadequacies of Malagasy medical students. According to the article, their knowledge of French was limited at best, and they were repulsed by the notion of dissection due to their belief in the "cult of the dead" (Kermorgant 1903: 182). By contrast, Rencurel noted that after extensive medical training and despite initial hesitations, Malagasy medical students "have also lost their traditional fear of the dead and do not back up in horror in front of a cadaver. They learned to dissect and to do an autopsy, and now that their original revulsion is gone, they desire to acquire knowledge and are curious to know the physical structure of the human body" (1897: 142). Other examples of cultural change within the medical school emerged in Rencurel's account. Gender difference, as conceptualized by Malagasy patients, was successfully erased in the examination room because women, initially resistant, eventually acquiesced to physical examinations in front of (male) students and doctors (142). In Sokheing Au's study of French colonial medicine in Cambodia (Indochina), administrators were also interested in finding ways to mitigate gender difference in order to bring female patients into hospitals and ultimately improve infant mortality rates. There, as in colonial Madagascar, administrators fretted over the "underpopulation" of the region (Au 2011: 138). The creation of a medical school was just one part of Gallieni's larger goal of forming the AMI (Assistance Médicale Indigène) in Madagascar, which trained a select group of Merina men to become doctors and eventually educated women to become midwives as well. Medical establishments spread from the island's center to its coasts. In his 1911 report on the AMI presented before the Congress of Eastern Africa, Lasnet openly admitted that Gallieni's "political goal" was for the AMI to win "the confidence of the natives" through modern medicine. His "economic goal" was to "increase the number of workers," which he hoped to expand tenfold in less than a century (Lasnet 1911: 3). In a Foucauldain ([1979] 2008) sense, biopolitical mechanics at work in colonial Madagascar were unequivocally fixated upon increasing the number of laboring Malagasy bodies.

Medico-Ethnographic Encounters in the Colonial Archive

It was in this imperial setting that Rencurel observed a *sarimbavy* in the Antananarivo Hospital in 1897. Rencurel defined *sarimbavy* as "a man who, from his exterior way of being, his way of life, became a woman" (1900: 563). The *sarimbavy* that Rencurel observed wore women's clothing, removed all facial hair, and engaged in the traditional economic activities of Merina women: sewing, carrying water, lace making, and weaving (563). The *sarimbavy*, who remained anonymous, came to the hospital requesting a certificate to prove that she/he was incapable of participating in the labor required of male colonial subjects; the *sarimbavy* told Rencurel that she/he was not "used to the bulk of men's work" (562).[6] Another medical examination was conducted with a different *sarimbavy* by Rencurel to better understand this native condition. For Rencurel, *sarimbavy* differed from other "inverts" in that they were "disgusted by any type of genital act whatever type it is" (566). *Sarimbavy*, Rencurel argued, did not have sex with men: "After a meticulous interrogation, and after having taken information from educated Malagasy people, I believe I can say that apart from some very rare exceptions, *sarimbavy* do not indulge in any acts against nature" (565). He even asserted that a new medical term, "asexual invert," should be created (566).

The central question occupying Rencurel's analysis was the same one that would be taken up by doctors and psychologists in Europe who read his report. Did *sarimbavy* represent innate inversion or environmental perversion? The discussion had recently arisen in reference to Europeans themselves; should such individuals be read as "inverts" who were innately predisposed to certain forms of gender/sexual difference, or were they "perverts" who have been conditioned into such proclivities? The answer for Rencurel was not mutually exclusive; in some cases Rencurel interpreted the etiology of the gendered/sexualized difference of *sarimbavy* as an internal "instinct," while for others he attributed it to "an imposed decision" by parents (563). In Rencurel's first case study, the father of the *sarimbavy* tried to bribe his "son" into abandoning feminine ways for money, but the *sarimbavy* did not accept (567). This narrative supports the innate theory, which Rencurel acknowledged: "The origin of this perversion is in the nature of the individual, in his ancestors, etc." (566). Yet the second and last case study in the article describes a *sarimbavy* (also anonymous) who started to wear girl's clothing when there was no female in the family to fetch water after the mother died (568). This narrative, which emphasizes external causes, contradicts his previous innate-inversion theory.

Two years after Rencurel first observed two *sarimbavy* in Antananarivo, Lasnet, a first-class colonial medical doctor, published an article in which he argued that *sekatra* were similar to the *sarimbavy* described by Rencurel, but that *sekatra* were more numerous within the Sakalava ethnic group than the *sarimbavy* were within the Merina ethnic group.[7] Lasnet also asserted that *sekatra* did not settle for simply resembling women, but that they "go much further in their intimate connections" (1899: 495). If the *sarimbavy* described by Rencurel were asexual, the *sekatra*, Lasnet argued, were sexual beings who were attracted to men: "When a man pleases them, they give him money to sleep with him and have sex in a cow horn filled with grease that they place between their legs; sometimes they have anal intercourse . . . because of their more delicate or puny appearance, one treats them like little girls, and little by little, they are considered to be real women, taking the costume, character and all the habits" (495). *Sekatra* constructed fake breasts by placing several pieces of fabric under their clothing and were accepted within their community; those who chose to ostracize *sekatra* risked having a hex cast upon them that could render them ill (495).

Back in Antananarivo, just a few years later, Rabary, a *sarimbavy*, arrived at Jourdan's medical office. Six years prior, Rabary had visited Rencurel to ask for a medical excuse to be exempt from the fifty days of corvée labor required of all male colonial subjects (Rencurel 1900). According to Jourdan, Rabary had again come to the hospital to request an exemption "from the personal tax" (1903: 808). As described earlier, Rabary, who remained anonymous in Renurel's article, is displayed in two typical anthropometric-style photographs, which feature both a frontal and profile perspective (811). Jourdan described Rabary's body, including genitalia, in explicit detail, and noted that men habitually approached Rabary to make sexual propositions but that she/he "always pushed them away" (809). Most significantly, perhaps, the article claimed that Rabary had no sexual drive due to underdeveloped physical senses: "He is missing certain reflexes given by sight, odor, touch, and taste necessary to enter into a desire for a voluptuous sensation. He doesn't desire, it's an indifferent asexual . . . his ancestors were maybe damaged from alcoholism or from syphilis" (812). Both Rencurel and Jourdan place the etiology of sexual difference primarily in the physical body of the *sarimbavy*. Laurent, on the other hand, would disagree.

Also based in Antananarivo, Laurent had just arrived in Madagascar at the time of his encounter with several *sarimbavy*; previously he had worked in Paris where he published a book on his research as a criminologist in Parisian prisons (Laurent 1890). His piece "The Sharimbavy of Madagascar" ended with his own brief obituary; shortly after completing his work in Madagascar, Laurent had passed away in Sudan. According to the statement, Laurent was "a curious man, who found problems surrounding the abnormal, the strange, and the criminal especially interesting" (Laurent 1911: 248). Laurent presented to the European reader two *sharimbavy*, Ramanantenasoa and Imanga. Laurent also included a photograph of five *sharimbavy* in the text, which I have previously described (243). He had met the *sharimbavy* when he visited them in prison, thanks to Mosnier, the prison doctor, who allowed Laurent to study the *sharimbavy* "from close-up" (243). Ramanantenasoa, the first *sharimbavy* Laurent described, is stated to have always preferred being in the company of girls and to wear women's clothing "from habit." Her/his head had been shaved, and Laurent insinuated that this occurred in the prison (244–45). Ramanantenasoa was in prison for the third time for not having paid the required taxes and claimed not to have had sexual relations with women, while prison guards told Laurent otherwise (245). Despite this, Laurent agreed with Rencurel that *sharimbavy* do not have sexual relations. Laurent stressed that a mother's desire for a girl created *sarimbavy*; he argued that if she has no other girls, a mother may dress her male child in girl's clothing and that eventually "he" will "forget his true sex" (247). *Sharimbavy* became difficult for Laurent to conceptualize because, according to him, they were not pederasts (they did not participate in oral or anal intercourse), nor were they "real" inverts, because they were conditioned into the role by kin from a young age. This particular emphasis on external perversion may have come from Laurent's mentor, Alexandre Lacassagne, who wrote the preface to Laurent's book on the degeneracy of men in Parisian prisons.

In describing the French school of criminology, Lacassagne notes that "we do not believe in this fatalism and in this original defect . . . it's the society that makes and prepares criminals" (Lacassagne 1890: iv). For Laurent, to become *sharimbavy* is to be subjected to external, perverting cultural practices. If being *sharimbavy* is not something biologically innate, then it is something that can be changed through external conditioning.

Making Meaning in the Metropole

The original ethnographic encounters between *sarimbavy* and French colonial doctors were mediated by certain social norms and metacommunicative conventions that determined how these encounters unfolded and how they were documented (Briggs 1986). This initial process of mediation meant that these medico-ethnographic texts were themselves already entextualized constructions (Bauman and Briggs 1990). The decontextualization and recontextualization of these accounts continued in mainland France where individuals republished and commented upon these "discoveries." After Rencurel's work was published in 1900, the anonymous reviewer F. F. wrote an article in *La Semaine médicale* that engaged with Rencurel's findings. The article focused on the need for a more nuanced sexological classificatory system given the increasing accounts of "inverts" whose diversity defied standard typologies. F. F.'s article repeated Rencurel's assertion that there were two different kinds of *sarimbavy* to consider: "Sometimes, in fact, the future Sarimbavy manifests spontaneously, from the youngest age, and despite the will of their parents . . . sometimes, on the contrary, these are parents which, having only boys, desire a girl . . . try to feminize their child" (F. F. 1900: 404). F. F. stressed the need to distinguish between different groups of *sarimbavy*: "There would probably be a place to distinguish, from a psychopathological point of view, between the 'congenital' Sarimbavy and those for whom the inversion isn't but a consequence of education that they received and existing conditions in which they found themselves" (405). While *sekatra* had sex with men, F. F. argued that this did not prove that homosexual desire was required of inversion; the "asexual" nature of the majority of *sarimbavy* called into question their sexological classification as "sexual perverts" (405).

Lasnet's findings on *sekatra* were again reprinted, without any comment, in the *Mercure de France* by Albert Prieur (1900). The journal *Mercure de France*, at this time, was associated with the Symbolist movement in France and published the first works of same-sex-loving André Gide and Colette. Michael Lucey asserts that the *Mercure de France* "was well known for its interest in literary attempts at representing same-sex sexualities" (2006: 76). Lasnet's attention to the sexuality of *sekatra* and their transcendental powers (their ability to cast hexes) created a compelling narrative. This instance of recontextualization speaks principally to the journal's readers, some of whose personal interests in sexual diversity would have drawn them to Lasnet's sexualized account of *sekatra* over Laurent's asexual interpretation of *sarimbavy*. In all of these instances, the local ethnographic description and context is minimized; the colonial frontier is presented as a scientific and literary laboratory.

Entextualized by the Anglophones

Across the English Channel, British sexologists were also grappling with the issue of sexual inversion. The most famous of them, Havelock Ellis, was sympathetic to the cause of "sexual inverts" in England for deeply personal reasons; his wife engaged in sexual relations with other women, and he was friends with several same-sex-desiring men, including Edward Carpenter (Weeks 2000: 25). In the 1901 edition of *Sexual Inversion*, Ellis drew from Rencurel's and Lasnet's accounts as well as the *Revue de Psychiatrie*, which had republished their findings. Ellis, like his French counterparts, was concerned with the question of etiology, although somewhat less so. While Ellis thought that *sekatra* "are apparently chosen from childhood . . . and brought up as girls," he asserted that *sarimbavy* "have sometimes been brought up as girls because their parents desired to have a girl, but in other cases the impulse toward feminine habits and vocations arises and persists in spite of the parents' opposition" (1901: 10). Ellis stated that *sekatra* engage in sexual relations with men, while *sarimbavy* have no sexual impulses whatsoever (10–11). These conclusions do not drastically differ from the positions taken by French colleagues, although Ellis was slightly less concerned with etiology and more interested in the universal phenomenon of "sexual inversion" cross-culturally.

On the other hand, two British intellectuals approached the issue in radically different ways from Ellis and the French sexologists. Both Edward Carpenter's and John Addington Symonds's references to *sarimbavy* and *sekatra* did not engage with medical discourse; this was likely linked to their own same-sex desire. They, like Ellis, highlighted the universal innateness of gendered and sexualized diversity, a perspective that differed, for example, from Laurent's comment that "before the arrival of Europeans amongst the Imerina, there were few or hardly any sexual morals, but there were no prostitutes and no sexual perversions" (Laurent 1911: 243). Unlike Laurent, Carpenter and Symonds did not insist that sexual perversion was a Western disease that should be surveyed as strictly in the French metropole as in the colony.

The poet and literary critic Symonds coauthored an earlier version of *Sexual Inversion* alongside Ellis and filled the role of historical expert, while Ellis provided the medical knowledge and expertise that gave the work legitimacy. Symonds's article "A Problem in Greek Ethics," which appeared in the appendix of the first edition, referenced the "Tsecats of Madagascar" ([1897] 1975: 186).

Symonds finished writing his article in 1873, well before the publication of any of the accounts provided by French colonial medical doctors, and while he personally had sexual relations with other men, they remained largely hidden from the public in the confines of his journals (Bleys 1995: 212; Weeks 2000: 26). Based on the spelling, Symonds likely obtained this ethnographic evidence either from Flacourt's seventeenth-century account or from another publication that cited it. However, Symonds used the *tsecats* of Madagascar to argue that "we are obliged, in fact, to separate . . . the true Hellenic manifestation of the paiderastic passion, from the effeminacies, brutalities and gross sensualities which can be noticed alike in imperfectly civilized and in luxuriously corrupt communities" ([1897] 1975: 187). *Tsecats* of Madagascar, then, were placed among the "gross" degenerates distinct from the perfected ancient Greek example of manly love that Symonds celebrated. For Symonds, *tsecats* were a "primitive" perversion whose existence overshadowed the cisgendered homosexuality of the Hellenic tradition.

Like Symonds's article, Carpenter's *Intermediate Types among Primitive Folk* (1914), did not draw from the francophone colonial medico-ethnographic accounts. Instead, Carpenter turned to an earlier travelogue by B.-F. Leguével de Lacombe. Leguével de Lacombe described *sekatses* as dancers who "imitated" women's voices, wore women's clothes and accessories, and were generally accepted within Malagasy society. No note was made regarding their sexual desire. Leguével de Lacombe asserted that they were "the poets or the bards of Madagascar; they improvise rhapsodies in praise of those who pay them" (1840: 97–98). He defined *sekatses* as "bastards," and argued that they could hardly be said to have parents, thus implicitly challenging the later argument that gender variance or conformity was enforced by mothers. Carpenter also drew from Flacourt when he described *sekatses* as "effeminate men who wore female attire and acted as women, thinking thereby to do God service" (1914: 41). For Carpenter, *sekatses* were active participants in the sacred, the artistic, and the imaginative. The image of a spiritual *sarimbavy* flourished in this interpretation. While Carpenter championed the talents and gifts afforded to "intermediate types," Symonds was only willing to promote gender-normative forms of same-sex desire. Ellis, Carpenter, and Symonds, though, all used the figure of the *sarimbavy* to articulate key arguments surrounding the universality of gendered and sexualized difference.

Eugenic Fervor across the Atlantic . . . and Back Again
The specter of the *sarimbavy* eventually materialized into bibliographic references in a few books and scholarly articles in the United States in the early twentieth century. By the time these medico-ethnographic accounts crossed the Atlantic, they had already been decontextualized and recontextualized multiple times, first in the ethnographic encounter itself, second in mainland Europe, and finally in

the anglophone readings of these accounts. Two of these articles, authored by Arthur MacDonald (honorary president of the Third International Congress of Criminal Anthropology of Europe), cited the article written by "Jourdran" (Jourdan) in 1903. In his article "A Sadistic Murder," MacDonald described a male medical student ("A") who killed two women in a church, was found guilty, and was sentenced to capital punishment for his crimes. Evidence showed that one of the women was both choked to death and sexually mutilated. Anthropometric evidence was provided; A's measurements were listed, including his height, length of left foot and middle finger, shape of chin, and place of birth: Canada (1906: 591). The article's purpose was clearly stated: "The present case may be of assistance in explaining this species of murder, which unfortunately seems to be increasing" (1906: 589). Like Laurent, MacDonald believed that an overall increase in perversions accompanied technological advancements in North America and Europe. MacDonald later folded his article into a report titled "Juvenile Crime and Reformation, Including Stigmata of Degeneration," which proposed to the United States House of Representatives the creation of a "laboratory for the study of the criminal, pauper, and defective classes." In the preface of his report, MacDonald provided his opinion that "governments should look after the moral health of the people with as much scientific foresight as they do the physical health of the people" (1908: 7). As but a mere reference in MacDonald's article and judicial committee report, this reference to *sarimbavy* may seem trivial. However, its utility as bibliographic evidence reveals how such forms of "deviance" were recontextualized in an American atmosphere of eugenic fervor.

Jourdan's account of *sarimbavy* made no reference to murder, of course; however, *sarimbavy* did conflict with the interests of the colonial state and were at times incarcerated, and their very difference produced an uncanny sense of disease in the colonial doctor and many Euro-American readers. While in Rencurel's article "the physical stigmata of degeneracy . . . are neither numerous nor very clear," (1900: 566), MacDonald was centrally concerned with the prominence of "moral stigmata," which he defined as "anomalies of character, especially in infancy, as bad impulses, violence, anger, strange vagaries of sensibility, refractory to all reform, and instinctively perverse acts" (1908: 290). Such "perverse acts" included "crimes against chastity and decency . . . incest, sodomy, exhibitionism, and other sexual perversions" (290). (Ironically, *sarimbavy* were described by Jourdan as asexual.)

The medicalized discourse of degeneration returned across the Atlantic back to England in the work of Dr. N. Lukianowicz, who wrote an article in 1959 titled "Survey of Various Aspects of Transvestism in the Light of our Present Knowledge." Lukianowicz drew from Ellis's description of *sarimbavy* in a section of the article devoted to a cross-cultural approach to "transvestism" and mentioned that *sarimbavy* "are usually brought up as girls, because their parents desired to have a girl" (Lukianowicz 1959: 55). Lukianowicz also engaged with the work of several American-based psychologists and sexologists who proposed various psychoanalytic (Mortimer Ostow), glandular (Harry Benjamin), and surgical treatments (Christian Hamburger) (58–60). Ultimately, Rencurel's vision of new typological possibilities for the classification of gendered/sexualized difference in Madagascar, and more specifically that of the "asexual invert," finally came true when Lukianowicz claimed: "With regard to its sexual aim, transvestism has been classified into . . . 1. Asexual, 2. Auto-mono-sexual, 3. Hetero-sexual, 4. Homo-sexual, and 5. Bi-sexual" (61).

Conclusion

Among the many boxes filled with archival materials on plants and nonhuman animals in the *Muséum National d'Histoire Naturelle* in Paris, I "discovered" in the French metropole a series of documents collected by the ethnographer Raymond Decary that revealed the story of another *sarimbavy* whose gender expression caused conflict with the colonial state (Decary, n.d.). Only the individual's last name, Razanajafy, is recorded. Razanajafy, who was from a suburb of Antananarivo and presumably illiterate, had signed the typewritten letter with a cross. The letter closed with "your humble and obedient servant," and explained that she/he had been ordered into the security general's office on July 6, 1939, and was commanded to cut her/his long hair. She/he was told to wear men's clothing and hairstyles from there on. Razanajafy wrote that she/he had been a *sarimbavy* since birth and translated it into French as a "false woman." Razanajafy continued by stating that she/he paid her/his taxes every year and never had any problems with the colonial administration. The letter was addressed to the governor, whom Razanajafy called "Father and Mother" and "protector of the weak." Razanajafy pleaded that she/he no longer knew how to present as a man and requested to be able to dress as before and to be able to grow her/his hair out. Razanajafy promised to continue paying taxes each year and reminded the reader that she/he was "always ready to fulfill [her/his] duty to France." The authorities decided that Razanajafy needed a medical examination before a decision could be reached, and on August 3 Razanajafy went to see Dr. T. C. Ricou. Ricou referred to Razanajafy as a "man-woman" and stated that as a fully developed male, Razanajafy belonged in the "social category of men" and had no sexual desire for men or women. Razanajafy's feminine tendencies, Ricou argued, were the result of having frequented women's spaces. By August 17 a decision was reached; in sloppy handwriting, it was documented that "no text condemns wearing the clothing of another sex as long as individuals don't . . . [unclear] . . . for immoral purposes." Razanajafy appeared before authorities on September 2 and was informed of their decision.

Only after reading through these documents several times did I make note of Decary's observation that Razanajafy was from a "worker's camp" in Avaratetezana. Had she/he too been forced to labor for the colony as a male-bodied subject? Perhaps, and it seems fitting, then, that the authorities would have tried to regulate Razanajafy's gender expression. While the original colonial corvée system was no longer functioning, it had been replaced by SMOTIG (Service de la Main-d'Oeuvre des Travaux d'Interêt) in 1926, which similarly recruited male subjects to labor for the colony (Sharp 2003). Genese Sodikoff astutely notes that SMOTIG was ruled by a "masculine culture" whose oppressive nature led many to desert and even inflict pain on themselves in order to be released from service, thus promoting "an atmosphere of confrontation and resistance" (2005: 420). Likewise, Razanajafy had willfully navigated bureaucratic channels in order to challenge colonial attempts at gender regulation. When Rabary visited Jourdan to ask for an exemption from the corvée, she/he also produced several documents to the physician, including one from Dr. Rasamimanana, the first European-trained Malagasy doctor (Boulinier 1995: 347), that certified Rabary's lack of "physical development" (Jourdan 1903: 808).

Here I want to move beyond an overly simplified dichotomy that attempts to "recover" or "save" queer lives—such as Razanajafy's—from a disturbing archive or that celebrates "agentive" acts of rebellious defiance (Arondekar 2009; Love 2007). Indeed, to salvage the stories of *sarimbavy* from a Western closet, blanket them in proleptic taxonomies, and free them from the grips of empire would be just as insidious as the colonial project to peg *sarimbavy* into European sexological theories. Instead of assuming that the subaltern speaks to the reader through this research (Spivak 1988), I hope to "learn to learn from below" (Spivak 2004)—that is, from the *sarimbavy* that occupy these archives—in order to allow for novel understandings of, among other phenomena, sex/gender systems in Madagascar and the French colonial project. As such, the illusory figure of the *sarimbavy* has challenged me to imagine both the possibilities and limitations of queer agentive acts within the structure of a colonial regime. Perhaps some readers will be similarly provoked. But, if nothing more, the figure of the *sarimbavy* makes a case for trans- studies scholars to engage more deeply with the kinds of translations and transformations inherent in transnational and transimperial modes of knowledge production.

Seth Palmer is a PhD candidate at the University of Toronto in the Department of Anthropology, the Mark S. Bonham Centre for Sexual Diversity Studies, and the Women and Gender Studies Institute. His dissertation project is concerned with the relationship between *sarimbavy/ sarindahy* subject formation and *tromba* spirit possession in western Madagascar.

Acknowledgment

All translations from French and Malagasy are my own. Archival research was conducted in the Archives Nationales in Antananarivo, Madagascar, the Archives d'Outre-Mer in Aix-en-Provence, and the Muséum National d'Histoire Naturelle in Paris. The project was funded by a Short-Term Doctoral Research Grant from the Centre for the Study of France and the Francophone World and a PhD Pilot Research Grant from the Department of Anthropology at the University of Toronto.

Notes

1. When referring to the "metropole," I describe a space that was imagined and constructed vis-à-vis the (non-European) "colony." Of course, metropolitan centers existed throughout the Indian Ocean well before the late nineteenth century.

2. This scholarship primarily draws from Derrida's concept of *hauntology*—that is, the ontology of haunting (1994).

3. *Sekatses/sekatra/saikatra/tsecats* has various regional meanings that include hesitant, infertile, or effeminate. In reference to male-bodied, gender-variant persons, *sarimbavy* is more common in contemporary usage.

4. See also Roux (1905) for a discussion of a *sarindahy* (gender-variant and/or same-sex-desiring female-bodied person).

5. The Merina are a typically lighter-skinned ethnic group whose ancestral lands are located in the central highlands and were privileged by the French administration.

6. The third-person pronoun in Malagasy, *izy*, is gender neutral. I avoid using gendered pronouns as much as possible, but when used I employ she/he to best reflect the Malagasy language.

7. See note 3 for a definition of *sekatra*.

References

Aldrich, Robert. 2001. "Homosexuality in the French Colonies." *Journal of Homosexuality* 41, no. 3: 201–18.

Alexander, M. Jacqui. 2005. *Pedagogies of Crossing: Meditations on Feminism, Sexual Politics, Memory, and the Sacred*. Durham, NC: Duke University Press.

Arondekar, Anjali. 2005. "Without a Trace: Sexuality and the Colonial Archive." *Journal of the History of Sexuality* 14, no. 1–2: 10–27.

———. 2009. *For the Record: On Sexuality and the Colonial Archive in India*. Durham, NC: Duke University Press.

Au, Sokheing. 2011. *Mixed Medicines: Health and Culture in French Colonial Cambodia*. Chicago: University of Chicago Press.

Bauman, Richard, and Charles L. Briggs. 1990. "Poetics and Performance as Critical Perspectives on Language and Social Life." *Annual Review of Anthropology* 19: 59–88.

Bleys, Rudi C. 1995. *The Geography of Perversion: Male-to-Male Sexual Behavior Outside the West and the Ethnographic Imagination, 1750–1918*. New York: New York University Press.

Boddy, Janice. 2011. "Bodies under Colonialism." In *A Companion to the Anthropology of the Body and Embodiment*, ed. Frances E. Mascia-Lees, 119–36. Malden, MA: Wiley-Blackwell.

Boulinier, Georges. 1995. "Ramisiray: Un des premiers docteurs en médicine malgaches." *Histoire des sciences médicales* 29, no. 4: 347–54.

Briggs, Charles L. 1986. *Learning How to Ask: A Sociolinguistic Appraisal of the Role of the Interview in Social Science Research*. Cambridge: Cambridge University Press.

Campbell, Gwyn. 1988. "Slavery and Fanompoana: The Structure of Forced Labour in Imerina (Madagascar), 1790–1861." *Journal of African History* 29, no. 3: 463–86.

———. 2003. "The Origins and Development of Coffee Production in Réunion and Madagascar, 1711–1972." In *The Global Coffee Economy in Africa, Asia, and Latin America 1500–1989*, ed. William Gervase Clarence-Smith and Steven Topik, 67–99. New York: Cambridge University Press.

Carpenter, Edward. 1914. *Intermediate Types among Primitive Folk*. London: George Allen.

Cole, Jennifer, and Karen Middleton. 2001. "Rethinking Ancestors and Colonial Power in Madagascar." *Africa* 71, no. 1: 1–37.

Cook Andersen, Margaret. 2010. "Creating French Settlements Overseas: Pronatalism and Colonial Medicine in Madagascar." *French Historical Studies* 33, no. 3: 417–44.

Cooper, Frederick. 1996. *Decolonization and African Society: The Labor Question in French and British Africa*. Cambridge: Cambridge University Press.

Dave, Naisargi N. 2011. "Abundance and Loss: Queer Intimacies in South Asia." *Feminist Studies* 37, no. 1: 14–27.

Decary, Raymond. n.d. "Dossier sur les sarimbavy." Fonds Decary (MS 2984/VIII), Muséum National d'Histoire Naturelle, Paris.

Derrida, Jacques. 1994. *Specters of Marx: The State of the Debt, the Work of Mourning, and the New International*. Translated by Peggy Kamuf. New York: Routledge.

———. 1998. *Archive Fever: A Freudian Impression*. Chicago: University of Chicago Press.

Ellis, Havelock. 1901. *Sexual Inversion*. 2nd ed. Philadelphia: Davis.

Eng, David. 2010. *The Feeling of Kinship: Queer Liberalism and the Racialization of Intimacy*. Durham, NC: Duke University Press.

Esoavelomandroso, Faranirina. 1981. "Résistance à la médicine en situation coloniale: La peste à Madagascar." *Annales: Histoire, sciences sociales* 36, no. 2: 168–90.

F. F. 1900. Untitled. *La Semaine médicale* 20: 404–5.

Feeley-Harnik, Gillian. 1984. "The Political Economy of Death: Communication and Change in Malagasy Colonial History." *American Ethnologist* 11, no. 1: 1–19.

———. 1991. *A Green Estate: Restoring Independence in Madagascar*. Washington, DC: Smithsonian Institution Press.

Ferguson, Roderick A. 2004. *Aberrations in Black: Toward a Queer of Color Critique*. Minneapolis: University of Minnesota Press.

Flacourt, Etienne de. (1661) 1995. *Histoire de la grande île de Madagascar*. Paris: Karthala.

Foucault, Michel. (1979) 2008. *The Birth of Biopolitics: Lectures at the Collège de France, 1978–1979*. Edited by Michel Senellart. Translated by Graham Burchell. New York: Palgrave Macmillan.

Freccero, Carla. 2006. *Queer/Early/Modern*. Durham, NC: Duke University Press.

Gallieni, Joseph. 1908. *Neuf ans à Madagascar*. Paris: Librairie Hachette.

Gallieni, Marthe. 1903. "L'Œuvre des dispensaires et des maternités à Madagascar." *Revue de Madagascar* 5, no. 2: 424–28.

Jacquier, Léonce. 1904. *La Main-d'œuvre locale à Madagascar*. Paris: Jouve.

Jennings, Eric. 2009. "Confronting Rabies and Its Treatments in Colonial Madagascar, 1899–1910." *Social History of Medicine* 22, no. 2: 263–82.

Jourdan, Edmond. 1903. "Psychologie des sarimbavy: Perversion sexuelle observée en Imerina." *Archives d'anthropologie criminelle* 18: 808–12.

Kermorgant, A. 1903. "École de médecine et hôpital indigène de Tananarive (Madagascar)." *Annales d'hygiène et de médecine coloniales* 6: 181–84.

Koerner, Francis. 1994. "La protection sanitaire des populations à Madagascar (1862–1914)." *Revue historique* 291, no. 2: 439–58.

Lacassagne, Alexandre. 1890. Preface to *Les habitués des prisons de Paris: Étude d'anthropologie et psychologie*. Paris: Masson.

Lasnet, Antoine. 1899. "Notes d'ethnologie et de médecine sur les Sakalaves du Nord-Ouest." *Annales d'hygiène et de médecine coloniales* 2: 471–97.

———. 1911. "Rapport au congrès de l'Afrique orientale sur l'assistance médicale indigène à Madagascar." Série H (carton 262e), Archives Nationale de Madagascar, Antananarivo.

Laurent, Émile. 1890. *Les Habitués des prisons de Paris: Étude d'anthropologie et psychologie*. Paris: Masson.

———. 1911. "Les Sharimbavy de Madagascar." *Archives d'anthropologie criminelle* 26: 241–48.

Leguével de Lacombe, B.-F. 1840. *Voyage à Madagascar et aux îles Comores 1823–1830*. Paris: Desessart.

Love, Heather. 2007. *Feeling Backwards: Loss and the Politics of Queer History*. Cambridge, MA: Harvard University Press.

Lowe, Lisa. 2006. "The Intimacies of Four Continents." In *Haunted by Empire: Geographies of Intimacy in North American History*, ed. Ann Laura Stoler, 191–212. Durham, NC: Duke University Press.

Lucey, Michael. 2006. *Never Say I: Sexuality and the First Person in Colette, Gide, and Proust*. Durham, NC: Duke University Press.

Lukianowicz, N. 1959. "Survey of Various Aspects of Transvestism in the Light of our Present Knowledge." *Journal of Nervous and Mental Disease* 128, no. 1: 36–64.

MacDonald, Arthur. 1906. "A Sadistic Murder." *Medico-Legal Journal* 24: 589–603.

———. 1908. *Juvenile Crime and Reformation, Including Stigmata of Degeneration*. Washington, DC: US Government Printing Office.

Merlin, J., B. Mafart, and J. L. Triaud. 2003. "L'assistance médicale indigène à Madagascar (1898–1950)." *Médicine tropicale* 63, no. 1: 17–21.

Muñoz, Jose. 2009. *Cruising Utopia: The Politics and Performance of Queer Futurity*. Durham, NC: Duke University Press.

Prieur, Albert. 1900. Untitled. *Mercure de France* 33: 490–91.

Puar, Jasbir. 2007. *Terrorist Assemblages: Homonationalism in Queer Times*. Durham, NC: Duke University Press.

Rajaonah, Faranirina. 1999. "La fête des enfants à Antananarivo pendant la colonisation." In *Fêtes urbaines en Afrique: Espaces, identitiés et pouvoirs*, ed. O. Georg, 113–30. Paris: Karthala.

"Rapport sur le fonctionnement de l'assistance médicale à Madagascar en 1902." 1903. Archives Nationales de Madagascar, Imprimerie Officielle de Tananarive.

Rencurel. 1897. "Organisation de l'école de médecine de Tananarive." *Archives de médecine navale* 68: 139–43.

———. 1900. "Les Sarimbavy: Perversion sexuelle observée en Émyrne." *Annales d'hygiène et de médecine coloniales* 3: 562–68.

Roberts, Mary Louise. 2002. *Disruptive Acts: The New Woman in Fin-de-Siècle France*. Chicago: University of Chicago Press.

Roux. 1905. "Note sur un cas d'inversion sexuelle chez une comorienne." *Bulletins et Mémoires de la Société d'anthropologie de Paris* 6, no. 6: 218–19.

Sharp, Lesley A. 2002. *The Sacrificed Generation: Youth, History, and the Colonized Mind in Madagascar*. Berkeley: University of California Press.

———. 2003. "Laboring for the Colony and the Nation: The Historicized Political Consciousness of Youth in Madagascar." *Critique of Anthropology* 23, no. 1: 75–91.

Sodikoff, Genese. 2005. "Forced and Forest Labor Regimes in Colonial Madagascar, 1926–1936." *Ethnohistory* 52, no. 2: 407–35.

Spivak, Gayatri Chakravorty. 1988. "Can the Subaltern Speak?" In *Marxism and the Interpretation of Culture*, ed. C. Nelson and L. Grossberg, 271–313. Basingstoke, UK: MacMillan Education.

———. 2004. "Righting Wrongs." *South Atlantic Quarterly* 103, no. 2: 523–81.

Stoler, Ann Laura. 2009. *Along the Archival Grain: Epistemic Anxieties and Colonial Common Sense*. Princeton, NJ: Princeton University Press.

Stoler, Ann Laura, and Frederick Cooper. 1997. "Between Metropole and Colony: Rethinking a Research Agenda." In *Tensions of Empire: Colonial Cultures in a Bourgeois World*, ed. Frederick Cooper and Ann Laura Stoler, 1–56. Berkeley: University of California Press.

Symonds, John Addington. (1897) 1975. "A Problem in Greek Ethics." In *Sexual Inversion*, by Havelock Ellis and John Addington Symonds, 163–251. New York: Arno.

Thompson, Virginia, and Richard Adloff. 1965. *The Malagasy Republic: Madagascar Today*. Stanford, CA: Stanford University Press.

Weeks, Jeffrey. 2000. *Making Sexual History*. Cambridge: Polity.

Toms and Zees

Locating FTM Identity in Thailand

JAI ARUN RAVINE

Abstract Who is Zee? Zee is a site of dissonance that helps illustrate how Thai and Western concepts of gender and queerness converge and collide. How Zee is frequently recognized as male but then constantly reiterated as female while embodying a certain gender ambiguity in language and appearance is a product of the slippage between geographically and culturally specific understandings of gender, which unfortunately causes Thai FTMs in both the United States and Thailand to experience isolation and alienation from Thai community, a silence camouflaged by that very ambiguity.
Keywords trans-; Thai; Thailand; FTM; *toms*; gender

Who's Zee? . . . I'm Zee" is the heading for a "Special Fashion and Exclusive Interview" with pop singer Zee Matanawee Keenan in a 2010 issue of *@tom act*, Thailand's tomboy lifestyle magazine (*@tom act* 2010). *Tom* and *dee*[1] (also referred to as *tom/dy/lez*) culture in Thailand has gained visibility over the past decade with the launch of *@tom act* in 2007 and the popularity of the Thai films *Yes or No* and *Yes or No 2* (dir. Saratswadee Wongsomphet, 2010, 2012) and *She: Their Love Story* (dir. Sranya Noithai, 2012), which feature *tom* and *dee* characters in relationships. Megan Sinnott's research on *tom* and *dee* culture notes the complexity of a possible cross-gender identification with masculinity coexisting at the same time as female embodiment among *toms* (2000: 97–98). However, *tom* identity cannot be completely equated with or translated as butch lesbian identity as it is defined within an American cultural context. In this article, I use Zee's popular persona and gender presentation as a springboard for locating female-to-male (FTM) transgender (trans) identity in Thailand as possibly included within, yet also completely separate from, the category *tom*.

The "About" section of the 25-year-old pop star's Facebook fan page lists sex and gender (in two different places) as "female" (Zee Matanawee Keenan's Facebook page). Yet Zee consistently uses *khrap*, the male particle for polite speech in the Thai language, and *phom*, the masculine "I" pronoun.[2] Zee is also often referred to as *sao laaw* (handsome lady). Traditionally used only to describe cisgender men, the word *laaw* (handsome) is a constant descriptor for Zee among Facebook fans. While some *toms* use *khrap* (or codeswitch between *khrap* and *kha*) and may also bind their chests, many refer to themselves as "she" when communicating in English, despite the fact that the Thai language has only one gender-neutral third-person pronoun (*kao*). In a recent comment to the music video for Zee's single "Deeply," a YouTube user writes, "My idol like him!!" and another (presumably Thai) user responds with, "Uh, yeah about that. He is actually SHE. Just thought you might wanna know" (Comments on "ส้วง"). References to Zee by viewers as male, followed by similar kinds of policing of gender pronouns, occur regularly in YouTube and Facebook comment threads.

Zee is a site of dissonance that helps illustrate how Thai and Western concepts of gender and queerness converge and collide. How Zee is frequently recognized as male but then constantly reiterated as female while embodying a certain gender ambiguity in language and appearance is a product of the slippage between geographically and culturally specific understandings of gender, which unfortunately causes Thai FTMs in both the United States and Thailand to experience isolation and alienation from Thai community, a silence camouflaged by that very ambiguity. "Before transitioning, I avoided using *kha* and *khrap* because I didn't want to use *kha*, and using *khrap* just got me strange looks," a Thai FTM in Bangkok shared with me. He continued, "With *di-chun*, I never used it because it was just weird for me and *phom* just got me strange looks as well. So I just became socially awkward and tend to not talk to anyone, or else they would think of me as a rude person." Hesitating to speak is a common thread, as is detachment, as we are forced to choose between two syllables, two identities. "I detached myself from [Thai] community when I was in the process of coming out," said a Thai American FTM in Los Angeles. In speaking about being Thai and being trans, he says, "I always had to feel like I had to choose one or the other. When I want to come back and interface with Thai community, I have to downplay my queerness. I feel that in Thai communities people do express heterosexist mentality in really explicit ways, it's space-taking."

While a full analysis of Zee's gender presentation and embodiment of masculinity in music videos and Instagram photos cannot be done here, it is my opinion that Zee appears more masculine-presenting than other *toms*, especially because of the way Zee is often pitted against a young cisgender man when vying for a young woman's love in music videos. When I was first introduced to Zee online, my initial thought was, "They look like a trans guy." I was struck immediately by the ways she appeared to be both *tom and* trans.[3] Zee's embodiment of masculinity became a site of affirmation for my own identity formation as a mixed-race Thai American transmasculine and gender-nonconforming person; it also informed the project that became *Tom/Trans/Thai*, a short film I created in 2011. For me, Zee became a sort of bridge. She/he[4] gave me hope that I might find some kind of context for FTM identity in Thailand as well as a sense of connection and lineage amid the isolation and alienation from Thai community that I and other Thai FTMs were facing. This article discusses the research surrounding my film, contemplates the resonance and dissonance between the categories of *tom* and *trans*, and gently opens a space for Thai FTM self-determination and community building.

Defining Scope, Acknowledging Limits

Tom/Trans/Thai is a seventeen-minute short film I created in Thailand in 2011. My original goals were to investigate the connections and disjunctions between *tom* identity and FTM identity, to interview Thai *toms* and Thai FTMs in Thailand and the United States, and to explore how concepts of gender are embodied, mobilized, and communicated transnationally. After applying for several different grant and fellowship opportunities, I was selected for a one-month residency at the ComPeung Village of Creativity in Doi Saket, Thailand, in March 2011, with the agreement that I would represent their Artist-In-Residency Program in the "Chiang Mai Now!" art exhibition at the Bangkok Art and Culture Centre with the project I would create. I had about twenty-five days to conduct interviews, shoot footage, and edit the film, which was installed from April 7 through June 9, 2011.[5] Due to these time and resource constraints, I had to condense much of my original plan. In addition to a short film, my original proposal included more substantial scholarly research, extensive interviews, a creative manuscript, and a live performance as well as a six-month to one-year timeline and a budget that included Thai language classes. My first and foremost goal was to become fluent in Thai in order to conduct interviews with Thai speakers. However, because I was awarded only a one-month residency to complete the film for exhibition, I was forced to conduct interviews in English, which led to a lot of difficulty with translation and limited what could actually be discussed and communicated between interviewees and myself. These time and language constraints as well as feelings of frustration and inadequacy affected the overall production of the film and how I grappled with the research questions I had originally set up for myself.

In making a film, I wanted to approach the silence around FTM identity in the Thai context by addressing *tom* and transmasculine[6] identities in Thai and Thai American communities and the transnational relationships between gender and language. I wanted to introduce the intersections between *tom* identity, FTM transgender identity, and Thai identity in a transnational context; to my knowledge, such a project had never been tackled before.[7] I interviewed eleven participants (in person, over Skype, or over email), many of whom were also *luk kreung* (half

Thai), who identified as *tom*, queer, gender-nonconforming, and/or on the FTM spectrum and lived in Chiang Mai, Bangkok, Australia, and the United States. Rather than present the interviews in documentary form, I translated them artistically into dance and movement in an effort to locate the difficulties of gender within the Thai landscape. My broader aim is to bridge critical discussions regarding gender-identity formation among *toms* and Thai FTMs living in Thailand and the United States by analyzing how gender and queerness are linguistically and culturally conceptualized and communicated. In other words, I look at how Thai people think and talk about gender, how they communicate and embody gender (i.e., Is gender talked about as a concept? Is gender talked about as an identity?), and the existing language regarding gender. I look at how language impacts cross-cultural recognition and connection between *toms* and Thai FTMs and how language contributes to the invisibility, isolation, and silencing of Thai transgender men and transmasculine people.

One of the reasons for doing this project is that whenever I articulate the words "transgender" and "Thailand" in the same sentence, people automatically assume I am talking about *sao praphet song* (also referred to as *kathoey*)[8] or male-to-female (MTF) transgender women. To date, *sao praphet song* have been the predominant focus, and more accessible subject, of popular research and film in the West. It is thus crucial to provide a counterpoint to the hypervisibility of *sao praphet song* by gently investigating the invisibilized existence of Thai transgender men. While *toms* are also hypervisible (and fashionable) in Thai popular culture, before embarking on this project I did not know if any FTM or transmasculine-identified Thais existed other than myself and three people in my personal network. When I asked Thai *toms* about FTM or transmasculine Thais, I was met with silence and confusion and with the astounding difficulty of translating the concepts "trans" and "FTM" in ways *toms* could understand. Conversely, Thai FTMs and transmasculine people (in both Thailand and the United States) often expressed a disconnection to Thai cultural belonging and acceptance because of the *tom/dee* gender binary and cultural constructions of gender, including the demands to gender oneself as either female or male and the heteronormative implications of language (i.e., gendered "I" pronouns [*phom/chun*] and gendered particles for polite speech [*khrap/kha*]). I felt frustrated by the failures of translation and the poverty of language, but I knew it was important to somehow locate transmasculinity in Thailand, if only for those three friends and myself. Thai FTMs had to exist somewhere. Where were they, and what factors made it difficult for us to find and recognize each other? If I recognized Zee as trans, what might the categories of *tom* and trans mean to each other? Why (and to whom) would such a transnational conversation be useful? How is the language we have for gender and the concept of gender itself transforming as a part of this process?

Interviews with Thai FTMs and Thai American queer and transmasculine people seemed to flow effortlessly and often felt surreal with the level of recognition and knowing that passed between us. I showed up to interviews with Thai *toms* with the same set of questions but immediately found them inadequate and often completely untranslatable. I was not fluent in Thai, but I also was not fluent in their experiences or cultural understandings of gender and what gender might mean for them. How could I ask them things that did not even seem to have language? I found that instead of trying to find the correct translation, I had to take time to make myself visible, and I always left feeling less visible, less able to make a connection than before.

During the process of making the film, I realized that perhaps my project was for all the queer and transmasculine Thais I interviewed who knew no other people like them, who were not sure about their relationships to Thai cultural belonging, who were completely silenced by language. I had attempted to read *tom* and FTM identities together, as transmasculinities, but I was seeing the immense divide between them. Many people I interviewed had experiences of being read as *tom* or of people trying to peg them as either *tom* or *dee*. Trying to explain that they were not *tom* was a painful process that exposed the failures of language and the failure of a category to accurately communicate who we are. While this article was originally born from my frustrations and limitations surrounding the film and from a need to process my personal experiences surrounding the interview process, it also gestures toward the need for further research concerning Thai transmasculinities, and again, it gently opens a space for Thai FTM (and gender-nonconforming) self-determination and community building.

Dissonance Resonates: Locating the Boundary between *Tom* and Trans

Zee was an important reference point in my interviews with both *toms* and FTMs in Thailand. The responses I received to the question, "Have you heard of Zee?" ranged from "Zee helped Thailand to know a good *tom*" to "I think she look like man. I don't like some say *khrap* like a man, I don't like. I think *tom* look like girl, must say *kha*. I say *kha*, not *khrap*. I don't like it." In our conversations, *toms* and *dees* actively inscribed the boundaries of *tom* identity (as embodied in appearance and speech), and it seemed that Zee was simultaneously within the circle *and* without. This mirrored the ways I both felt included within the intimacy of a *tom* "boi's club" *and* was also always outside, struggling to find language with which to name myself. In this section I give context for why locating FTM experience in Thailand was initially difficult through a discussion of issues that arose in my interviews with Thai *toms* and by touching on factors that may impact *toms'* knowledge of and desire for medical transition.

One day I went to interview a *tom* who owned a restaurant in Doi Saket, a town about thirty minutes from Chiang Mai. I had eaten dinner there a few days prior and had set up an interview time with her then. When I arrived for the interview and showed her the Thai translation of my "call for participants," which had translated "transmasculine" as *ying bpen chai* (literally, woman is man), she became outwardly confused. She had thought I was a cisgender guy when we first met, and asked several times in Thai if I was a boy or a girl. I was extremely uncomfortable, not only due to the question itself but also because of our limited language capabilities—the language barrier was silencing me. More than not wanting to respond, I did not know how to respond in terms that she would understand. She also struggled to articulate her answers; often I found myself apologizing with *mai kow jai* (I don't understand) as she switched to English and grappled for words that, stacked together, might amount to her meaning. I thought she was rather distant and short of words during the interview, and her girlfriend did most of the translating. At the end of the interview she asked if I was a boy or a girl again, so I said *puu ying* (woman). She replied, "So you are like a *tom*!" Identifying me as someone "like" her, she then said she would be glad to be interviewed again, any time.

This happened in another interview with a group of friends—some *tom*, some *dee*—at a bar in Chiang Mai. Halfway through our conversation, the younger sister of a *tom* I had previously interviewed said, "I just realized you are a girl! I thought you were a man!" The discussion reached a point where I explained the physical effects of my testosterone injections and that FTM transition was not only about bottom surgery. Later, while we were chatting after the conclusion of my questions, one of the *toms* at the table asked me, "So, when did you know you were like a *tom*?"

During another interview with a *tom* in Doi Saket, I passed as another *tom* until midway through our conversation, when I chose to out myself as trans and queer, which caused her a lot of confusion. The energy in the room shifted, and I wondered if I had upset her in some way. Despite her difficulty understanding my definitions of queer, which she read as lesbian and as not being strict about active and passive roles during sex, afterwards she seemed fine with it and returned to the idea that I was "like" her, was another *tom*, and was a friend. She proceeded to ask if I had a girlfriend, and why I did not have one. "You don't want one? Because you can find a good girl."

During the opening reception of the exhibition at the Bangkok Art and Culture Centre, I noticed that a person I read as *tom* was sitting on one of the beanbag chairs watching my film. We made eye contact and began talking. Part way through our conversation, she asked, "You, boy or girl? When you were born, boy or girl?" When I answered, she revealed, "Me, too. I always knew that I liked ladies. But you, you look like a guy, a lot."

These episodes made it clear that I had not taken into consideration the ways in which I would be perceived by interviewees and how these perceptions would influence the quality of our connections and understandings of each other. Despite the many ways *toms* adapt masculinity, and despite the fact that some *toms* (to me) seem to pass as male, none of the *toms* I interviewed had heard about transgender men. They were at times resistant and critical of the concept. Even though some Thais read me as a cisgender man or a *tom* before interviews occurred, after my attempts to explain my personal identification all returned to the word *tom* in order to make a connection with me. Many *toms* explained the nature of being *tom* (what might be defined as their "gender") in terms of knowing they had always been attracted to feminine women. *Tom* (as a "gender") is then defined in terms of sexual attraction, or one's sexuality. Masculine gender presentation and attraction to feminine women seem to be one and the same—one directly follows the other. Because the Thai language does not differentiate between the words "sex" and "gender" (both are translated as *khwam phet*), articulating gender as separate from sexual preference in my conversations with Thais was one of my first obstacles and became a complicated task.

Because I felt the need to locate transmasculinity in Thailand in order to feel a sense of Thai cultural belonging, I searched and grasped for a sense of connection with other *toms*. While I tolerated their questioning of my assigned sex and the discomfort that it caused, I felt a complicated and contradictory sense of elation *and* alienation when they repeatedly recognized me as "like" them. I felt silenced by the assumption that I desired feminine women in the same way I felt silenced by the demand to choose between *khrap* and *kha*. I delicately asked about what I had only just learned was called *tom*/gay, *tom* and *tom* pairings,[9] but I was afraid to appear too strange and possibly lose my sense of connection with *toms*. The geographically and culturally specific ways in which I conceptualized my queerness and my gender (as someone who has come into being as a queer and trans person of color in the San Francisco Bay Area) were lost on and illegible to most Thais.

I was also not prepared for how my strong sense of identification with other gender-nonconforming and transmasculine Thais somewhat overshadowed my connections with *toms*. Mostly this was due to language and cultural context. All the trans and gender-nonconforming Thais I met spoke English, and to a certain extent I believe that their identification as trans or gender nonconforming was made possible because of their fluency in English and familiarity with certain US-derived cultural concepts. Even though the terms *tom* and *dee* are derived from English words, they have a specific cultural context in Thai; however, "trans" and "gender nonconforming" have a limited linguistic and cultural context when translated into Thai, and much of the popular knowledge around "trans" relates to trans women.[10] While *sao praphet song* or transfeminine identities in Thailand are structured around the taking of birth control pills, surgeries, and the idea of passing as a cisgender woman, *tom* identity has no relation to hormones or surgeries and is generally not concerned with passing as a cisgender man.

When I asked *toms* if they had ever heard of transgender men (to accommodate the translation, I asked if they had ever heard of women changing their sex to be men, or if they knew *toms* who took male hormones), most replied with theorizations of their own personal identity, saying they did not want to change their bodies, or with a discussion about the meanings of *tom*. One participant theorized being *tom* as coming to terms with having a female body, that using *khrap*, binding one's chest, and using the men's restroom were not really all they were hyped up to be, and that when a *tom* finds someone, that person will love them for who they are, despite and because of having a feminine, yet masculine, body. This is interesting alongside the vantage point of one Thai FTM participant living in Bangkok, who was the only Thai FTM in Thailand I was able to meet in person. My call for participants had been posted with the tags "Thai," "trans," and "genderqueer" on tumblr, and a few of my interviewees, including this one, connected to me through this tumblr post.[11] During our Doi Saket-to-Bangkok Skype call, he said that most Thai people think of FTM transition as only involving surgery and that they do not know about the possibility of taking hormones. This was true of the *toms* in the group conversation at the Chiang Mai bar; they talked about top surgery not being desirable and being worried about how bottom surgery would impact their experience of orgasm. They were very curious about how taking hormones had physically changed my own body; when I said that I had grown some muscle, one *tom* said, "I want it!" In addition, the options for getting access to testosterone therapy in Thailand at the time were very limited and expensive. The Thai FTM in Bangkok said that his injections were six thousand baht per shot. Information about FTM transition (at least in 2011, at the time of this initial writing) is only made public in Thai media through news stories about non-Thai FTMs coming to Thailand for gender reassignment surgeries, and thus FTM transition itself becomes folded into the industry of tourism and Western (or non-Thai) influence and consumption. This definitely impacts how *toms* come to understand FTM identity and experience and in turn influences how they choose to embody gender.

How *toms* choose to embody gender and how they are able and allowed to embody gender are also affected by larger national discourses around Thai masculinity. One *tom*'s reasoning for why it is acceptable to be *tom* in Chiang Mai involved an explanation of the ways in which masculinity differs in different regions within Thailand, and it involved comparing masculinity in Thailand to that in other countries like the United States and Australia. According to this participant, a softer or more effeminate masculinity is accepted in Chiang Mai among men than in Bangkok or more metropolitan areas of Thailand. She cited an article in *Matichon* (a Thai newspaper with a relatively progressive leaning) that discussed the ways in which Thai women have more cultural power within the family unit (i.e., when men and women marry, men go to live in the women's houses) and more sensitivity and *ot-ton* (patience) than men.[12] According to this participant, being *tom* in Chiang Mai is accepted because it is accepted that women can take on the power associated with masculinity and that men have to have, as she said, a "small voice" and have to be, to a certain extent, subordinate to women.

It is interesting to relate this to larger racialized imperialist discourses around Asian masculinity. During our Doi Saket–to-Portland Skype call, one Thai American participant (and tumblr contact), in response to a question about what fears and insecurities they have about their bodies and about masculinity, said that they pass as a guy in many public spaces because, being Asian in the United States, it is more accepted to be an effeminate guy and because Asian masculinity, within this discourse, is read as effeminate and subordinate to White masculinities. Thai *toms* are often read as cute and friendly, perhaps because their adaptation of masculinity—"softer," more sensitive—is less threatening to maleness as a whole. Zee performs a level of cuteness as a *tom* that is acknowledged and highly celebrated by her fans (Facebook fan page comments are cluttered with exclamations of *naa-rak* [cute] in both Thai and English). However, as was the case with the *tom*'s point of view noted in the beginning of this section, the fact that Zee looked too much like a man meant that she/he had stepped out of bounds. Even though a degree of masculinity, strength, and power is accepted for Thai women, there are also many prescribed cultural codes for femininity, which affect both *sao praphet song* and *toms* in different ways. Being female in Thailand is about being *rieb roy*, which roughly translates as "extremely proper and polite"; according to one *tom* participant, if you want to be a girl, you will not be anything but *rieb roy*. Aren Z. Aizura (2009) writes about "the circulation of feminine beauty as a standard-bearer for Thai nationalism, and as emblematic of Thai governmental aspirations to modernity and status as a developed nation, while retaining the specificity of a 'traditional' Thainess" (305). I believe that Thai transgender men may be rendered invisible in Thai discourse because of how they reject and refigure the femininity embedded in the ideal of Thainess.

Recognition Disorients: Locating FTM Experience outside Language

In early April 2011, the young Thai FTM participant living in Bangkok, whom I had previously interviewed via Skype, met me on the ninth floor of the Bangkok

Art and Culture Centre. We sat there together watching my film, almost entirely in silence. I remember feeling elated, yet also strangely at ease. Afterward, we walked around Siam Square and got a couple of Singha beers at the 7-Eleven. We sat on the corner and talked for what easily could have been the entire night. We discovered we both liked parks and carried water bottles and that Thai people do not like to go to parks and do not carry water bottles. Were we Thai or what? My film project had miraculously opened up a space for the both of us to meet. When he left, I lingered on the Skytrain walkway and watched a "Hello Korea!" dance competition taking place in front of the MBK mall below. I felt that, if nothing else, I had made this film for him.

The final section of this article is about my conversations with other FTM and transmasculine-identified Thais. It has been difficult to write. At first this difficulty seems odd. My struggles with Thai *toms* (with translation, constant definition, and a feeling of erasure) were somehow more concrete and substantial than the disorienting sense of sameness, family, kinship, fullness, and possibility that I felt with the Thai FTMs and queers I had hoped, but never dreamt, I would meet. These people were articulating and braiding together parts of myself that had been buried deep, were giving voice to things for which I had never before found language. Also, nearly all of the FTMs I interviewed were also mixed race, like myself. I was seeing myself, and being seen, as if for the first time. My encounter with Thai FTMs and queers mirrors the moment my new friend, the young Thai FTM mentioned above, realized transition was actually possible. I asked him to elaborate on this moment, which he mentioned in our interview, and in a later email communication to me he wrote: "Well, I think the only thing I could remember is that I saw [this] (trans)guy wearing a blue shirt, sitting in front of a camera talking about testosterone and how he was transitioning. Before I came across this vid, I didn't know anything about transgender or FTMs. My belly just felt really strange, it was a feeling of hope, hope that I can really live my life as a boy and be happy." Recognition can be disorienting. Translating what I know and feel intuitively as our truths into a text that can be communicated and analyzed conceptually has been the hardest part of the process. In my film, I moved away from spoken and written text into dance and movement as modes of translation for precisely this reason. But here in the final section of this article, I challenge myself to notate and share some points of our inner landscape—namely, disconnection, exclusion, removal between and among categories of gender, ethnicity, and nationality, but also excitement and hope that Thai FTM community can be found.

I began my interviews with Thai FTMs with the question, "How do you connect to being Thai?" I wanted to know how being queer and/or trans was a barrier to connecting with and finding a sense of belonging in Thai community and being accepted by our Thai families. This usually opened up a discussion around the intersectionality of gender, ethnicity, and nationality as well as feelings of exclusion and disconnection from the categories of *tom* and Thai. One gender-nonconforming, ethnically Chinese participant said, "It's becoming more of a question of how do I disconnect with being Thai, especially when the word Thai signifies a lot of things that I don't really connect with." While I talked with people who identified as FTM, transmasculine, gender nonconforming, and queer, who identified with varying degrees of masculinity, all still felt constricted by and disconnected from *tom* as a category and because of this did not know of, or had yet to find, community with any other queer and trans-identified Thai people. Our distances to being Thai mean we do not find each other.

While being half Thai removes me from being fully or "authentically" Thai already, I feel that my identification as queer and trans enacts a further removal, causing me to make more of an effort to find a way to be Thai across all that distance—I have to search. Thai Americans often felt that their gender or gender-nonconforming presentation excluded them from Thai cultural belonging. Sometimes gender and ethnicity inhabit completely separate communities and parts of our identity such that they are unable to exist simultaneously. The Thai transmasculine-identified person living in Portland (whom I mention above) also spoke about being queer and being Thai as not the same thing, as not connecting. This person was preparing to visit their family in Thailand in the coming months and felt that in order to go there, they would have to take a break from being a trans person. Ultimately, they felt it was more important to get to know their community and build relationships with their family there, so they decided to stop taking testosterone in order to make the trip. Because they felt so separate from Thai identity, they decided it was important to search for it and go to Thailand, even though it meant having to present as a cisgender woman and having to choose between being Thai and being trans. This was a hard decision for them to make, and they felt that while they wanted both their gender and ethnicity to coexist, they could not.

I already knew it was difficult to be both trans and Thai: for Americans it required proving Thai cultural belonging and being legible as Thai, whether that was through being able to speak Thai or having access to and being accepted by Thai community. But was it difficult to be both *tom* and Thai? This latter question failed to translate in my interviews with *toms*, because *toms* living in Thailand did not experience their gender and ethnicity as mutually exclusive in the ways that Thai and Thai American FTMs and I constantly expressed and had to negotiate. The Thai transmasculine person living in Los Angeles (whom I mentioned earlier) also talked about the ways in which his gender, ethnicity, and nationality engaged with each other as a "constant negotiation." Many *toms* had a strong sense of self and of their community and had pride in being both Thai and *tom* without separation, although their ethnicity and gender, or their legibility as Thai, came into question only when they traveled outside Thailand, without the presence of *tom* communities. They commented on the high visibility of *toms* in Chiang Mai and Thailand at large and pointed out that they did not feel the need to hide. Even though Thai society might not entirely accept *toms* as politicized beings with a discrete, collective "identity," it still held them; unlike FTMs, they had a community rooted in a shared Thai cultural belonging. The lack of a place or available cultural role in Thailand for Thai FTMs often meant "picking a side," or choosing to be either Thai or trans, when it came to finding community.

In contrast to *toms'* visibility and strong sense of community, the two trans guys living in Thailand with whom I spoke in 2011 were extremely isolated, what with the complete lack of information in the Thai media about the possibility of FTM transition, other than the Internet, and with how *toms* had difficulty understanding their need or desire to "pass" as male. The Thai FTM in Bangkok said that because there is "no word for trans guy in Thai," it is "difficult to explain that I identify as male to Thais. They just don't get the concept." Both of the trans guys I interviewed were seeing doctors who had never had FTM patients before.

For myself and other Thai Americans, the ways in which we construct and conceptualize our gender identities within a QTPOC (queer and trans people of color) framework and community clashes with Thai constructions of gender and binary thinking, rendering us illegible as Thai. Many transmasculine Thais disidentified with *tom* identity and consequently with being Thai, because they did not see themselves in that culture. Being Thai (and having Thai mothers) conflates Thai identity with femininity, rendering our gender transition as a transition away from being Thai. For those of us who are half white, our queerness often makes us more white, or more American. Thus our trans identification distances us from femininity and Thai identity and makes us "whiter." The participant living in Portland said, "I looked more Asian when I was a girl" and that "presenting more masculine made me Whiter," a sentiment that resonated with me. They also shared that their gender is dependent on the context in which they find themselves. While they were often read as a cisgender guy, they missed being a part of women's community and women-of-color spaces and found a giant rift between their woman-of-color and Thai identities and their genderqueer, trans, and white identities. When we "transition," we sometimes alienate ourselves from women-of-color spaces or from our Thai identity, because sometimes the spaces in which we encounter trans community are white dominant. They said, "I don't see my kind of queerness or transness coexisting with my kind of Thainess." There was no narrative for being all these things.

Since the making of the film and the initial writing of this essay, Bangkok has started to become more widely known for providing FTM gender reassignment surgeries, although this information does not seem to be made publicly available to Thai people. Instead, it is disseminated and passed on through FTM communities and networks outside Thailand, feeding the medical tourism industry and empowering non-Thai trans men, while Thai trans men remain in the dark. This dichotomy is further troubled by the publication of an English-language article, "A Tricky Transition: Two Female-to-Male Transsexuals Open Up about the Difficulties They Have Faced with Their Sexuality, Families, and Winning Acceptance" (*Bangkok Post* 2012). The article is the first of its kind that I have seen to profile the lives of Thai trans men. Surprisingly, it manages to use all the politically correct language concerning "transgender" experience in an American context while curiously making no mention of the hypervisible *tom/dee* community in Thailand. The English-speaking expatriate community in Thailand is very large and powerful enough to have English-language Thai publications like the *Bangkok Post* available, which are specifically geared toward an expat readership but are inaccessible to non-English-speaking Thais. This may explain why this article about Thai trans men exists while Thai people remain resistant to their existence. One of the two people profiled in the article, Kritipat Chotidhanitsakul, "began administering testosterone injections on himself after extensive internet research about F2M transitions, and a failed attempt to gather medical information on the topic within the country." He was "shocked when the medical practitioner in question Googled the brand of testosterone and the dosage he had brought along for him to see." Kritipat "dates straight women whom he often has to explain the term transman to." These were the same issues that the Thai FTMs I interviewed were facing.

Recently, Kritipat (nicknamed "Jimmy") started the Transmale and Alliance Association of Thailand (FTM Thailand), which has its own Facebook group and is the cause for much excitement. I even stumbled upon a photo of Zee with Jimmy, which means some of these discussions around *tom* and trans identity and embodiment must have already begun. I have also discovered the existence of a gender-neutral "I" pronoun (*ka-pa-jao*) and a gender-neutral particle (*haa*), and while I am not sure how popular these are in common speech among trans people in Thailand, it is at least a start. There is so much more I had hoped to discuss that I could not do here, much more that can be mined from my interviews and research, and much more that I have yet to learn and desire to know. As I listen to Zee's new single and scroll through the Transmale Alliance Association of Thailand's Facebook posts, my belly feels strange. I no longer see the failures of language—I see a beginning.

Jai Arun Ravine is the author of แล้ว *and then entwine: lesson plans, poems, knots* (2011) and the director of the short film *Tom/Trans/Thai* (2011), which has screened at the Bangkok Art and Culture Centre (Thailand) and CAAMFest 2013 (San Francisco), among others.

Acknowledgments

Some of this material previously appeared in a different form as the essay "Tom/Gay, Trans/Queer: Mixed Translations Across Thai and Thai American Trans-masculinities," an excerpt of which was published by Emerson Whitney online at *Wild Gender*.

Notes

1. In "Masculinity and *Tom* Identity in Thailand," Megan Sinnott writes, "In contemporary Thai, *tom* is a term derived from the English word 'tomboy' and refers to masculine-identified women who have sexual attraction towards and relationships with feminine-identified women, who are called *dee* (from the English word 'la*dy*')" (2000: 94). I would modify this statement by adding that *tom* is used by masculine-presenting female-bodied Thais to refer to themselves and that *dee* or *dy* is used by feminine-presenting female-bodied Thais to refer to themselves. Some *dees* identify as heterosexual, while others may date both *toms* and straight cisgender men. The shorthand *tom/dy/lez* (*lez* being derived from the English word "lesbian") is currently in use by @*tom act*, on the web, and in social media.

2. In the Thai language, gender is self-assigned in everyday speech by the use of gendered "I" pronouns—*phom* for men and *di-chun* or *chun* for women—as well as the particles *khrap* (for men) and *kha* (for women), which are used at the ends of sentences or as shortcuts for affirmative responses (i.e., "yes"). *Chun* is also often used by men in popular music, but for FTMs it does not suffice as a gender-neutral option.

3. In speaking of transfeminine–identified women of color in New York, David Valentine writes, "But I am beginning to wonder about how Nancy and her friends fit into 'transgender' alongside Andrew, Riki, Cindy, or Cherry, each of whom has their own way of mapping differences and similarities between themselves and others" (2007: 9). Valentine's interest in looking at "transgender" as a category "and how it is setting the terms by which people come to identify themselves and others" (21) helped me think about how *tom* might fit into trans (as in the case of Zee), and how trans might fit into *tom*.

4. I have not been able to determine what pronoun Zee would use to self-describe in English. Even though Facebook fans use "she," the fact that Zee consistently uses *phom* and *khrap*, and may also have had top surgery and be taking hormones (though this is hearsay), I use "she" and at other times "she/he" to replicate this ambiguity.

5. Since then, the film has been installed at Sabina Lee Gallery (Los Angeles) and was screened at CAAMFest 2013 (San Francisco), Pitzer College (Claremont, CA), and My People Film Series (Pittsburgh), among others, and taught in college courses throughout the United States. For more information, see Ravine 2011.

6. In this article I use "transmasculine" to describe those who identify as being on the FTM spectrum, including those who identify completely as male or as something other or between. For the purposes of this article I do not use it in reference to *tom* identity. At other points in the article, my usage of FTM includes transmasculine and gender-nonconforming people.

7. I was also interested in making connections to more recent research on transmasculinities in other areas of Southeast Asia, including the Philippines, Taiwan, and Vietnam, but these connections were not able to be made within the scope of the article in its present form.

8. I use *sao praphet song* instead of *kathoey* to refer to trans women in the article. My reasoning follows LeeRay Costa and Andrew Matzner,

> *Sao braphet song* are more commonly known in Thailand and the West by the terms "*kathoey*" and "*lady boy*." In this book we use the term *sao braphet song* because various Thai we spoke with felt that this term was more polite than *kathoey*. Since the term *kathoey* is ambiguous, i.e., it can have positive or negative connotations depending on the context and position of the speaker and can be interpreted as a slur, we decided to use the more neutral *sao braphet song*. (1997, 1)

9. One participant directed me to a website that is no longer available. Subsequent participants mentioned that they had heard about the same website but had not personally met anyone who identified that way.

10. The word *kathoey* was originally used in reference to nonnormative behaviors on the part of both men and women, and while it has come to be translated as a variety of words in English, including "homosexual," "transsexual," "transvestite," and "sterile," it is currently used only to describe gay men or trans women and is often used as a slur. See Sinnott (2000: 103).

11. I am grateful to whoever posted my call for participants on tumblr, which helped me connect to several participants and Thai FTMs even after completing the film.

12. I have not been able to find this *Mathicon* article or a translation of it.

References

Aizura, Aren Z. 2009. "Where Health and Beauty Meet: Femininity and Racialisation in Thai Cosmetic Surgery Clinics." *Asian Studies Review* 33, no. 3: 303–17.

@*tom act*. 2010. "Special Fashion and Exclusive Interview with Zee." July–August.

Bangkok Post. 2012. "A Tricky Transition: Two Female-to-Male Transsexuals Open Up about the Difficulties They Have Faced with Their Sexuality, Families, and Winning Acceptance." October 8. Reposted by the Thai Transgender Alliance, www.thaitga.com/index.php/library/news/198-female-to-male.

Comments on "ลึง (Deeply): ZEE [Official MV]." youtu.be/cfK385VC3sw (accessed January 4, 2014).

Costa, LeeRay, and Andrew Matzner. 2007. *Male Bodies, Women's Souls: Personal Narratives of Thailand's Transgendered Youth*. New York: Haworth.

Ravine, Jai Arun, dir. 2011. *Tom/Trans/Thai*. jaiarunravine.wordpress.com/tomtransthai (accessed March 8, 2014).

Sinnott, Megan. 2000. "Masculinity and Tom Identity in Thailand." In *Lady Boys, Tom Boys, Rent Boys: Male and Female Homosexualities in Contemporary Thailand*, ed. Peter A. Jackson and Gerard Sullivan, 94–116. Chiang Mai: Silkworm.

Transmale and Alliance Association of Thailand (FTM Thailand) Facebook page. facebook.com/groups/ftmthailandofficial (accessed March 8, 2014).

Valentine, David. 2007. *Imagining Transgender: An Ethnography of a Category*. Durham, NC: Duke University Press.

Zee Matanawee Keenan's Facebook page. www.facebook.com/zeefc (accessed March 8, 2014).

The Technical Capacities of the Body

Assembling Race, Technology, and Transgender

JULIAN GILL-PETERSON

Abstract This essay travels with the testosterone molecule to pursue a theory of racialized and trans embodiment as technical capacities of all bodies, not only of the trans-of-color subject subordinated to racially normative and gender-normative white and cisgender bodies (though the hormone molecule is implicated in those relations). It focuses on technology to think race and transgender *together*, from a common conceptual ground, rather than as separate strands of thought recombined through an intersectional or cyborg hybridity framework.

Keywords transgender; body; race; hormone therapy; technology; capacity

W hen the US Congress added synthetic testosterone to Schedule III of the Controlled Substances Act in 1990, it did so avowedly to curb sports doping. But as Toby Beauchamp (2013: 59) points out, Congress's attempt to secure and regulate the bodily mobilities that synthetic hormones enable is a case study in transgender studies' importance to questions that implicate *all* bodies in their biopolitical investment by the state. Beauchamp asks us to consider, in addition to synthetic hormone therapy for trans[1] bodies, what "a discussion ostensibly about *inanimate* objects—chemical substances—tell[s] us about the gendered, racial, and national stakes of hormone regulation" (59; emphasis added). I begin with an extension of this insight, by revaluing the ostensible inanimateness of the chemical molecule. Congress ranks synthetic hormones relatively low on what could be called the national animacy hierarchy, codifying the hormone molecule as a substance analogous to recreational drugs: able to be abused but possessing no relevant agency prior to human consumption. If synthetic testosterone is treated as a technical object, however, we can ask different questions of it: what dynamism inheres in the actual molecule? How and at what scales does its circulation increase or decrease the capacities of various bodies to affect and be

TSQ: Transgender Studies Quarterly ★ Volume 1, Number 3 ★ August 2014
DOI 10.1215/23289252-2685660 © 2014 Duke University Press

affected (Deleuze and Guattari 1987: 283–84)? And how do the testosterone molecule's material itineraries reshape transgender studies' understanding of the relation of race to transgender through the lens of technology?

The itineraries of the testosterone molecule as a technology trace something emergent, something greater than its literal sum total—they trace an ecology. An eco-logic of testosterone attends to the Greek root of ecology, *oikos*, meaning a home, natural habitat, or milieu (Guattari 1989: 147). The testosterone molecule has many homes, each one occupied simultaneously and yet inhabited differently. It circulates in the flesh of the human body, modulating the endocrine system; it circulates as a politicized and regulated medicine in an apparatus of institutional healthcare, access to which is severely unevenly distributed in the United States; it circulates on markets both licit and illicit, commodified and trafficked; it circulates as a linguistic signifier, caught in the vocabulary of trans subjectivity and politics; and it circulates as a chemical index of environmental toxicity, one among countless drugs flushed through the industrial water system into rivers and oceans (see Ward and Blum 2012; Don, Mendoza, and Pritchard 2008). As those endocrine disruptors accumulate in water, plant, and animal bodies, eventually reingested by humans, the molecule does not so much restart a linear cycle as act differentially—ecologically: the hormone molecule never quite strikes each of its homes in the same way, and both the technical object and its milieu are continuously transformed by each iteration of its travels.

Not all of these itineraries are enabled by human action or even by the unintended effects of human agency. Indeed, some of testosterone's ecological homes are built by the actions of so many countless molecules themselves, saturating environments in which their presence can be deduced only spectrally through its effects, as when they render river systems toxic to populations of fish. To say that the testosterone molecule circulates in an ecology is to take notice of its dynamism as a technology rather than treat it as a domesticated tool synthesized and used by humans for rational or irrational ends. Approaching the hormone as a technology whose circulation maps out an ecology underscores that although the human subject, the subject of transgender and race, is one of its homes, it is not the only one—and that "matters" (Cheah 1996) a great deal, in turn, to our understanding of both transgender and race, because from the very beginning of endocrinology as a medical technology the body and its technical capacities have bound sex and gender to race through hormones.

This essay travels with the testosterone molecule to pursue a theory of racialized and trans embodiment as technical capacities of all bodies, not only of the trans-of-color subject subordinated to racially normative and gender-normative white and cisgender bodies (though the hormone molecule is implicated in those relations). It focuses on technology to think race and transgender *together*, from a common conceptual ground, rather than as separate strands of thought recombined through an intersectional or cyborg hybridity framework (see Puar 2012; LaMarre 2012: 79–80). The hormone is what the French thinker of technics Gilbert Simondon (1958: 52) calls "a technical object," the threshold between the human and the machine as well as between race and trans; it relates trans to race through their enmeshed embodied processes while nevertheless maintaining their positive difference.[2] As an emergent ecology, the total circulation of testosterone molecules on the planet functions as what Timothy Morton (2013) might call a hormonal hyperobject, one too massively distributed in time and space to be apprehended by human consciousness as a totality yet not for that diminished in its insistent, if spectral, presence. Rather than being too overwhelming, this ecology finds its consistency in the fact that the circulation of the hormone molecule is always technologically mediated. Through technology, thought opens onto the racialization of trans bodies via a common analysis that does not subordinate race a priori or retrospectively to the conceptual protocols of theories of transgender embodiment but rather attends to how they both receive their historical animacy from an endocrinological engagement with the body's hormonal technicity.

Recent work in transgender studies has explored the value of what gets left out in privileging the human subject and culture over technology and nonhuman agents. Aren Aizura (2012) examines the population level of biopolitics in transnational transgender migration and immigration, while Beatriz Preciado (2013: 33–34) playfully maps the dimensions of the "pharmaco-pornographic" arrangement of the contemporary biopolitics of sex and gender. Lucas Crawford (2008) speculates, mobilizing Gilles Deleuze and Félix Guattari, on the affectivity of a transgender Body Without Organs, while Eliza Steinbock (2013: 116) adds that "affect and the force of curious thinking may offer a livability that is not available by other means" to transgender studies. And in a unique contribution to posthumanist thought, Myra J. Hird (2008a) speculates on "animal trans," transplanting transgender to nonhuman life. Accounts of the cross-species becoming of trans now include essays on spiders, starfish, and horses (Hayward 2008, 2011) in a textual field that yields a dynamic theory of trans as an expansive term for a general "somatechnics," as Susan Stryker and Nikki Sullivan put it (2009). This essay adds to these emergent conversations by leveraging technicity to rethink not only transgender but also its relation to the racialized body. It mobilizes, in turn, Jacques Derrida's (2002, 2005) work on originary technicity, Deleuze and Guattari's (1987) writing on affect, and Simondon's (1958) philosophy of technicity to accent the different forces that each of them offers to transgender studies as well as to feminist, queer, and critical race theories of embodiment. Turning then to a case of contemporary transgender biopolitics, the theoretical strands of the essay are reexamined through the hormone molecule in an analysis of the medicalized emergence of the transgender child through puberty-suppression therapy.

This is both a materialist and a speculative essay.[3] Its departure from the sometimes more recognizable position of the "lived experience" of political subjects who identify or are categorized as trans or of color is not meant to replace, dilute, or transcend any of those objects of analysis. The ecological travels of the hormone molecule do nevertheless insist on a different map of what counts as political than that which is given by the juridical subject of right enforced by the European Enlightenment and its colonial regimes. After exploring the potentiality of technology for thinking trans and race as technical capacities of the body, this essay concludes by dwelling within the modes of politics whose itineraries, including that of the testosterone molecule, it shadows.

Transgender as an Originary Technicity

Humanism is predicated on a strict categorical separation and implicit hierarchy of the body over technology. As Bernard Stiegler explains, the consequence of this ontological distinction is that "the analysis of technics is made in terms of ends and means, which implies necessarily that no dynamic proper belongs to technical beings" (1998: 1). The ontological separation of technics and living beings underwrites the notion of an integral human body, according to which the incorporation of technology is a fall from the original wholeness of birth.

This ontological separation is important to the category transgender because it informs any thinking of "body modification," a phrase whose temporal spacing suggests the prior existence of a "body" that can only be modified after the fact, by means of technology as a tool, as the extension of the human beyond its biological originality. This strict separation is one reason it has made sense to argue that, whatever the empiricism of the existence of two biological sexes (and there is more than enough evidence to dismiss sexual dimorphism [see Hird 2008b]), the capacity to proliferate a multiplicity of psychic genders via technocultural modification of bodies according to rational human agency is the strength of transgender (see Butler 1990: 8–10; Salamon 2010). Yet this is also a transgendered political subjectivity derivative of the European Enlightenment's version of human agency that presumes a set of universalisms in defining the subject. Monique Allewaert's (2013: 20) work on ecology and "parahumanity" in the colonial tropics adds that the enlightened human as political subject, in addition to being historically exclusionary, may never have taken root, even as an ideal, within subaltern modes of personhood in the "modern" Americas.

The restriction of transgender agency to psychic identity also renders the matter of the trans body passive, inaccessible, and ultimately separate from the subjectivity that is meant to be its anchor, leaving the possibility open for transphobic devaluation. As the "border wars" in American feminism over the inclusion and exclusion of trans women remind (see Enke 2012), if the capacity to transition from one recognized gender to another—or to suspend legible gender by inhabiting its in-between—requires an intentional modification of a preexisting body, then trans subjects can be cast under suspicion as not "truly" what they claim to be, as imperfect copies of an original. The use of technology to modify the body can be deployed against its authenticity, as a means of devaluing the trans body by measuring only its resemblance to the presumed natural cisgender body.

To avoid vulnerability to this transphobic, humanist reaction, I follow Stryker and Sullivan (2009) in proposing trans as an expression of the originary technicity of the body. Technics and its specific technologies, rather than subordinate to the rational subject, can be thought of expansively, as life touching itself. Derrida's affectionate engagement with Jean-Luc Nancy in *On Touching* (2005: 216) provides such an account in its meditation on "eco-technics," the technics of the body. For Nancy, the body touching itself is the fundamental example of how living beings are constituted by their differential technical capacities. In *Corpus*, Nancy (2008: 63) writes evocatively that "the body is the plastic matter of a spacing out without form or Idea," which Derrida glosses in *On Touching* as a "plasticity and technicity 'at the heart' of 'the body proper' . . . an irreducible *spacing*, that is, what spaces out touching itself, namely con-tact . . . this spacing makes for the trial of noncontact as the *very* condition or experience *itself* of contact" (Derrida 2005: 221; emphasis in original). Touching is conditioned by the radical impossibility of touching oneself or the other, the elusiveness of pure, unmediated presence in contact between flesh.

Later, Derrida continues that it is through Nancy's account of the irreducibility of the spacing or *différance* in touching that

> this *technical* supplementarity of the body [is] acknowledged [as] essential and necessary, as it seems to me that one should always do. . . . It goes without saying that "essential originarity" is conveniently translating this "law" into a classical language that precisely meets its limit here. For this supplementarity of technical prosthetics originarily spaces out, defers, or expropriates all originary properness: there is no "the" sense of touch, there is no "originary" or essentially originary touching before it, before its necessary possibility—for any living being in general, and well before "the hand of man" and all its imaginable substitutes. (223; emphasis in original)

To speak in terms of originary technicity does not merge the technical and the somatic but maintains the productive *différantial* relation through which the spacing of life by its technical modes both effaces the purity of origin of the body while making available its energetic deferrals and associated media for what Nancy terms "incarnation": the "organic articulation" of the body by technics (2008: 221). Originary technicity is an account of *how* living beings differ from themselves—a definition of *how* it is to be alive (not what it is or means). "As a self-relation," Derrida (2002: 244) explains, "as activity and reactivity, as differential force, and repetition, life is always already inhabited by technicization." Technology is not added to living beings. Life reaches beyond itself and returns to itself, touches itself and the world around it, in order to grow and change, to differ from itself over time, through an impure and yet necessary technical disposition.

If forms of trans embodiment are expressions of the originary technicity of the body, then body modification cannot be transphobically exceptionalized as a betrayal of the human's integrity. For example, sex reassignment surgery—or, indeed, all desired surgeries, whether deemed "elective" or "medically necessary"— are a participation in the body's open-ended technical capacities, the ways in which its physical matter, biological systems, and affective components exceed conscious will through receptiveness to change as difference, as nonidentity. The intervention of the surgeon's technologies is not opposed to the body's systems but rather informs and is informed by them. Hormone therapy, likewise, is a participation in the technical capacity of the endocrine system. The difference between synthetic hormone therapy and the endocrine system's autonomic functioning is that hormone therapy involves a subject's technological intervention upon its own body—a situation akin to Nancy's example of the skin touching itself.

In the Austrian endocrinology circles that first produced the gonadocentric theory of the body's sexed and sexual development in the 1910s and 1920s, the categorical splitting of the gonads into a separate reproductive gland (producing sperm or eggs) and "puberty" gland (producing testosterone or estrogen) medically unhinged biologically defined sex and sexuality from reproduction for the first time by proposing a hormonal plasticity separate from the function of the gametes (Logan 2007: 690, 698–703). This separation of sex, in both its somatic and psychic manifestations, into an actionable field that could be modified by removing or transplanting gonads was the medical intervention into the body's technicity that made possible the eventual concept of sex reassignment and cross-sex hormone therapy. By understanding the endocrine system as receptive to change through variable hormone circulation and environmental change that could be affected by medicine, early endocrinologists recognized even before the synthesis of hormones that medical technologies of sex gain their relative animacy from the body's own technicity, not in opposition to or by transcending it.

Treating endocrine therapies as an example of the originary technicity of the body does not collapse life and technics into an undifferentiated organism.

Drawing on a passage by Deleuze and Guattari engaged with Simondon, the trans subject intervening technologically upon its body can be understood as what they name the artisan. The artisan appears in *A Thousand Plateaus* (Deleuze and Guattari 1987: 408) to explain Simondon's critique of hylomorphism, the philosophical separation of active form from a passive or homogenous matter upon which form is impressed by human activity. In a hylomorphic account of hormone therapy, the rational mind impresses the ideal form of gender upon the substrate of the passive body through scientifically determined hormone dosage. The hylomorphic account of the work of the artisan follows analogously: the carpenter impresses the form of furniture she wishes to build upon the passive material of the wood.

"But Simondon demonstrates that the *hylomorphic* model," Deleuze and Guattari note, "leaves many things, active and affective, by the wayside" (408; emphasis in original). The artisan works on the wood, but the wood also works on itself and on the artisan, affecting the final object. The wood's "implicit forms," the virtual potential it carries as living matter, are what make it topologically receptive to being shaped by the artisan. These implicit forms are the torsions of the wood fibers that guide the tools and action of the artisan at the level of technique. Then there are its variable affects: "wood that is more or less porous, more or less elastic and resistant" (408). Rather than the artisan's violently imposing the form she has imagined onto the wood, Deleuze and Guattari propose, "it is a question of *surrendering to the wood*, then following where it leads by connecting operations to a materiality. . . . What one addresses is less a matter submitted to laws than a materiality possessing a *nomos*" (408; emphasis added). Not only do the wood's affects condition what the artisan can and cannot do, but the artisan must syncopate with their rhythms, acquiesce to their vibrant materiality, in order to "make" anything.

Following Derrida, the activity of the wood can be understood as its technical capacity for differentiation as living matter. The technique of the artisan is not a violent imposition upon the wood, because the wood shares with the artisan an originary technicity, as two distinct living beings entering into relation. Transposing this example back to hormone therapy, the trans subject is likewise an artisan, and the material with which the subject is engaged is the flesh of the body, with the hormone molecule serving as the interface relating the two without opposing them or collapsing their distinction. The body is not a passive substrate ruled by a transgendered consciousness but an open technical system with its own implicit forms, its own affects that enable and restrict the capacity of the subject to change the body with hormones (see Preciado 2013 for a first-person account). Hormone therapy as a strategy of trans embodiment is a unique expression of a living body's capacity to reach beyond and back toward itself through technics.

This material becoming entails the possibility of creative failure, too: to exceed itself and swerve in unexpected ways. The body undergoing hormone therapy cannot be separated in kind from other living beings in this respect and devalued as impure, for it is not of a different kind of technicity than a cisgendered body, even if their respective becomings are radically distinct.

If "trans," then, signals the technical capacity of the body to modify its gender—if gender is defined by technical modes that are not external or purely prosthetic—then technicity is also the link to understanding racialized embodiment without recourse to an intersectional or cyborg framework because, as the next section explores, the same endocrinologists who first separated genetic and embodied forms of sex through hormones bound their clinical research to a racialized body. Technicity, then—the capacity that Simondon (1958: 72) describes as "the intermediary between form and matter"—is how bodies assemble themselves simultaneously as racialized and gendered while preserving what makes each distinct.[4]

Race is Technical

Social constructivist theories of race share with analyses of transgender as a psychic identification the humanist hierarchy of the body over technology. In what Arun Saldanha (2006) might call the deontologization of race, race becomes a form of phenotypic false consciousness, an irrational lamination over the body—literally, only "skin deep." This approach offers a durable critique of the ongoing biologization of race in the West and its colonial enterprises (see Chun 2012: 40–47). Nevertheless, if race is "merely" a bodily fiction, it follows that it must eventually be subtracted from the human, that antiracist and postcolonial projects must share the goal of restoring the body to an unraced form. To maintain the bodily integrity of humanism, not only must it be purified of technology, it must be purified of race (see Latour 1993). Although social constructivism rejects any ontology of race, then, it nevertheless affirms a humanist ontology that is politically, ethically, aesthetically, and technologically immiserating. Humanism is immiserating because it dismisses and excludes with suspicion anything that is not of its ideal body, and it is immiserating because it seeks the subtraction of race from itself. Humanism interpellates minoritarian subjects into a racial melancholia that risks reinforcing the hegemony of whiteness as a totality through stubborn opposition to it (see Viego 2007). As a consequence, humanism is also less able to account for how the universal body of the human without a race is already de facto occupied by the unmarked white body in narratives of transcendence like American "post-racial" discourse (Nyong'o 2009: 1–6). Finally, humanist theories of race produce a regulatory ideal of political agency derived from European modernity. As Saldanha puts it, this version of race as politically actionable "refers to the cultural *representation* of people, not to people themselves" (2006: 9).

If race is an effect of signification and regimes of visuality, Saldanha draws attention to the unresolved question of "how signification comes to have any effect at all, if not through the materiality of signs, bodies, and spaces" (9) Instead, Saldanha argues, "race must . . . be conceived as a chain of contingency, in which the connections between its constituent components are not given, but are made viscous through local attractions. . . . Nobody 'has' a race, but bodies are racialised" (12). If race is mapped out in its "machinic geography," the implication is that "race should not be eliminated, but *proliferated*, its many energies directed at multiplying racial differences to so as to render them joyfully cacophonic" (21). In a sympathetic essay that aims ambitiously to "wrest the concept of race away from reactive dialectics and give it over to its full positivity," Amit Rai (2012: 64) terms his ontologically embedded account "race racing." Rai's method is "to diagram race as sets of intensive variations in ecologies of sensation distributed unevenly and with uneven effects across populations," so as not to separate race from what it can do to rearrange the historical forces that produce and manage its various forms (70). For Rai, race racing emphasizes the potential for experimentation and mutation in the historically given "habituated sensations" of living in racialized bodies, redefining the resources of antiracist politics (73–74).

The common question of the *how* of race—how racialization materially happens—and what it might look like were it to migrate away from humanism can be historically finessed in its relation to transgender through technicity. Race is technical to the extent that technicity gives race the force of its history, the history of technologies of racialization. In media studies, the growing ubiquity of digital technology has prompted consideration of race *as* technology. Beth Coleman's (2009: 178) eponymous essay works toward "extending the function of *techne* to race" in order to evaluate the range of agentic potentials that resides in race's repurposing. Coleman asks of her readers "to rest with the formula: race as a technology—as a prosthesis of sorts—*adds functionality to the subject*, helps form location, and provides information" (194; emphasis added). Race as a technology entails an affirmation of the capacity wielded by all subjects to retool the future of racialization in a less exploitative, less violent, and less racist way than humanism offers in its zero-sum game of subtraction. Wendy Hui Kyong Chun's 2012 essay "Race and/as Technology" adds two questions that build on Coleman's work: "Can race be considered a technology and a mode of mediatization, that is, not only a mechanism, but also a practical or industrial art? Could 'race' be not simply an object of representation and portrayal, of knowledge or truth, but also a technique that one uses, even as one is used by it?" (38). Race, Chun suggests, could and should be made to do more in the service of the overcoming of systemic forms of violence. If there is a value to thinking of "race as prosthesis," as Chun puts it (49), it is that technicity is, following Derrida, an active capacity of living beings that makes this "prosthesis" inseparable from the body. To ignore its political capacities is a lost opportunity.

Both Coleman and Chun are careful to emphasize that the framework of race as technology is to think of race on aesthetic and ethical terms rather than on ontological terms, since for them ontology amounts to the biologizing question "what *is* race?" In light of Derrida's careful exposition of the word *originary* and Saldanha and Rai's Deleuzian ontology of difference, this essay's treatment of race as technical leads to a slightly different conclusion. If race has any ontological consistency, it is expressed in historical, arbitrary, and contingent forms derivative of technicity; race is defined by historical change and a lack of origin in the sense in which Derrida glossed the originary noncontact of touching. Race has *not* always existed; it is not required for human life. Indeed, race is literally no-thing. It is a historically inherited capacity for embodied techniques that, by virtue of being technical, carries with it the immanent ontological capacity of technics to swerve toward antiracist projects, toward futures that are not prescribed by the Enlightenment and colonialism. Race is aesthetic and ethical, but both of those are made ontological by technicity if by ontology we ask "what is the *becoming* of race?" instead of what race "is."

The distinction between ontological technicity and historical technologies is important when considering that sex and race have been entangled in the medical body from the very beginnings of endocrinology. In their 1920 paper "Climate and Puberty (*Klima und Mannbarkeit*)," Austrian endocrinologists Eugen Steinach and Paul Kammerer, the same figures who defended the hormonal plasticity of sex and gender, read anthropological literature alongside their heat experiments on rat gonad development to argue that higher temperatures stimulated the "interstitial tissues" that produce sex hormones, leading to an earlier onset of puberty and hyper–sex drive in colonized populations in tropical climates (quoted in Logan 2007: 694–95). Not only did they correlate race, through climate, to sex and sexuality, but they also argued that the endocrine system was the mechanism through which environmental information affecting the body was transmitted to subsequent generations, rejecting genetic determinism. Anticipating the post–World War II shift from scientific racism to humanist theories of cultural difference, Kammerer in particular deployed endocrinology in his subsequent work in the service of a "humane" form of racial hygiene he termed "rejuvenation," according to which knowledge of the endocrine plasticity of the body's development through sex and puberty would lead to an enlightened cultivation of the body politic, a hormonally conscious "socialist anatomy" of racial improvement in line with his Marxist politics (714). The endocrine system, as a vehicle of chemical information that serves as interface between the environment, the body, and its heritable acquired characteristics, produced a medical body from the very beginning that bound sex to race and sexuality through the hormone molecule's technical capacities to affect both biology and culture.

If both transgender and race benefit from treatment as technical capacities of the body, it remains to explain how it is they retain their differences in this framework as well as how they are made more or less available at various ecological scales by systems of normalization and regulation. Given the historical binding of sex to race through endocrinology's definition of puberty, the administration of populations through a contemporary hormonal biopolitics of transgendered puberty provides an opportunity to think transgender and race together.

The Administration of Transgender and Race:
Biopolitics and Puberty Suppression

Biopolitics addresses what Michel Foucault (1990: 141) enigmatically terms "the entry of life into history," the investment in and administration of the biological life of bodies and populations by the modern state and, increasingly, by neoliberal modes of capital that subsume the body down to its material and affective scales (Hardt and Negri 2001). Biomedicine is at the forefront of the contemporary biopolitics of sex, gender, sexuality, and race (see Rose 2006), and the transgender child is emerging as one of its newest anchors.

Puberty suppression therapy is increasingly administered for children under sixteen diagnosed with Gender Identity Disorder (GID) in the United States, Canada, and Europe (Cohen-Kettenis et al. 2011: 843). Through monthly injections or an implant device inserted under the skin, doses of a gonadotropin-releasing hormone (GnRH) analog bind with receptors in the pituitary gland to prevent it from releasing the luteinizing hormones (LH) and follicle stimulating hormones (FSH) that would otherwise trigger the release of sex hormones. If a child has not yet begun puberty, the therapy will do as its name suggests and prevent puberty from beginning, but it can also be administered to halt puberty after it has started. The procedure is, as its medical literature emphasizes, "reversible": once the GnRH medication is stopped, puberty begins or continues, regardless of age. Once a psychotherapist has assented to the "readiness" of the child per the diagnostics of GID, cross-sex hormones can be administered, and the child will undergo puberty as the desired sex (Cohen-Kettenis and van Goozen 1998: 247).

Puberty suppression therapy is touted by endocrinologists for reasons contested both in medical circles and in public debates over gender identity in childhood (see Lambrese 2010). Relying on a definition of puberty as a special period of somatic development segregated from an already consolidated core gender identity, the therapy's goal is to prevent the morphogenesis of "secondary sex characteristics," a concept adapted from nineteenth-century sexology by American researchers on transsexuality and gender identity in the 1950s and 1960s (Meyerowitz 2002: 127). Yet the therapeutic aim in preempting puberty is not only somatic but also psychological. Undergoing puberty in a wrongly sexed body is frequently described as "a nightmare," and the case is made that puberty suppression will prevent anxiety, depression, and suicidal ideation in adolescence (Cohen-Kettenis and van Goozen 1998: 248; Cohen-Kettenis et al. 2011: 846). Its second goal is a "more 'normal' and satisfactory appearance" after transition—a far more gender-normative capacity for passing and "realness" than has been available for adult transition (Giordano 2008: 580).[5] In some cases, FTM children who undergo puberty suppression therapy will not need top surgery as part of sex reassignment surgery, and MTF children will not need to manage the residues of voice change, facial hair, and a visible Adam's apple. Height can also be hormonally adjusted so that FTM and MTF adults fall within the statistical averages of men and women after puberty (Gibson and Cattlin 2010).

Puberty suppression therapy emerged in a Dutch clinic in the late 1990s (Cohen-Kettenis and van Goozen 1998: 246), but GnRH analog therapy predates it both in treatment of adult trans patients (to stop the production of endogenous sex hormones before administering cross-sex hormones) and in treating "precocious puberty." The latter in particular opens onto the biopolitics of sex, gender, sexuality, and race. The Tanner scale, the five-point diagram of "normal" puberty progression used to evaluate whether its onset is "precocious" and when to begin suppression therapy in trans children, is an astoundingly normalizing device: its visual and anthropometric standards were created out of median statistical analysis in the 1960s (Carel and Léger 2008: 2366). In bodies classified as male, the size of the phallus remains the most important measure, whereas for bodies classified as female, breast size and age of menstruation are emphasized. In order to minimize the arbitrariness of determining "when" puberty is supposed to take place, medical studies have produced variously phallocentric explanations of precocious puberty: one 2006 article in the *American Journal of Human Biology* (Matchcock and Susman), for instance, gives as a possible cause of precocious puberty in girls the absence of a father in the household. Puberty's medical management is also highly racialized in the United States, where black and Latina girls are medically categorized by a supposedly "earlier" puberty than white girls, echoing the much older colonial hypersexualization of and medical interest in the genitals of the black and brown female body (see Gilman 1985).

Having framed trans and race as differential technical capacities of the body, a biopolitical analysis highlights how those capacities are impaired and administered by systems of governance like healthcare rather than being guided by the free will of an Enlightenment-derived subject. Puberty suppression therapy is a hormonal technology for naturalizing the gender-normative appearance of the body and for racializing puberty, as its second use in treating "precocious puberty" emphasizes. In its use to suppress puberty for transgender children, the stakes are similarly biopolitically entangled across the body, technology, and the politics of sex, gender, sexuality, and race. Puberty suppression therapy is rarely covered by insurance plans in the United States, and the cost of a monthly injection is about $1,500, while the yearly implant option is about $15,000—and this does not include the associated costs of regular blood work to check hormone levels and of follow-up appointments. Given the enforced precarity of the lives of many transgender children, particularly of color, puberty suppression therapy's normalization as a medically necessary procedure covered by insurance might increase their relative bodily capacities through the amplified circulation of hormones.

At the same time, biomedical therapeutics of transgender childhood are not only normative in their fixation on suppressing puberty in order to achieve a "real" (real-looking) transition, but their technicity is also eugenic—given that race and puberty are historically entangled categories of endocrinology. The technological capacity to defer and medically produce the temporality of puberty recasts trans adults as insufficiently developed, awkwardly childish bodies, privileging a developmentalist understanding of the human body's sex as the ideal anchor of transgender medicine. In the biopolitics of puberty suppression therapy, trans and race are copresent technical capacities, but in the sense of having been partially captured and programmed by the state and medical institutions in a logic of improvement that echoes the "rejuvenation" theories of early twentieth-century Austrian endocrinologists. A supple and adaptive politics of puberty suppression therapy must begin, then, by recognizing the ontological-technical and historically technological entanglement of transgender and race.

Conclusion: The Technical Politics of Transgender and Race

A potential technical politics of transgender and race that affirm originary technicity and mobilize historical technologies to engage the debilitating effects of contemporary transgender biopolitics could be an ecological politics that does not prioritize the juridical subject of right enforced by the Enlightenment. In the case of healthcare, attention to its uneven distribution at the population level asks transgender studies to speculate on forms of autonomy that could wrest it away from the valuation of neoliberal capital and into the hands of not only trans-of-color bodies but all bodies. The neoliberal rationality according to which synthetic hormones are prohibited as performance enhancement for athletes, require years of prohibitively expensive medico-psychiatric diagnosis for transgender patients and yet already permeate the environment in a geopolitics of toxicity suggests the concrete utility of ecological experimentation with a politics of hormones in which the molecule contributes a technical and therefore political dynamism (see Bennett 2009).

The political capacity of technicity allows the hormone molecule to serve as the nonhuman threshold between nature and culture, between transgender and race, and opens onto a form of politics in which neither transgender nor race is subordinated to the other's politics or separated, requiring resuturing through a belated intersectionality or hybridity. Rather, trans and race carry with them historically conditioned potentials for retooling the body and the body politic. In this technical politics, it matters that the testosterone hormone circulates at multiple ecological scales, for a hormonal politics of transgender and race cannot attend to the question of access to healthcare without also attending to the racialization of black femininity through precocious puberty, the accumulation of endocrine disruptors in water supplies home to wildlife, and the humanist devaluation of performance enhancement through recourse to a "naturally" athletic body in organized sport. The ecological itineraries of the testosterone molecule prompt in their technicity a slight but vitally different version of Audre Lorde's ([1984] 2007) important formulation: it's not so much that "the master's tools will never dismantle the master's house" but that the tools are not technically defined by their use by any master, human or otherwise. The tools enter into relation with living beings—are their mode of self-elaboration—but also preserve a partial, irreducible autonomy of their own, available for different political becomings. Transgender and race are assembled together, technologically mediated, and they can always be assembled differently.

Julian Gill-Peterson is a doctoral candidate in American studies at Rutgers University. His dissertation, "Queer Theory is Kid Stuff," examines the emergence of the gay and transgender child. He is also a coeditor of "The Child Now," a forthcoming special issue of *GLQ: A Journal of Lesbian and Gay Studies*.

Acknowledgments

This essay benefited from the generous attention of the 2012–13 Rutgers Institute for Research on Women Seminar, "Trans Studies: Beyond Hetero/Homo Normativities," including the IRW's fellowship support. Particular thanks go to Yolanda Martínez–San Miguel and Sarah Tobias. My thinking in this essay took its first forms with guidance from Jasbir Puar, Patricia Clough, and Ed Cohen. I am also indebted to Stephen Seely, Jean-Thomas Tremblay, and Rebekah Sheldon for reading drafts. Aren Aizura generously shared his time both at Rutgers and at *TSQ*, encouraging this project's itinerary, and the anonymous readers' reports and special-issue editors made invaluable contributions to revisions, for which I am grateful. Any shortcomings in this version are my own.

Notes

1. In this essay, I employ both "trans" and "transgender." By "trans," I mean to accent an expansive conceptual reach of the term in contexts other than subjectivity or identity, particularly in thinking of trans as a technical capacity of the body. When I employ "transgender," it is in reference to populations or bodies categorized as such as well as to the field of transgender studies.

2. "L'objet technique est au point de rencontre de deux milieux" (The technical object is the meeting point of two milieus [Simondon 1958: 52]). This volume, like most of Simondon's work, has yet to be officially translated into English. All translations are therefore mine.

3. By speculative, I mean that the aim of this essay is the active creation of new values through materially engaged thinking rather than the reactive critique of or opposition to existing values.

4. "La technicité . . . est comme l'intermédiare entre forme et matière."

5. The sheer intensity of this investment in normative gender presentation and reductive sexual dimorphism is staggering in its blatant disavowal of anything that does not conform to the standards of the idealized cisgendered body, recuperated and naturalized through a narrative of growing up into adulthood.

References

Aizura, Aren. 2012. "Incalculating Transgender Justice (against the Nation-State)." Rutgers Institute for Research on Women Distinguished Lecture, October 18.

Allewaert, Monique. 2013. *Ariel's Ecology: Plantations, Personhood, and Colonialism in the American Tropics*. Minneapolis: University of Minnesota Press.

Beauchamp, Toby. 2013. "The Substance of Borders: Transgender Politics, Mobility, and US State Regulation of Testosterone." *GLQ* 19, no. 1: 57–78.

Bennett, Jane. 2009. *Vibrant Matter: A Political Ecology of Things*. Durham, NC: Duke University Press.

Butler, Judith. 1990. *Gender Trouble: Feminism and the Subversion of Gender*. New York: Routledge.

Carel, Jean-Claude, and Juliane Léger. 2008. "Precocious Puberty." *New England Journal of Medicine* 358, no. 22: 2366–77.

Cheah, Pheng. 1996. "Mattering." *Diacritics* 26, no. 1: 108–39.

Chun, Wendy Hui Kyong. 2012. "Race and/as Technology, or How to Do Things with Race." In *Race after the Internet*, ed. Lisa Nakamura and Peter A. Chow-White, 38–60. New York: Routledge.

Cohen-Kettenis, Peggy T., et al. 2011. "Puberty Suppression in a Gender-Dysphoric Adolescent: A 22-Year Follow-Up." *Archives of Sexual Behavior* 40, no. 4: 843–47.

Cohen-Kettenis, Peggy T., and S. H. M. van Goozen. 1998. "Pubertal Delay as an Aid in Diagnosis and Treatment of a Transsexual Adolescent." *European and Adolescent Psychiatry* 7, no 4: 246–48.

Coleman, Beth. 2009. "Race as Technology." *Camera Obscura*, no. 70: 177–207.

Crawford, Lucas. 2008. "Transgender without Organs? Mobilizing a Geo-affective Theory of Gender Modification." *WSQ* 36, no. 3–4: 127–43.

Deleuze, Gilles, and Félix Guattari. 1987. *A Thousand Plateaus*. Translated by Brian Massumi. Minneapolis: University of Minnesota Press.

Derrida, Jacques. 2002. "Nietzsche and the Machine." In *Negotiations: Interventions and Interviews, 1971–2001*, ed. Elizabeth Rottenberg, 215–56. Stanford, CA: Stanford University Press..

———. 2005. *On Touching—Jean-Luc Nancy*. Stanford, CA: Stanford University Press.

Don, Jeff, Martha Mendoza, and Justin Pritchard. 2008. "Pharmaceuticals Found in Drinking Water, Affecting Wildlife and Maybe Humans." *Associated Press*, March 18. hosted.ap .org/specials/interactives/pharmawater_site/day1_01.html.

Enke, A. Finn. 2012. "The Education of Little Cis: Cisgender and the Discipline of Opposing Bodies." In *Transfeminist Perspectives in and beyond Transgender Studies*, ed. A. Finn Enke, 60–85. Philadelphia: Temple University Press.

Foucault, Michel. 1990. *An Introduction*. Vol. 1 of *The History of Sexuality*, translated by Robert Hurley. New York: Vintage.

Gibson, Bethany, and Anita J. Catlin. 2010. "Care of the Child with the Desire to Change Gender—Part I." *Pediatric Nursing* 36, no. 1: 53–59.

Gilman, Sander. 1985. "Black Bodies, White Bodies: Toward an Iconography of Female Sexuality in Late Nineteenth-Century Art, Medicine, and Literature." *Critical Inquiry* 12, no 1: 204–42.

Giordano, Simona. 2008. "Lives in a Chiaroscuro: Should We Suspend the Puberty of Children with Gender Identity Disorder?" *Journal of Medical Ethics* 34, no. 8: 580–84.

Guattari, Félix. 1989. "The Three Ecologies." Translated by Chris Turner. *New Formations*, no. 8: 131–47.

Hardt, Michael, and Antonio Negri. 2001. *Empire*. Cambridge, MA: Harvard University Press.

Hayward, Eva. 2008. "Lessons from a Starfish." In *Queering the Non/Human*, ed. Noreen Giffney and Myra J. Hird, 249–64. London: Ashgate.

———. 2011. "Spider City Sex." *Women and Performance* 20, no. 3: 225–51.

Hird, Myra J. 2008a. "Animal Trans." In *Queering the Non/Human*, ed. Noreen Giffney and Myra J. Hird, 227–48. London: Ashgate.

———. 2008b. *Sex, Gender, and Science*. London: Macmillan.

LaMarre, Thomas. 2012. Afterword to *Gilbert Simondon and the Philosophy of the Transindividual*, by Muriel Combes, 79–108. Cambridge, MA: MIT Press.

Lambrese, Jason. 2010. "Suppression of Puberty in Transgender Children." *American Medical Association Journal of Ethics* 12, no. 8: 645–49.

Latour, Bruno. 1993. *We Have Never Been Modern*. Cambridge, MA: Harvard University Press.

Logan, Cheryl A. 2007. "Overheated Rats, Race, and the Double Gland: Paul Kammerer, Endocrinology, and the Problem of Somatic Induction." *Journal of the History of Biology* 40, no. 4: 683–725.

Lorde, Audre. (1984) 2007. "The Master's Tools Will Never Dismantle the Master's House." In *Sister Outsider*, 110–13. New York: Ten Speed.

Matchcock, R. L., and E. J. Susman. 2006. "Family Composition and Menarcheal Age: Antiinbreeding Strategies." *American Journal of Human Biology* 18, no. 4: 481–91.

Meyerowitz, Joanne. 2002. *How Sex Changed: A History of Transsexuality in the United States*. Cambridge, MA: Harvard University Press.

Morton, Timothy. 2013. *Hyperobjects: Philosophy and Ecology after the End of the World*. Minneapolis: University of Minnesota Press.

Nancy, Jean-Luc. 2008. *Corpus*. Translated by Richard A. Rand. New York: Fordham University Press.

Nyong'o, Tavia. 2009. *The Amalgamation Waltz: Race, Performance, and the Ruses of Memory*. Minneapolis: University of Minnesota Press.

Preciado, Beatriz. 2013. *Testo Junkie: Sex, Drugs, and Biopolitics in the Pharmacopornographic Era*. Translated by Bruce Benderson. New York: Feminist.

Puar, Jasbir K. 2012. "'I Would Rather Be a Cyborg Than a Goddess': Becoming-Intersectional in Assemblage Theory." *philoSOPHIA* 2, no. 1: 49–66.

Rai, Amit. 2012. "Race Racing: Four Theses on Race and Intensity." *WSQ* 40, no. 1–2: 64–75.

Rose, Nikolas. 2006. *The Politics of Life Itself: Biomedicine, Power, and Subjectivity in the Twenty-First Century*. Princeton, NJ: Princeton University Press.

Salamon, Gayle. 2010. *Assuming a Body: Transgender and Rhetorics of Materiality*. New York: Columbia University Press.

Saldanha, Arun. 2006. "Reontologising Race: The Machinic Geography of Race." *Environment and Planning D* 24, no. 1: 9–24.

Simondon, Gilbert. 1958. *Du mode d'existence des objets techniques*. Paris: Montaigne.

Steinbock, Eliza. 2013. "Groping Theory: Haptic Cinema and Trans-Curiosity in Hans Scheirl's *Dandy Dust*." In *The Transgender Studies Reader 2*, ed. Susan Stryker and Aren Aizura, 101–18. New York: Routledge.

Stiegler, Bernard. 1998. *Technics and Time, I: The Fault of Epimitheus*. Translated by Richard Beardsworth and George Collins. Stanford, CA: Stanford University Press.

Stryker, Susan, and Nikki Sullivan. 2009. "King's Member, Queen's Body: Transsexual Surgery, Self-Demand Amputation, and the Somatechnics of Sovereign Power." In *Somatechnics: Queering the Technologisation of Bodies*, ed. Nikki Sullivan and Samantha Murray, 49–64. London: Ashgate.

Viego, Antonio. 2007. *Dead Subjects: Towards a Politics of Loss in Latino Studies*. Durham, NC: Duke University Press.

Ward, Jessica L., and Michael J. Blum. 2012. "Exposure to an Environmental Estrogen Breaks Down Sexual Isolation between Native and Invasive Species." *Evolutionary Applications* 5, no. 8: 901–12.

Decolonizing Transgender

A Roundtable Discussion

TOM BOELLSTORFF, MAURO CABRAL, MICHA CÁRDENAS,
TRYSTAN COTTEN, ERIC A. STANLEY,
KALANIOPUA YOUNG, and AREN Z. AIZURA

Abstract This roundtable discussion took place between August 2013 and January 2014 through e-mail. Eventually, two questions were posed, and participants individually e-mailed their responses in. The questions were posed in the hope of making space for a number of scholars, activists, and culture makers to take the pulse of transgender studies' political possibilities and limits and to talk practically about methods for creating change.

Keywords transgender; trans- people; gender; decolonization; knowledge production

This roundtable discussion took place between August 2013 and January 2014. We started off as a cc e-mail list; everyone introduced themselves, then sent responses to questions. When time constraints became pressing, two questions were posed, and participants individually e-mailed their responses in. The questions were posed in the hope of making space for a number of scholars, activists, and culture makers to take the pulse of transgender studies' political possibilities and limits and to talk practically about methods for creating change.

Aren Z. Aizura: *What does decolonizing mean to you: personally, politically, intellectually?*

Micha Cárdenas: For me, decolonization is a foundation and support structure for my political and theoretical work. I feel as a settler living in the Americas—a site of the murder of over one hundred million indigenous people in the founding of contemporary nation states—that a politics that accounts for decolonization is the only possible ethical stance today. I also firmly agree with Eve Tuck and K. Wayne Yang's article "Decolonization is Not a Metaphor" (2012), which states that decolonization movements must be centered in actual struggles of indigenous

TSQ: Transgender Studies Quarterly ★ Volume 1, Number 3 ★ August 2014 **419**
DOI 10.1215/23289252-2685669   © 2014 Duke University Press

people, be they aesthetic, political, theoretical, or a mix of those categories, which are not so easily separable. Toward that end, I have worked in solidarity with the EZLN in Chiapas, Mexico, for many years, but my current practice focuses more on questioning Western systems of rationality and how they have limited our conceptions of political possibility by creating models of identity such as gender, race, and sexuality, which are individual and distinct as opposed to communal, connected, and networked ontologies of the Nahua people as described by Diana Taylor and Gloria Anzaldúa. I see my work for prison abolition and against gender oppression as part of a project to dismantle tools of colonization and build new postcolonial possibilities.

My work has taken place in a transnational and hemispheric frame, working toward connections in artistic and political practices across the Mexico/ United States border with the "Transborder Immigrant Tool," understanding transgender experience in global networks of virtual worlds in "Becoming Dragon," and considering gender, race, and sexuality in transnational spaces such as airports, border checkpoints, and international art and academic spaces in "Becoming Transreal." Currently, with "Autonets," I am focused on creating networks of safety between trans women of color, two-spirit people, sex workers, and disabled people in Toronto, Detroit, Bogotá, and Los Angeles. Autonets works toward decolonization by learning from digital networks and then creating ways of replicating them in embodied methods that do not rely on digital technologies or the European binary logics they reproduce.

I met up with Aren [Z. Aizura] at the recent Critical Ethnic Studies Association Conference in Chicago, where there was a deep discussion of decolonization going on. Jin Haritaworn cited Eve Tuck and K. Wayne Yang's article "Decolonization is not a Metaphor" (2012) to raise some incredible questions about the intersections of decolonization and transgender studies. They questioned the sudden popularity of interest in decolonization in academic journals whose study might not benefit from a decolonizing framework or whose work might not benefit decolonization struggles, going so far as to say that some people's interest in decolonization may be a self-serving way to add more lines to their CVs, and pointed out how much activist-oriented scholarship treats oppressed people in an interchangeable way, where who is being oppressed is not as important as the appearance of doing work that is saving *someone*. They discussed recent struggles in Berlin in the transgender community that focused unquestioningly on white male trans people, leaving trans women of color and low-income people with less access to education out of the conversation. Haritaworn used this example to point to the problematic ways that queer and queer of color organizing attempt to encompass trans struggles in ways that work against decolonization struggles. Personally, I feel that decolonization has deep, shared interests with transgender studies in resistance to pathologization by the medical-industrial complex and Western notions of gender and sexuality, which can be understood as systems of control and genocide.

Tom Boellstorff: In terms of decolonization and postcoloniality, my thoughts are above all shaped by my many years of work in Indonesia. That's taught me to attend to the specificities of colonialisms (Dutch colonialism in Indonesia, for instance, took on a very specific cast over three centuries) and also the way in which colonial legacies and resistances are so often about stances of complexity, imbrication, the forging of new possibilities not predicated on stances of purity or exclusion. It also leads me to attend to the relationships between when people use terms like *colonial* or *decolonization*, and so on, in a more metaphorical versus a more literal sense, and the advantages and dangers of those slippages.

Kalaniopua Young: For me, decolonization has been an important part of my daily life. Both in terms of what interests me as an oʻiwi mahu (Native Hawaiian transgender woman), as a person, and as a trans/queer scholar-activist, the concept opens up (rather than forecloses) various ways of rethinking power and relationships. In my current work, I look at how my own positionality as an oʻiwi mahu ethnographer articulates a decolonial space for rethinking ethnographic and anthropological research. This decolonial space is an important practice of defining autonomous futures in the intellectual merging of decoloniality and transgender studies.

Trystan Cotten: One of the things that continually comes up in my research is how to present some of the dismal data on trans experiences in Africa(n) Diaspora without reinforcing an idea of Western racism of the continent and black/brown peoples as backward, primitive, and uncivilized. At the same time, however, I still struggle with my positionality in my work, by which I mean both my own cultural and social class limitations of my questions and theoretical frameworks *and* the socioeconomic power imbalance between myself and my subjects. This latter issue resonates with me because it gets to a question I've been concerned about since the 1990s, when queer theory was starting to distinguish itself from LGBT studies: the question of who benefits from our knowledge production in the academy. Huge contradictions exist between the social class that we as researchers and intellectuals live and that of the trans subjects whose lives we rely on (and mine) for intellectual resources. For me, this is a question of de/colonizing trans knowledge production. Many institutions and entities profit from trans lives (universities, publishers, academics and intellectuals, the media, corporations, and so on).

While we mine their lives and suffering to produce important, critical knowledges, I don't see many trans people's lives improving. We researchers, most of whom are not trans, profit from doing work on or addressing trans issues and people, while the majority of trans people (around the world) are disempowered, disorganized, and doing poorly. And this is a gap I want to both problematize and think of creative strategies to address. I want to be careful not to dismiss academic knowledge production. That's too simplistic and reactionary and doesn't shed any light on the problem. At the same time, I don't want to shy away from this question, because I think it's important to ask who is profiting from knowledge production and what roles we might play in decolonizing these relationships of production. I also want to situate this question within a larger discourse reexamining queer (and trans) production and consumption and how certain elements have been appropriated, co-opted, and converted into mainstream normative interests of global capitalism. I think the commodification of trans both follows the tendency analyzed in queer culture/politics and also contradicts it in unexpected, interesting ways.

I was especially struck by Micha's point about the sudden popularity of decolonization in queer and trans theory. I've thought about that too and discussed it with Jin as well. It came up recently in Berlin a few weeks ago among friends and family. In addition to the sudden interest in decolonization, we also felt that intersectionality and disability studies (crip theory) are two more areas that had become chic to explore in theory without really producing a substantive politics that benefits colonized, disabled, and migrants.

Mauro Cabral: I'm an intersex and trans* guy from a Latin American country (Argentina), academically trained as a historian and philosopher, who works full time codirecting an international trans* organization (GATE). From that position, decolonizing has different meanings to me. In the context of that conversation, I would like to focus on three of those meanings.

First of all, of course, I speak a colonial language: Spanish is my mother tongue. Nonetheless, and as do many other intersex people, I share the experience of *estrangement* from my "own" language produced by gendering violence—in the same sense in which Austerlitz, the character in W. G. Sebald's novel, was an (ethico-political) foreigner in its (his?) "own" mother tongue. Moreover, I am forced to speak and write in a different language, which has its own colonial relationship with the other languages in the continent that I inhabit. Even to be able to have this conversation with friends and colleagues who share the same commitment with decolonization, I must write in English just to be part of the interchange. In both cases—and actually, in *all* cases—decolonizing means the call to produce, or at least attempt to produce, short-circuits in language: the kind of *minor* language that Gilles Deleuze and Félix Guattari read in Kafka, but also the interdictions, the "interruqtions" (a beautiful word created by valeria flores) in the genericized ontology of the language.

The second meaning is associated with some particular affective economies of theory—and in particular, those of *resentimiento* (resentment) and *resistencia* (resistance)—every time decolonization is intertwined with my positionality as a trans and intersex reader: how to decolonize trans and intersex lives and deaths from the imperium of queer theory and other similar academic enterprises? How to counteract, for instance, the ways in which Judith Butler (2004) colonizes David Reimer's life and . . . suicide? Decolonizing is therefore intensely related with finding ethical, political, and theoretical tools to challenge the production of trans* and intersex people as "proper objects," "privileged examples," and, in general, valuable goods in the theoretical primitive accumulation of flesh?

The third meaning is more related with my own line of work at GATE: as someone deeply involved in the poetics and politics of depathologization. Decolonizing trans* and intersex experiences—of embodiment, identity, expression, sexuality, and so on—from biomedical regulations implies, today, to go beyond scientific classifications to reach their translation into the logics of international capitalism. We are told—and we frequently confirm for ourselves—that these are key times of reform: both DSM-5 (*Diagnostic and Statistical Manual*) and, in a few years, ICD-11 (*International Classification of Diseases*) will codify trans* issues in different and hopefully less pathologizing ways. In the same sense, different laws and regulations around the world seem to move toward a different organization of bodies and identities. Some countries, like Nepal and Australia, already allow people to use different nomenclatures than *M* or *F* in their passports. Other countries, such as mine, allow people to reinscribe themselves as *M* or *F* regardless of their bioanatomies: which is to say, rendering *M* or *F* mere nominalist inscriptions. The liberal appearances of these changes must be approached, however, from a critical perspective—as they exemplify the intense process of recolonization of personal identity through biometrical technologies.

Aren Z. Aizura: *What are some strategies to make transgender or trans studies–themed knowledge production serve the interests of trans and gender-nonconforming people who are most marginalized, both within the academy itself and within the world at large? Why are they important?*

Mauro Cabral: This is a key question—provided that it articulates a painful paradox: on one hand, and for a long time, many of us have desired, intensely, the emergence of a specific academic field focused on trans issues, and finally it exists. On the other hand, it is what it is: an academic field, whose emergence is related to its compliance with academic standards. It means that even when trans studies came to make justice to the relegated place of trans issues and knowledge within broader academic fields (including queer theory), it is at risk, all the time, of (re) producing injustice—starting with geopolitical injustice.

In the first place, and so far—after the publication of two *Transgender Studies Readers*—the very label of "trans studies" seems to be intrinsically associated not only with the academy but also with an academy that reads, writes, and speaks in English—and that colonizes the rest of the world in pursuit of "cases." This geopolitical fact implies the need to translate the question, once again, geopolitically. How could trans studies serve the interest of those people who are most marginalized from the academic-industrial complex? Once again, the question is paradoxical: the "most marginalized" people are part of the economies of that complex—reified as objects of interest (and that's why some of us entertain the possibility of calling a strike of objects to challenge academic appropriation of trans*-lived *surplus*). Reification has, however, a negative impact on those who enjoy the privileged position of subjects in the field—and they are forced, from time to time, to exhaust audiences in remote locations articulating theories lacking any connection with the local realities that they asseverate to interpret.

In the current state of affairs—characterized by their chronic exclusion from education, employment, housing, and health, to begin with—I am seriously concerned about the concrete possibilities of the field in terms of trans* people's meaningful involvement in most countries and academic systems in the world. A couple of examples from Argentina: (1) Some trans activists who fiercely struggled to dismantle institutional transphobia while studying—and, in many cases, while surviving, at the same time, familial and social rejection—are now considered to be *too old* to be able to continue their academic careers, as they are over thirty. The same institutions that they challenged and changed and that recognize their history of exclusion and their commitment to inclusion fail to recognize the specific temporality of their struggle. As Sara Ahmed (2012) puts it, those institutions really believe in the performative effect of their own pronunciation as trans* welcoming—and reject any further interpellation in terms of the material conditions for that welcoming. (2) For more than a decade, the field of legal studies was challenged by trans activists—most of them *travestis*, who where extremely poor sex workers with equally limited access to education. These activists not only challenged legal understandings on trans* issues, they also imagined a revolutionary gender identity law and got that law passed. However, when the first book on the law was published, it only included them as *voices*—which is to say, their testimonies. Analysis was provided by the same scholars who denied the very possibility of the law until it was passed. The reason? Trans* people can change the world—but we can't change the rules of academic writing.

I'm absolutely confident about the theoretical and political imagination of trans* people—but I'm not confident at all about the capacity of the academy—including the trans* academy—to be challenged by them.

Eric A. Stanley: In prison abolitionist organizing, which has constituted the majority of my more legible political work for the last decade, we often use the term "most directly impacted" in an attempt to get at these same sets of questions. The problem is, of course, that identity is always relational and that under the sensibilities of neoliberal inclusion, at best we often end up with representational change and abandon our demand for structural transformation. I think, or I would at least like to hope, that we might be able to have both, as they necessarily prefigure one another.

We might be able to trace this representational-over-structural change in the current excitement over *Orange Is the New Black*, and in particular the casting of Laverne Cox as Sophia Burset, an incarcerated black trans woman on the show. Casting trans women of color as trans and non-trans characters is vital if we are to disrupt the structuring logics of antitrans and antiblack visual culture. However, left out of almost any discussions around the show itself is that there are not any formerly incarcerated people playing incarcerated people. This omission shows the ways in which some identities (as an example, formerly incarcerated trans women of color) cannot yet make it to a public discussion. This is not suggested as a read but as perhaps an invitation and a way of remembering that there is never a "perfect" representation that can apprehend the full complexities of lived experience. This is perhaps a long way of saying that understanding the category of "the most impacted" must always be a process in which we cannot understand our work to ever be done.

Returning to Antonio Gramsci's conceptualization and Gayatri Chakravorty Spivak's radical rereading of the subaltern might also be helpful in thinking about the political immediacy of these questions. The category of the subaltern as that which necessarily resides outside the grasps of hegemony—or, put another way, as beyond the scope of incorporation—helps remind us that once those who previously inhabited that category are brought into representation, they no longer occupy the same relationship to the periphery. This is not to say that they have more access to the somewhat clunky term *privilege* but that, under the ordering of the political, there remains something and someone outside our view. What, then, might be a political, academic, representational project that works or at least attempts to work at bringing down the political order as such? That would be my dream of an insurgent trans study that refuses its own complicity in the brutality of exclusion. However, I fear my dream is rather quickly being lived as the unfolding nightmare of a trans studies invested in the proper objects of the colonial academy.

I do, however, see the work of an insurgent trans studies already being practiced in many spaces. One example is *The Spirit Was . . .* , the archive Reina Gossett (2014) has built that both gathers up histories as an activist project and also attempts to foreground accountability to the communities it represents. Gossett's work, of course, still resides outside the more formalized confines of the academy. It is not that I believe her work should be smuggled in, but that we must allow it to radically transform, which is to say undo, the academy as such.

Micha Cárdenas: Year after year, statistics on violence against LGBT communities show that transgender women of color are the number one targets of violence (see Giovaniello 2013; Laver 2011). One strategy for serving the interests of trans and gender-nonconforming people is to focus scholarship on violence prevention. While the concept of the "most marginalized" is deeply problematic, it is clear to me that transgender women of color exist within a matrix of oppressions that allow us to be murdered on a very frequent basis. As such, I support the leadership and scholarship of transgender women of color within and outside the academy as a means to combat violence against us. These trends of violence are tied to different countries' histories of colonialism, and while black transgender women are commonly targeted for violence in the United States, indigenous women are more frequently murdered or missing in Canada. There are many of these intersections to be addressed, such as incarcerated, sex working, and HIV-positive trans women of color. Working for justice for trans women of color is a decolonizing effort, as it works against shared histories of colonial violence against black, latina, Asian, and mixed-race women, from slavery as a form of external colonialism, to settler colonialism in the Americas, to the neocolonialism of the drug war. To work for decolonization, these efforts for justice should center the leadership of two-spirit people and non-Western non-binary people such as the muxe of Mexico.

In *Invisible Lives* (2000), Viviane Namaste describes in detail ways that scholarship can be "reflexive"—that is, ways that scholarship can be accountable to transgender communities instead of merely talking about us without improving our lives. Namaste describes many ways that trans people are made invisible, erased, in queer theory, activism, administration, and culture, saying, "Queer theory is limited theoretically insofar as it only offers an application of poststructuralist thought, in addition to its restricted conception of text. The field's neglect of the social and economic conditions in which transgendered people live makes it of questionable political import" (39). Namaste proposes the concept of reflexive sociology, a sociology that studies society but also looks to the research populations' opinions of the findings in order to make them more accurate, saying, "Many scholars limit their studies to the medical and psychiatric production of transsexuals, neglecting other important features of everyday life. Significantly, this inquiry advocates a type of sociological theory and practice that is created primarily for academics, not for members of the research population, not even for legislators, jurists, social policy experts, or the administrative personnel of community based organizations that work with the individuals under investigation" (37). She looks at specific case studies to show how TS/TG people are erased by the administrative workings of health care providers, gender identity clinics, and HIV treatment programs. Namaste describes many ways that trans people are made invisible, erased, in theory, activism, administration, and culture. Namaste's book *Invisible Lives* is based on the goals of producing scholarship that can have meaning for trans people, that can address the lived realities of trans people, and that can create concrete social change. Recent transgender studies books like *Normal Life* by Dean Spade continue Namaste's work, while updating it with a discussion of how databases are being used as new forms of violent administration of trans people's lives. While the situation for trans people today is very different than at the time of her writing, her work provides an important model for transgender studies that can act in transgender people's interests.

Kalaniopua Young: I am excited for trans studies–themed knowledge production and the potential for this emerging field of study to serve the interests of gender-nonnormative people who are themselves marginalized by structural violence. Part of my excitement stems from the possibility of mobilizing this field toward a more revolutionary standpoint, one that can better avoid the trappings of identity politics by rooting activist scholarship to community-based social-justice efforts that operate from the bottom up. Activist scholarship in this way serves as a critical tool for grounding intellectual pursuits in the academy to grass-roots movements that are seeking, demanding, and creating change for front-line communities who are most marginalized. One such movement, or shall I say event, particularly relevant to this discussion is the annual international Transgender Day of Remembrance (TDOR).

According to a recent article commemorating the fourteenth anniversary of the international TDOR, 265 people from around the world were reported killed in 2012 due to antitrans violence. Sadly, this number reflects a rising trend in the number of antitrans murders. In 2011, for example, the number of antitrans murders was recorded at 221 and at 211 the year before that. While jarring, quantitative figures alone do not reflect the actual number of deaths, due to inadequate reporting capabilities and other failures in data collection, nor do they capture the ubiquitous senselessness with which governmental forms of systemic violence dispose of many more trans and nontrans folk alike through various kinds of slow death: cuts to welfare and education, the criminal-industrial complex, gentrification, environmental racism, and land dispossession, for example, facilitate perhaps an even more insidious and targeted form of inequality among all gendered subjects that while more general are no less cruel.

TDOR is a memorial event for transgender, two-spirit, and gender-nonconforming people killed by antitrans violence. But it is also so much more.

Its growing transnational popularity around the world suggests that there is something significant happening here that transcends the social and cultural lines of gender liminal identity. The proliferation of the event is particularly empowering. Typically, these events are organized by random, devoted volunteer groups and are hosted at common public sites: legislative buildings, city parks, college campuses, city halls, churches, and community centers. As such, TDOR events provide a great opportunity for bridging the academy and the community by collectively addressing antitrans violence through a collaborative and reflective effort to affirm trans life as lives that matter.

As a veteran co-organizer for a number of TDOR events in several US cities including Olympia, Austin, Portland, and Seattle, for me TDOR has come to symbolize an increasingly important site for public resistance and a potentially strategic site for mobilizing an activist-based transgender studies education that can better organize and account for an intersectional analysis of antitrans violence. For example, it can assist in articulating, analyzing, and accounting for the intersections of race, class, and gender within the context of antitrans violence. This is an important endeavor, for while trans women of color suffer the highest number of casualties due to antitrans violence, a cogent analysis of their disposition at the dangerous nexus of race, gender, and class receives little if any attention at TDOR events. Further, volunteer organizers for TDOR events tend to generalize antitrans oppression and thus fail to account for the complexities that tacitly institute such violence in the first place. As Kortney Ryan Zeigler (2012) points out, "the goal of eradicating gender oppression as a necessary step in the transgender movement is one that is failing to keep trans people of color alive."

Thus while TDOR creates a space for resisting gender violence, there is oftentimes little attention paid to how such violence disproportionately affects trans women of color. This discrepancy presents an important opportunity for trans studies scholars who can collaborate with TDOR organizers on and off campus to create a more robust resistive stance in politicizing antitrans death as part of larger systems of injustice and systems of gender violence that is both classed and racialized. Without a cogent analysis of how systems of race, historical trauma, and social, environmental, and economic disparities play into antitrans violence, the experiences of transgender women of color in particular remain unaccounted for while we become a quantifiable body count for a largely white, middle-class trans movement.

As many of us involved in the planning and facilitation of such events are aware, antitransgender violence is anti-men and anti-women, and as such, the recognition that state violence obscures our subjective connections should remain paramount to any effort seeking to shift the TDOR function from one of mourning to one of activist-based action. The structural violence of gender oppression affects everyone, whether self-identified as men, women, asexual, and/or gender or sexual liminal.

Still, even with a nuanced recognition of gender-violence operations among diverse communities that traverse identity categories, it is interesting to note that trans women of color still remain differentially and disproportionately pipelined into bare life, premature death, and antitrans violence. In this sense and in line with Judith Butler, I suggest that we must all work to vehemently oppose state violence and facilitate a horizontal politics recognizing the undue distribution of precarity as but one important site of opposition against systemic inequality and disenfranchisement. As she points out, "Precarity cuts across identity categories as well as multicultural maps, thus forming the basis for an alliance focused on opposition to state violence and its capacity to produce, exploit and distribute precarity for the purposes of profit and territorial defense" (Butler 2009: 32). Similarly, Devon Peña, in discussing Mesoamerican diasporic subjectivities, suggests, "There has never been a louder giant sucking sound than the screed violently heralded by the shift of wealth that has led us to the current class composition of the USA in which 371 families have as much wealth as 150 million of the rest of us. We are Basement America. And it is time to dig out" (2012).

TDOR, in collaboration with trans studies scholar-activists, I argue, has the potential to offer this kind of counterhegemonic collective space to do just that—to dig us out. Through grassroots efforts of public mourning, for example, we begin to affirm the sacredness of life and our continuing responsibilities to stewardship in terms of our relationships to one another as humans as well as to more than humans (land, animals, and so on). Common spaces of mourning offer us an opportunity to more effectively honor our people and commit to politicizing the social, environmental, and economic injustices that leave the most disenfranchised to endure disproportionately the burden of antitrans hate and violence.

One notable observation from this year's TDOR list of people killed in antitrans violence that struck me especially is the fact that the majority of those killed this year as well as last are trans women of color. This is important to note because while we are all inoculated within a generalized state of precariousness, the realities of precarity afforded to trans women of color highlight an especially egregious form of hateful state violence that renders us subject to a mortifying reality of bare life.

In the courts, for instance, a man can kill a trans woman of color, claim ignorance about her gender identity, and receive a reduced sentence. Then, when a trans woman of color like Cece McDonald defends against a violent attacker, she is criminalized and imprisoned. That the systems of so-called blind justice in this country imprison trans women of color for fighting to defend their lives only further oppresses all of society, because we are all tied to a shared legal commons. While it may be that trans women of color are particularly slated for legal injustice because we do not ascribe to white gender norms, the fact that the system of law criminalizes us for who we are and not what we do means that as transgender women of color we bear more than our fair share of a systemic failure that belongs to all of us. As trans revolutionary Leslie Feinberg reminds us, "CeCe McDonald is sent to prison. . . . [Meanwhile] the Emancipation Proclamation specifically spelled out the right of Black people to self-defend against racist violence" (quoted in Rivas 2012).

In the 1960s, trans women of color including Marsha "Pay it no Mind" Johnson and Sylvia Rivera stood at the forefront of the Stonewall Riots. They resisted arrest by brutal, corrupt police officers then targeting gender-nonconforming folks in Greenwich Village. The two street trans icons, along with other trans and queer folk, helped to kick-start what is now known as the gay rights movement. Around this same time, mahu activists in Hawaii struggled alongside their brothers and sisters at the forefront of an indigenous land dispute in cities like Waianae and Waimanalo, Oahu, as the state of Hawaii began evicting dozens of Kanaka Maoli (Native Hawaiian) families from their ancestral homelands.

The resilience of trans women of color has much to teach the world. Today, trans women of color are at the forefront of various human rights struggles. Hinalei Moana Wong, a mahuwahine activist, for instance, the cultural director for Halau Lokahi, a charter school in Honolulu, leads children in understanding *kuleana* (responsibility), TEK (traditonal ecological knowledge), hula, and Olelo Hawaii (Hawaiian language), contributing to broader collaborative efforts for environmental, economic, and social justice. Janet Mock, an African American raised in Hawaii, has developed an important critical media literacy campaign to address the rampant mistreatment of trans folk in media representations. Her successful Twitter campaign aptly named "girls like us," for example, addresses unbalanced media coverage of trans people and critically undermines the ways in which mainstream media programs represent and portray trans folk, especially trans women of color. In 2009, Sass Sasot, a Pinay trans activist and poet, testified before the United Nations Human Rights Commission and spoke out against the increasing mistreatment of trans people around the world, calling upon global leaders to end antitrans violence by enacting protective policies.

In order for trans studies–themed knowledge production to be effective, it must serve the interests of the most marginalized within our communities; it must be connected to community-based grassroots movements while working to create opportunities for the most marginalized among us to feel like their lives, their well-being, and their ideas matter. As trans studies activist scholars, we must work rigorously to ensure that we are doing everything in our capacity to bring these lives, these ideas, and these stories to the forefront of our pedagogical and intellectual engagements in the academy and in the world at large.

Trystan Cotten: My data call for a *transectional* framework: a framework that looks at the multiple transitions (or movements) they're engaged in as *intersecting* realities that shape my informants' lives—and not just what *kind* of life they may have but how long they live and whether they get to live at all. Let me explain by referring to my research.

In the oral histories I've collected of black and brown bodies in Africa (and the diaspora), gender and gender transitioning form only *one* dimension of people's lives. And it's not always the most salient thing in their daily struggle to feed and house themselves, but that also doesn't mean it's irrelevant, either. In fact, gender—whether it's a matter of gender presentation, the longing for relief from sex/gender incongruence, or something else—is very important in my subject's daily struggle, especially when it combines with their poverty, citizenship woes, geographic displacement, and ethnic warfare. But they don't single out this struggle as the most salient because of their problems with ethnic cleansing, racial profiling, sweatshop exploitation, and poverty. What is more, they tend to explain violence against trans people within the context of these other problems. Most of my informants in Zambia, for example, cite the colonial religions, Islam and Christianity, as the primary discourse informing state persecution of LGBT people and neocolonialist exploitation (through International Monetary Fund structural adjustment policies) as hardening their disempowerment. My informants in Nigeria also see the historical battle for control over oil production as a factor that fuels—pardon the pun—ethnic tensions, misogyny, and LGBT phobia.

In addition to decentering "gender/transition," I've also learned to shift my conceptual framework from trans *identity* to trans *migrations and movements*, because, again, that's what the data call for. A lot of my subjects are migrants. They're very poor and displaced from home due to any number of factors, including state violence against LGBT, ethnic cleansing, neocolonialism, religious persecution, and homelessness. Because they're constantly on the move in terms of their gender, geography, social class, and even their race, ethnicity, and nationality, I've moved away from relying on discursive analysis alone to understand how their identities are constituted differently from trans in our Western cultural contexts. In fact, this focus isn't even important in my research anymore, because it's not important to my subjects, and I'm keenly sensitive to Vivian Namaste's critique of how much academics are out of touch with the everyday struggles of trans people and what's important to them rather than the industry. When I write about my informants, I want to produce work that's true for them and that's really about *them* rather than about what *I* think is interesting to explore about them. It doesn't work for me to explore questions about whether gender is socially constructed or performative with my informants. Rather, they're concerned about getting enough food, shelter, and clothing and avoiding racial/ethnic profiling. When they flee persecution, it's not only because of their gender and/or sexuality but also because of their ethnicity, nationality, and religion. So I've taken a different approach, one that integrates global political economic analysis into a transectional framework that treats multiple movements intersecting, contextualizing, and mutually constituting one another.

Only after musing on this question have I come to realize that what academics in Western contexts think is important regarding trans identities and issues doesn't translate very well to other contexts, especially for Africans of trans experience. And I've learned to revise my methods, objects of analysis, and interpretive frameworks in order to write about my subjects' lives with some accuracy and integrity.

Tom Boellstorff: While still woefully underrepresented, the increasing centrality of trans studies–themed knowledge production is incredibly exciting; it benefits everyone through its enrichment of theoretical and empirical conversations. I cannot overemphasize the importance of this: the insights of trans studies occur in research communities shaped by a dizzying range of disciplines, and they will continue to be of great value to a whole range of topics. This broad relevance serves the interest of supporting marginalized trans and gender-nonconforming persons.

Trans studies–themed knowledge is being produced by both transgender- and cisgender-identified persons, in a manner that can potentially transform the fraught, medicalizing, and disempowering historical pattern wherein trans people were solely objects of knowledge. Just as straight-identified persons can produce excellent queer theory, and male-identified persons can produce excellent gender theory, rejecting the model by which trans and gender-nonconforming people are treated as pathologized objects of knowledge need not entail a model by which only such people are considered legitimate producers of transgender or trans studies–themed knowledge. Shifting between these two models would remain within an essentialist horizon and thereby reproduce a self/other binarism for knowledge production. It would reverse polarity without destabilizing the polarity itself.

This speaks to a set of beliefs regarding binarisms in general (not just the self/other binarism) that I see as one of the greatest contemporary barriers to conceptual innovation in both trans and queer studies. These include the idea that binarisms are inherently oppressive, limiting, and distorting; the idea that forms of fluidity, blurring, hybridity, and multiplicity are inherently less oppressive, limiting, and distorting; the idea that binarisms are inherently produced by systems of dominating power; and the idea that moving away from binarisms is inherently a form of resistance or liberation.

One thing we can gain from greater attention to trans and gender-non-conforming people who are most marginalized is a more contextual and polyvalent understanding of binarisms. For instance, the self/other binarism has multiple genealogies but originates above all in the colonial encounter. As many scholars of colonialism have noted, decolonization involves not just replacing the figure of the colonizer with the figure of the indigenous but recognizing messy entanglements of colonizer and colonized in emergent assemblages of embodiment, culture, and politics. For the language of constitutive authenticity is itself a legacy of colonial thinking.

I would suggest that for trans studies as for any other research community, work should be evaluated on its own terms, even as we keep in mind its conditions of production and circulation. By using the phrase "on its own terms," I imply neither elitism nor navel gazing, for the terms of research always have a politics and serve a range of interests, acknowledged or not. Rather, I question assuming that interests are self-evident and thus that serving those interests should be a condition for knowledge production—or that serving such interests always equates with an oppositional stance. There needs to be a space for research whose applicability and significance is not known at the outset. Emergent forms of knowledge production are vital for addressing emergent forms of culture and power. For instance, how are we to theorize persons who change gender and now wish to be identified as cisgendered men or women? Do they suffer from false consciousness; are they insufficiently or incorrectly political? Such dilemmas of course recall debates in other communities and scholarly conversations, from critical race theory and feminism to disability studies, and the possibilities for productive conversation are truly immense.

Here we return to messy imbrications, complicities, intimacies. A central tenet associated with the neoliberalization of the academy has been the growing demand that knowledge serve practical interests. (Many of these same forces also require interdisciplinarity as a condition of funding.) So the goal of serving the interests of trans and gender-nonconforming people who are most marginalized emphatically does not necessarily represent a move away from neoliberalism. It is more entangled than that. Serving the interests of any marginalized community is a laudable goal, but what these interests are may not be clear, even to community members. There are competing interests in any community. And interests can be theoretical. I have seen from experiences in HIV/AIDS prevention and treatment the negative consequences of the idea that people are dying, we need to act now and don't have time for theory. Because while it is true that people are dying, are suffering, and we need to act, the assumption that such action cannot be theoretical has led to a range of exclusions and retrenchments that have worked against goals of social justice.

Anthropology has something to offer here. It is unfortunate that anthropology is read far less in the humanities than the other way around. It is even more unfortunate that when discussed in the humanities, anthropology is often reduced to the methodological and representational practices associated with "ethnography" or critiqued for its links to colonialism. But all disciplines (from literature to statistics) are shaped by colonial discourse, and anthropology is more than ethnography. With regard to this discussion, it bears noting that anthropology has a long tradition of questioning Eurocentrism. Of course individual anthropologists can be Eurocentric, but, from a disciplinary standpoint, universalizing claims about gender, the family, economics, aging, or any other aspect of the human are suspect if based on data gathered only in the United States, only in English, and so on. In addition, anthropologists have long critiqued the self/ other divide as a condition of knowledge production. Ethnographic methods are predicated on the insight that one can learn other ways of being. That does not mean one has total knowledge (not least because no culture is monolithic in the first place) but that one can step outside the cultural contexts with which one is familiar. Learning another language, even to fluency, is not the same thing as speaking that language as a mother tongue. Yet in learning another language—or more broadly, learning another culture, always partially—one has gained something, can potentially communicate across difference and rework the grid of similitude and difference itself.

If my ruminations on these fascinating questions reveal anything, it is that we are on the threshold of an exciting new period of scholarly and activist innovation in trans studies, one that is profoundly interdisciplinary and deeply informed by a long history of excellent prior work. *TSQ* is poised to make an important contribution to this new period of innovation, and I look forward to enjoying the scholarly conversations it will foster.

Aren Z. Aizura: *How is transgender circulating transnationally? What are the implications of this for future trans and gender-nonconforming research and political projects?*

Micha Cárdenas: The transnational circulation of the idea of transgender is a colonial operation, spreading Western ontologies and logics such as Western medicine; the idea of the individual, unchanging self; and the binary gender system. In contrast, one can look to non-Western conceptions of gender nonconformity such as two-spirit people and shamans who can change form. While the term *two spirit* has many different local meanings, in some contexts it refers to people who have multiple genders, either simultaneously or over time. The example of Gloria

Anzaldúa is instructive here: in *Borderlands / La Frontera: The New Mestiza* (2012), she writes about being "mita' y mita'," half male and half female. Further, she sees her transformations in a decolonial framework. When she says things such as, "I know things older than Freud, older than gender," she points out the limited Western epistemologies of self on which concepts such as gender depend (48). In contrast, she describes nonhuman transformations such as becoming serpent, which are inseparable from her crossings of gender, race, language, and nationality. Anzaldúa's ability to enact these multiple transformations defies secular colonial conceptions of bodies that can be categorized by a binary gender system, as can be understood when she writes, "In the etho-poetics and performance of the Shamans, my people, the Indians, did not split the artistic from the functional, the sacred from the secular, art from everyday life" (88).

Recently, I have begun co-coordinating an effort to create an international network of trans women of color, focusing on a gathering of this network in Detroit, Michigan, in June 2014 at the Allied Media Conference. My co-coordinators are Lexi Adsit, b. binaohan, Askari González, and Sam Maria Andazola. Here is an excerpt from our collective statement about this gathering, which the Allied Media Conference organizers have told us they believe is a historic gathering:

> We know that trans women of color are magical, powerful, skilled, and wise, yet there is still no international network joining us together to address the struggles we face. This network gathering seeks to change that. . . .
>
> This network gathering will seek to connect diverse and dispersed trans women of colour so that we can begin to build the bridges, networks, and resources necessary to transform our communities using media and technology. Our network gathering will focus on sharing wisdom and skills between the Trans Women of Colour already living/working/existing on the front lines through a combination of workshops, skill shares, and networking activities. We hope that all of the people involved will walk away with not only the knowledge and connections needed to make change in their own communities, but with an international network of Trans Women of Colour that will aid us all in creating real and lasting change. Trans Women of Colour exist at an intersection of oppression that has resulted in our high levels of poverty, unemployment, incarceration, death (Black and/or Latina trans women make the majority of names on the global Trans Day of Remembrance list), among other serious problems too numerous to name. While we have intentionally chosen to use "Trans Women of Colour" this Network Gathering is inclusive of non-binary trans feminine people of colour as well, which includes, but isn't limited to, people of colour who identify as bakla, hijra, fa'afafine, third gender, genderqueer, provided that they/we understand that this gathering will focus on and centre the most vulnerable in our community—Black, Indi-

genous, and/or Latina trans women, binary or not, sex workers, incarcerated people, disabled people, immigrants. If you or your organization can provide support for this effort and would like to be added to our list of supporters, please contact us at twoc.amc@gmail.com. (International Trans Women of Color Network 2014)

Mauro Cabral: Again, and acknowledging how narrow this approach could be, I would like to center my answer in three very specific topics related to the broader issue of the transnational circulation of transgender and its implications.

I am deeply concerned by the circulation of transgender as a new commodity in both the theory and practice of human rights. That circulation seems to heavily depend on a "necropolitical" reduction of trans* people to potential or real victims—with a concrete and negative impact in trans* people's ability to participate meaningfully in decision-making processes affecting us. We are never supposed to be in the room—except as corpses, or bodies in danger of extension, exhibited for progressive consumerism, frequently oriented toward funding. And even when trans* issues—often codified, in a reductive way, as "gender identity issues"—occupy a growing portion in international LGTBI activism, that expansion is not translated into the circulation of critical knowledge produced by trans* people.

A second issue related with your question that seems very important to me is, precisely, the need to analyze the transnational circulation of transgender as a *corpus*, as a certain number of texts and theories, names and definitions, statistics, analysis, and interpretations. That circulation is heavily determined by geopolitics in a crude imperial capitalist landscape—and we, down *here* or far away *there*, circulate across the transnational routes of the industrial-academic complex, reified as the objects of colonial knowledge. Many denominations circulate currently as examples of a geographically neutral category—transgender, or trans*—and terms such as travesti, hijra, fa'afafine, and meti or katoey become doubly local, localized in their own culture and in relation to the international scope of transgender as a culturally nonspecific umbrella term.

Undoubtedly, transnational circulation has a particular meaning for trans* people: that of legal or illegal migration or even exile. Many trans* workers from Latin America survive—and die—in North America and Europe, carrying with them not only experiences that reject medical and legal colonization in their own countries. Many other trans* people travel internationally looking for transitional health care that is not available or affordable in their own countries. And, of course, many of us migrate in pursuit of academic opportunities that, again, are neither available nor affordable in our own countries. I would love to see these three lines, these three circuits begin to intersect, to struggle, to collide, to talk.

Tom Boellstorff: Historically, it was primarily cisgendered heterosexuality that circulated transnationally. Transgender and homosexuality circulated as abject deviancies that played a constitutive role in shoring up forms of normality but that were not themes of circulation in their own right, so to speak.

Obviously, not all things assigned the Latin-derived prefix *trans-* are reducible to each other. Yet we now find multiple, intersecting ways that transgender circulates transnationally, all with novel dimensions but also deep histories that shape present contexts. Three are of particular note. First, there are forms of migration of trans and gender-nonconforming people. Such migration can take the form of elite jet-setting, but more often it is economic migration seeking an escape from poverty or political migration seeking an escape from persecution. It is not always "transnational" (for instance, Indonesian *waria* frequently migrate between islands of the archipelago in search of employment), and when transnational, it can be within regions (say, neighboring countries in Latin America or from Indonesia to Malaysia) or across the globe. Second, there are forms of mass-mediated circulation of ideas, images, experiences, practices, and so on. This has been a long-standing focus of my own work, and it is fascinating to note the impact of online technologies in this regard. Third, there is the circulation of trans studies itself as a set of research and activist communities. While raising questions of inequality (for instance, the domination of Euro-American academics or English-language scholarship), such transnational scholarly and activist connection has also fostered productive forms of coalition building, collaboration, and learning.

With regard to the transnational circulation of transgender, two other general issues loom large from my perspective. First is the importance of accounting for spatial scales other than the transnational. How is transgender localized? Urbanized? How does it articulate not just with nationality but with regionality? (I have considered this question, for instance, with regard to the relationship between transgender and Southeast Asia as well as Indonesia.) What about archipelagic, networked, and atmospheric geographies that trouble the framework of nested spatial scales altogether? Second is the importance of accounting for spatial scaling itself as a social process. Most often this has been linked to capitalism, but that is clearly only part of the story. In particular, how is trans productive of spatial scales?

Tom Boellstorff is professor of anthropology at the University of California, Irvine. His publications include *The Gay Archipelago: Sexuality and Nation in Indonesia* (2005), *A Coincidence of Desires: Anthropology, Queer Studies, Indonesia* (2007), *Coming of Age in Second Life: An Anthropologist Explores the Virtually Human* (2008), and (with Bonnie Nardi, Celia Pearce, and T. L. Taylor) *Ethnography and Virtual Worlds: A Handbook of Method* (2012).

Mauro Cabral is the codirector of GATE (Global Action for Trans* Equality), based in Buenos Aires, Argentina. He is the editor of *Interdicciones: Escrituras de la intersexualidad en castellano* (2009), the second volume of which is forthcoming.

Micha Cárdenas is a Provost Fellow and PhD student in Media Arts and Practice at the University of Southern California and a member of the Electronic Disturbance Theater 2.0. She works at the intersection of movement, technology, and politics. Her coauthored publications include *The Transreal: Political Aesthetics of Crossing Realities* (2012) and *Trans Desire/Affective Cyborgs* (2010).

Trystan Cotten is associate professor of gender studies at California State University, Stanislaus. His areas of research are transgender surgery and medicine, and gender, sexuality, race, and migration in Africa and the African diaspora. His latest book is *Hung Jury: Testimonies of Genital Surgery by Transsexual Men* (2012).

Eric A. Stanley is a President's Postdoctoral Fellow in the Departments of Communication and Critical Gender Studies at the University of California, San Diego, and an editor of *Captive Genders: Trans Embodiment and the Prison Industrial Complex* (2011). Eric's other writing has been published in the journals *Social Text*, *Women and Performance*, and *American Quarterly*.

Kalaniopua Young is a radical Native Hawaiian transgender woman scholar-activist of color, a more-than-survivor of cis-sexist racial violence, and a community organizer with United Territories of Pacific Islanders Alliance in Seattle. As a doctoral student in the Department of Anthropology at the University of Washington, her forthcoming dissertation, "Re-thinking the Passage Home," is a critical ethnography that examines the daily lived experiences of frontline Kanaka Maoli (Native Hawaiians) houseless and home-free communities in Waianae, Oahu, a critical site for observing ongoing US settler colonialism, indigenous resistance, and survivance in the nation's largest outdoor homeless encampment.

Aren Z. Aizura is an assistant professor in gender, women, and sexuality studies at the University of Minnesota. He is the editor of the *Transgender Studies Reader 2* (2013). His work has appeared in *Medical Anthropology*, *Inter-Asia Cultural Studies*, and *Asian Studies Review* as well as in the books *Queer Bangkok*, *Transgender Migrations*, and *Trans Feminist Perspectives*.

References

Ahmed, Sara. 2012. *On Being Included: Racism and Diversity in Institutional Life.* Durham, NC: Duke University Press.

Anzaldúa, Gloria. 2012. *Borderlands/La Frontera: The New Mestiza.* Boston: Aunt Lute.

Butler, Judith. 2004. "Doing Justice to Someone: Sex Reassignment and Allegories of Transsexuality." In *Undoing Gender*, 57–74. New York: Routledge.

———. 2009. *Frames of War: When Is Life Grievable?* New York: Verso.

Giovaniello, Sarah. 2013. "NCAVP [National Coalition of Anti-violence Programs] Report: 2012 Hate Violence Disproportionately Targets Transgender Women of Color." *GLAAD Blog,*

June 4. www.glaad.org/blog/ncavp-report-2012-hate-violence-disproportionately-target
-transgender-women-color.

Gossett, Reina. 2014. *The Spirit Was . . . .* thespiritwas.tumblr.com (accessed April 15, 2014).

International Trans Women of Color Network. 2014. "International Trans Women of Color
Network Gathering at AMC2014." www.indiegogo.com/projects/international-trans
-women-of-color-network-gathering-at-amc2014 (accessed April 15, 2014).

Lavers, Michael. 2011. "Seventy Percent of Anti-LGBT Murder Victims Are People of Color."
Colorlines: News for Action, July 18. colorlines.com/archives/2011/07/70_percent
_of_anti-lgbt_murder_victims_are_people_of_color.html.

Namaste, Viviane. 2000. *Invisible Lives: The Erasure of Transsexual and Transgendered People.*
Chicago: University of Chicago press.

Peña, Devon. 2011. "The Shifting Balance of Class War." *Environmental and Food Justice* (blog),
March 23. ejfood.blogspot.com/2011/03/shifting-balance-of-class-war.html.

Rivas, Jorge. 2012. "'Free CeCe' Graffiti Left on County Jail Building CeCe McDonald Was
Held In." *Colorlines*, June 6. colorlines.com/archives/2012/06/free_cece_graffiti_left_on
_county_jail_building_cece_mcdonald_was_held_in.html.

Tuck, Eve, and K. Wayne Yang. 2012. "Decolonization Is Not a Metaphor." *Decolonization: Indigeneity, Education, and Society* 1, no. 1: 1–40.

Ziegler, Kortney Ryan. 2012. "Why Centering Race in Transgender Advocacy is Key to Equality
for All." *Huffington Post: Gay Voices*, November 19. www.huffingtonpost.com/kortney
-ryan-ziegler-phd/why-centering-race-in-transgender-advocacy-is-key-to-equality-for-all
_b_2156775.html.

Multiraciality, Haunting, and "People Like Us"

KARMA R. CHÁVEZ

The Biopolitics of Mixing: Thai Multiracialities and Haunted Ascendancies
Jinthana Haritaworn
Farnham, UK: Ashgate, 2012. x + 189 pp.

Academic and popular interest in multiracial or mixed-race identities has grown immensely over the past two decades in both European and North American contexts. In part, this interest is in response to the increased number of mixed-race people visible in public spheres and their efforts to achieve formal recognition of mixed-race status. The interest also reflects persistent racial anxieties and concerns over racial definitions as well as the lingering though reinvented eugenicist discourses that haunt racial understandings in the Western world. Jinthana Haritaworn's recent book, *The Biopolitics of Mixing*, helps to make sense of the complex ways in which discourses of multiraciality operate through the lens of Thai multiracialities in Germany and Britain, two countries often regarded as having different racialized histories and presents. Based primarily on empirical data from interviews with people of part-Thai parentage, interwoven with analysis of media texts, policy debates, and scientific discourse, Haritaworn's book packs a dense and invigorating theoretical punch. Specifically, Haritaworn draws upon and contributes to queer theories, theories of biopolitics and necropolitics, intersectionality and whiteness, and disability studies, among others. Proposing the figure of the "multiracial subject" who has been imagined as "an ideal candidate to usher in the post-race future, simply by virtue of hir 'mixed' parentage" (1), Haritaworn carefully investigates how the promise of multiracial inclusion often escapes the reach of multiracial people while it simultaneously justifies the exceptional, multicultural, and tolerant status of imperial nation-states. Still, the

TSQ: Transgender Studies Quarterly ★ Volume 1, Number 3 ★ August 2014
DOI 10.1215/23289252-2685678   © 2014 Duke University Press

promise is alluring, as many of the people Haritaworn interviewed seemed, at least partially, to feel compelled by or drawn into inclusionary discourses even as they often recognized inclusion's tenuousness and slipperiness.

The Biopolitics of Mixing begins with the familiar question, "Where are you from?"—a question often directed toward multiracial people who phenotypically appear as racially ambiguous in order to place their origins. In chapter two, the first analysis chapter, interviewees recount several of these encounters where their multiracial bodies were subject to this racializing gaze. The interviewees had a variety of methods for responding to or subverting these instances of what Frantz Fanon called "dissection," some of which justified the question and others that confronted it. Against common thinking, Haritaworn argues that it is important to shift from seeing racial ambiguity as a property of particular bodies and from putting multiracial people in charge of subverting the entire race project; instead, these instances of dissection should compel us to view multiracialization as a "set of practices, technologies and power relations" that are produced and able to be altered (28).

Many of Haritaworn's interviewees did not experience these instances of dissection as especially violent. In fact, some of them claimed that their multiracial identities were viewed in positive and celebratory ways. This paradox comprises the subject of chapter 3, as Haritaworn traces the transition from the historical eugenicist assumption that mixed-race people were degenerate to the present lauding of multiraciality as a sign of beauty, health, and intelligence, a mobilization of what Haritaworn calls "bioracial discourses" (54). Haritaworn shows how the ghosts of eugenics haunt this contemporary celebration, as the newly validated are uplifted at the expense of those whose "differences" render them invalidated. The fourth chapter picks up directly on this point as Haritaworn argues, "bioracial knowledges and the identities that draw on them are centrally about disability" (71). Haritaworn shifts from a discussion of the interviews to an exploration of popular science and the British program, *Is It Better to Be Mixed Race?* Through a careful analysis of this media text of popular science journalism hosted by a British South Asian scientist, Aarathi Prasad, and featuring the work of many scientists and doctors, Haritaworn lays out the ways in which the arguments about mixed-race superiority are profoundly ableist. The purported benefits of the multiracial subject's "genetic diversity" include physical, artistic, and intellectual aptitude. Further, it is not merely racial polarities that are desirable but sexual ones, as only certain respectable (and married) interracial heterosexuals can reproduce this highly abled, happy, multiracialized child, who becomes the central character in this narrative.

The ascendancy of the happy multiracial subject has another constitutive outside: those people of color who refuse mixing altogether, especially "Muslims."

In the fifth chapter, Haritaworn invokes the haunting figure of the "marginal man" from early twentieth-century sociology: a product of miscegenation who belongs nowhere and is confused about his own identity (92). Even as multiraciality is celebrated, the pathologization of the trauma experienced by the unhappy mixed-race person remains present in "psy discourses"—the sciences pertaining to emotion and conduct. Within such discourses, happiness is best assured through conformity, and often academics and activists have sought to be counted by the state as one way to conform, be included, and orient toward the tolerant, hybrid nation. The problem is that this ascendancy and the fantasy of the hybrid nation depend on the isolation and exclusion of those who are not mixed enough or in the right ways, namely, black people in countries like the United States and Muslims across the Western world.

Further, and as is seen in chapter 6, the select ones who approximate assimilated happy subjects may still be recognized as traumatized subjects, a tension difficult to negotiate. To address this tension, this chapter returns to the interview subjects, starting with a consideration of the way in which their happy stories trumped their sad ones in metronormative narratives of cities "as exceptional places of tolerance and diversity" (114). These happy narratives, however, are not merely about the dissection encounter; instead, they help to indicate the boundaries of belonging within post-race communities. To see those boundaries, Haritaworn puts the narratives in conversation with Rey Chow's notion of "coercive mimeticism," or the idea that the multicultural person is expected to approximate Western culture's preconceptions about them (114). This chapter then shows how the happy narratives are repeated both by those with some privilege (i.e., having one white parent and/or economic stability) and also within a context of cultural pressure and reading to embody certain expectations. The other to this happy narrative that kept returning in Haritaworn's research is the "Thai prostitute," a figure taken up in chapter 7. In that chapter, Haritaworn addresses the automatic assignment of Thai multiracial subjects to the realm of victim or prostitute, which then impacts sexual and gender negotiations. This leads Haritaworn to insist on paying attention to the Thai prostitute and how she haunts gender and sexuality for feminized subjects in particular in order to restore sexual agency and return the excluded to diasporic, queer, and feminist spaces.

Haritaworn ends their[1] book on a hopeful note, offering up the idea of "people like us," "forged by sexually and gender non-conforming people in Malaysia to describe positions that cannot easily be named, and whose likeness is felt rather than classifiable" (147). Recognizing the risks of taking terms from one context into another, Haritaworn still finds it important to offer this phrase so it may "resonate through the imaginary space" of the book—imaginary because there is no material space for all the figures in the book to actually reside (147).

Haritaworn invites readers to treat the figures who haunt the positive images of multiracial subjects as people like us, those to whom we should be accountable without fearing the unassimilable difference that haunts us all.

This book offers much to appreciate even as some of its claims may make less sense to readers in a North American context. For example, while the "Where are you from?" question can certainly be directed toward multiracialized people in the United States to imply a questioning of national belonging, the same question also has a strong regional component in the United States. The vast geographic distances that separate states and regions lead to different accents and cultural norms among people of all races, making the question "Where are you from?" a familiar one across the United States that may have less to do with race and national belonging than the European contexts of this book. Of course, this is one of the book's great strengths—it decenters the North American context.

This book is valuable for many, many additional reasons. First, while debates over the value and utility of intersectionality rage on in cultural studies circles, Haritaworn's book simply evidences, in beautiful fashion, the need for intersectional analysis and what critical intersectional approaches can continue to illuminate about complex social and political processes. If you are a teacher looking to show your students what an intersectional analysis should look like, this is your book. Second, this book provides an exquisite illustration of how to do multisite research without engaging in a comparative approach. The *relational* approach advocated here (and extended from the work of David Theo Goldberg) offers insight into the similar and different ways in which multiracial discourses operate in Germany as opposed to Britain, but it goes beyond any comparison, drawing also upon North American theoretical frameworks and discourses to reveal the related logics of raciality, ability, and reproduction that undergird these different national contexts. This approach then not only complicates an understanding of nation-states as discrete entities, but it also reveals the deep logics of empire, colonialism, and exceptionalism that manifest in related ways within ostensibly different contexts through the figure of the multiracial subject.

Third, Haritaworn's methodological self-reflexivity is stunning. They clearly show how the place in which they began the research and the kinds of questions they wanted to ask led to gaps in the research design, specifically surrounding discourses of transgender or genderqueer subjectivities and also disability. Unlike authors who simply apologize for the absence and move on (and I am indicting myself in this critique), Haritaworn works to fill in the gaps left from the interview portion of the research with analysis of media texts, policy debates, and scientific discourse. The apology would have been an easier route to take. But the admission followed with diligent action makes for a much stronger and more persuasive research study. The actions Haritaworn takes do not negate the fact that transgender and disabled subjects were not present in Haritaworn's thinking when designing the research project, and they also do not serve to entirely center such subjects, which may lead some readers of a transgender studies journal to pause. Yet I think an alternative response is more appropriate. Haritaworn's reflexivity and in-process research modifications indicate one reason why transgender and disability studies are so important: these bodies of knowledge push scholars toward more rigorous and nuanced intersectional research. Haritaworn's research also reveals that it is difficult to ignore the importance of transgender and disabled critiques and subjects when dealing with the logics of multiraciality, which implicate and draw upon abled and gendered discourses. For these reasons, Haritaworn's book is not only on the cutting edge of scholarship on multiraciality, but it will be a crucial addition in many cultural studies courses for both its methodological and its theoretical innovations.

Karma R. Chávez is an assistant professor in the Department of Communication Arts and the Program in Chican@ and Latin@ Studies at the University of Wisconsin–Madison. She is the author of *Queer Migration Politics* (2013).

Note
1.   Haritaworn prefers gender-neutral pronouns, such as they/them/their.

Animating Contemporary Culture

CYNTHIA WU

Animacies: Biopolitics, Racial Mattering, and Queer Affect
Mel Y. Chen
Durham, NC: Duke University Press, 2012. xi + 297 pp.

Mel Y. Chen's *Animacies* is an impressive monograph that brings together a staggering array of conversations in the fields of posthumanism, animal studies, environmental justice studies, queer affect theory, critical ethnic studies, disability studies, and cognitive linguistics. This thoroughly researched book highlights the heretofore unexplored connections among racialized difference, nonhuman animality, and metallurgical toxicity with an eye toward unpacking the insidious and often invisible disciplinary forces in modern life. Noting that "many contemporary discourses continue to disavow, if not simply ignore, the possibility of significant horizontal relationships between humans, animals, and other objects . . . [such that] the category 'animal' often comes with a segregating frame that opposes 'human' to 'animal'" (50), Chen's study seeks to redefine the terms on which contemporary global society might redress the fraught effects of neoliberal capital.

To be sure, scholars before Chen have made inroads into some of this thinking, but none have as yet launched such a compelling case for the decentering of the human in contemporary critical thought. The sense that one gets after reading this book is not that this is yet another reminder for producers of cultural theory about the benefits of diversifying, so to speak, beyond the human. Rather, we are left feeling that a wholesale demotion of human animals from the apex of any hierarchy is the only option left. In fact, *Animacies* does away with the pecking orders of bare life (and nonorganic "lifeliness") altogether and casts everything nonlinearly under the realm of biopower.

TSQ: Transgender Studies Quarterly * Volume 1, Number 3 * August 2014   **445**
DOI 10.1215/23289252-2685687   © 2014 Duke University Press

Chen's book is difficult to characterize in terms of its scope, be it with the artifacts that are summoned for analysis or the intellectual genealogies from which it emerges and intervenes. The unruly nature of *Animacies* appears to be intentional and, moreover, essential to this monograph, which can be better regarded as a series of interrelated meditations than as a conventionally structured, comprehensive study. In this, it aligns itself well with transgender studies, a field that by necessity builds its archive through queerings and refusing categorical taxonomies. The archive Chen assembles for this book consists of a wide range of ephemera, from news accounts in mainstream media outlets, to the language of LGBTQ activism, to nineteenth-century political cartoons grappling with the nation's changing racial landscape, to live-action and animated film, to advertisements and packaging for consumer items, among other related texts. *Animacies* is not so much an analysis of any one of these primary sources in a way meant to resemble historical or any other institutionalized forms of scholarship but—following recent methods adopted by affect theorists—a sustained exploration of the logics of feeling as they are installed in everyday life. In other words, the book is performative. Not only does it make a claim about the pressing need for a politics that queers human-centricity and other forms of order, its disciplinary disruptiveness is also queerly nonnormative as its structure mirrors its argument.

Animacies is divided into three parts, each organized around a single concept. Part 1, titled "Words," is where Chen's formal training in linguistics most saliently reveals itself. Drawing on the work of Bernard Comrie, Mutsumi Yamamoto, Michael Silverstein, and others, Chen establishes the grounds on which "animacy," as a "quality of liveness, sentience, or human-ness of a noun or noun phrase," would possess "grammatical, often syntactic consequences" (24). In doing so, this characteristic of the unit of language invokes and manages its "affective potency" (30). This foundational framework establishes the grounds for a critical reimagining of the genealogy of the term *queer*.

Part 2, organized around "Animals," begins by unpacking J. L. Austin's theory of performative speech acts. According to Austin, speech acts that are performative—that call a condition into being through their utterance—are not inherently so but function in this way only because there is an already existing social apparatus that legitimates them. Otherwise, they are merely farcical—as in "*a marriage with a monkey*" (Austin quoted on 94; Chen's emphasis). Locating in Austin's reference to a monkey an animacy that is laden with the weight of racialization and colonialism, Chen calls for a refashioning of the conceptual possibilities of the word *queer* to encompass the blurring of lines between human and nonhuman animal. The objects of analysis in this section are far ranging. Late nineteenth-century illustrated images of Chinese migrants to the United States rub shoulders with late twentieth-century film and installation art.

In "Metals," which constitutes part 3, Chen makes a strong case for the liveness of chemical elements alongside humans and nonhuman animals. Using the panic issuing from the United States in recent years about toys and food items made in China, Chen traces the transformations that the collective imagination has undergone with its thinking about lead: from a chemical agent to which poor and lower-working-class African Americans are exposed to one that insidiously infects white, middle-class consumers of baby products. Chen's chapter on mercury becomes the basis for an extended meditation on, first, present-day agitation surrounding vaccines and autism and, second, personal experience of environmental illness that may or may not have its etiology in exposure to mercury through vaccines or dental fillings. The effect is a reclamation of toxicity as a subversively queer political strategy—as that which can "intervene into the binary between the segregated fields of 'life' and 'death,' vitality and morbidity" (218).

As with any work innovative enough to be considered field changing, *Animacies* prompts discussion. As a way of engaging in these conversations with the author, I would like to present some questions that arise when considering this book in light of its claims. First, given that its central argument is that a queerly enabling politics can emerge from dissolving the boundaries among humans, nonhuman animals, and chemical elements, I want to ask about the stakes of resisting humanism's pull for some of the contingents that feature most saliently in this study. As Chen points out, the act of dehumanizing people of color and disabled people—in effect, likening them to animals—has historically been a damaging tactic that divests them of agency. Although Chen's suggestion that we reclaim a connection with animality rather than continue to assert full human status is a provocative one, I wonder about the political efficacy of this strategy for those who do not yet have the comfortable privilege of having their humanity assumed. Would the queer conceptual interfacing between humans and nonhuman animals (in addition to inanimate objects) only achieve its greatest subversive potential in cases where the barriers separating them are thickest to begin with? Can everybody afford in equal measure to turn away from human-centrism at this moment in time? Does everyone benefit from this maneuver to the same degree or in the same way?

Second, I want to press Chen further in the chapter on mercury that follows the one on lead. The analysis of the cultural logics of lead is impressively sustained and comprehensive in its reach, unpacking in detail the changes over time in the racial, class, gender, and sexual valences of lead exposure as well as the racialized panics that color contemporary discourse about lead. Chen's chapter on mercury, while insightful in its own right, might extend some of the concerns from the one preceding it, particularly when it comes to the racialized and class-based dimensions of mercury exposure. Might we think about the Asian-raced cast that mercury toxicity takes—different from but also similar to the one that falls upon lead—especially when the environmental spill at Minamata Bay in Japan is most readily associated with it? Also, while Chen rightly points out that lead exposure has been coupled with the poor and lower working classes in the United States, indexing the figure of the black child ingesting peeling paint inside abject living quarters, might a similar analysis be performed with mercury, which is found in greater concentrations among the seafood-consuming wealthy? How do the class connotations register here? Or do they?

Altogether, *Animacies* provides us with fresh, provocative insights into the queer possibilities of kinship and intimacies with some of the most overlooked forms of material existence. Readers will find much to admire in this book.

Cynthia Wu is an assistant professor of American studies in the Department of Transnational Studies at the University at Buffalo. She is the author of *Chang and Eng Reconnected: The Original Siamese Twins in American Culture* (2012).

Transgressive Truth Telling

LARA ROSSANA RODRIGUEZ

Testo Junkie: Sex, Drugs, and Biopolitics in the Pharmacopornographic Era
Beatriz Preciado
Translated by Bruce Benderson
New York: Feminist Press, 2013. 432 pp.

Within the field of trans- studies, a heterogeneous body of artists, activists, scholars, and pornographers have been coming together in order to address within their respective projects, performances, collaborations, and disciplines: what is the potential of the trans-body in the twenty-first century? Beatriz Preciado's *Testo Junkie*, translated from the French by Bruce Benderson, wrestles with this question, among others, in order to theorize the body in transition as it moves within and against a Western landscape corrupted by pharmacopower and pornpower. Preciado (who is fluent in Spanish, English, and French) delivers a theoretically cogent and compelling account of the "pharmacopornographic" regime as it functions under capitalist, colonizing practices; throughout hir analysis, the author maintains that these forms of control do not produce docile, self-surveilling subjects but instead seductively aid in their design. To use the words of contemporary artist Mike Mills, *the cops are inside us.* In the same spirit, the author of *Testo Junkie* claims, "In the pharmacopornographic age, biopower dwells at home, sleeps with us, inhabits within" (207). Throughout *Testo Junkie*, Preciado labors to describe with fascinating precision how we all, to our sexopolitical detriment, have consented to living in "hormonal straightjackets" (118). According to the author, committing to a lively mesh of biotechnophilic performative practices may be our best bet for refusing the prescriptive, prepackaged, hormonally regimented genders we have been sold.

As dystopic as things may seem, Preciado's rogue approach to hir topic allows hir to advance hir argument in terms no less sharp than they are original.

As a varied and increasingly techno-gendered public endeavors to negotiate the pharmacopornographic era, where "the body swallows power" in pill form, Preciado anticipates the molecular and political potential of the testo junkie as a noncompliant biosynthetic trafficker of gender (207). *Testo Junkie* investigates: to what ends can the trans-body inhabit and alter these super-endocrinologically managed times, and in addition, how might cisgendered subjects come to queer their own relationships to gender by choosing to undermine the prescriptive regimes that regulate the dispensation of hormones? Cis, it seems, was never so cis to begin with. Preciado's philosophical inquiry, equal parts seducer's diary, mourning diary, and cyborg manifesto is a formidable treatise on gender that, under the auspices of T, anticipates the potential of the new insurrectionary trans-feminist-punk politics to come.

One important aspect of Preciado's treatise is that the author never allows the body to lag behind as s/he endeavors to put to words the various haptic knowledges arriving to every organ, every orifice. Within *Testo Junkie*, the author often supplements a discussion of these knowledges with hand-drawn diagrams and winding word maps in order to provide some charismatic visuals for the intersecting and often contradictory knowledge flows as the author has perceived them; typically, these diagrams depict how various bodies of knowledge intersect and come to constitute some of the problematic logic and assumptions informing the relations between sex, power, pornography, and endocrino-politics. Ultimately, these conflicting knowledges and divergent styles of knowledge reporting collide to stunning effect.

For instance, in the text's introduction, Preciado asserts that the book is "a body-essay. Fiction, actually" (11). Well, which one is it, BP? But the genre ambiguity asserted by the author is a way of enacting and textually embodying the pleasures that accompany gender ambiguity: the refusal to capitulate or identify singularly once and for all informs the narrative and the performative swerves made possible by testosterone, taken by the author in the form of Testogel. These swerves propel the feminist philosopher to confront the difficult question, "What kind of feminist am I today: a feminist hooked on testosterone, or a transgender body hooked on feminism?" (22). As Preciado narrates hir 236-day T-trial, the author fluently integrates a historical account of the production of hormones with dizzying, testosterone-induced reflections and critiques of Judith Butler, Gilles Deleuze, and Michel Foucault in order to question the classics. The effect of such a method is a hybrid work in which ficto-criticism meets the philosopher in the bedroom as s/he immerses hirself in hir object of study, T, and its many intersecting and attendant histories.

In order to examine the biopolitical narratives that accompany the history of hormones, rather than assert T equals X (masculinity, machismo, maleness),

Preciado observes, "T is only a threshold, a molecular door, a becoming between multiplicities" (143). Beyond this threshold is the reader who receives the confessions of Preciado's self-intoxicated "I" submersed in the city, always lucid, always in transit. Such a narrator promiscuously transitions across genres in order to repair the damage done by moralizing pogroms, referred to as "somato-political fictions"—fictions that legislate the political limits of the body. Preciado's "body-essay," on the other hand, opposes the oppressive somato-political fictions by embracing a trans-cyberpunk style of reportage, one that imagines beyond the limits of a coherent, unified, and universal narrative "I" in order to claim: "I'm the residue of a biochemical process . . . I am T" (140). As a reader bears witness to Preciado's process, this poststructuralist narrative may read surprisingly for some like William Gibson's *Neuromancer* spliced with Samuel Delaney's *Times Square Red, Times Square Blue*. "Neither *testo-girl* nor *techno-boy*," one wonders if the testo junkie is beyond gender when s/he is transformed into "a port of insertion for $C_{19}H_{28}O_2$," (140). The body as "somatic filter" has never sounded so sexy nor spoken so eloquently (237). *Testo Junkie* makes a bold case for writing under the influence; such a practice involves the scholar's submitting to the rush of the high that comes with ingesting intellectually provocative content. In this case, testosterone is presented as one of the possible political fuels for an emerging techno-somatic transgressive politics.

Moreover, when the difficult challenge of recombining disparate discourses in desperate times presents itself, the testo junkie exhorts: "Blend" (133). Blend methods, blur genders, for "we must reclaim the right to participate in the *construction* of biopolitical fictions" (352). One might come to value in such radical acts the *transing* of scholarship, in which an author, rather than disclosing his or her identity or disciplinary home, moves within a work from one genre to another, from one language to another. As Susan Stryker, Paisley Currah, and Lisa Jean Moore have written in their introduction to the "Trans-" issue of *Women's Studies Quarterly*, transing "assembles gender into contingent structures of association with other attributes of bodily being" (2008: 13). In the transmission of knowledge, from one body to another, we need not restrict ourselves to one mode of truth seeking or telling. In order for new kinds of counterknowledges to proliferate, Preciado exhorts the theoretical urgency with which novel narrative strategies must continue to be deployed.

The author makes no secret of the fact that such strategies as are brought to bear in this project are largely indebted to and intertwined with hir friend Guillaume Dustan and hir lover Virginie Despentes, (referred to in the text as GD and VD, respectively). Both GD and VD (GD, deceased at the book's beginning, VD, disturbingly alive throughout) contribute to the urgency with which Preciado fucks, thinks, and writes. Conversely, if one were to reread VD's *King Kong*

Theory (2010: 17) where Despentes writes, "I wanted to live like a man, so I lived like a man," it would be equally apparent the intellectual impact Preciado had on Despentes. GD, however, remains a more elusive figure, perhaps especially so for the English reader, as most of his writing, with the exception of the controversial autobiographical work *in my room* (1996), has yet to be translated into English. Dustan died in 2005, and although the circumstances of his death remain unclear (was it an AIDS-related accidental overdose or a suicide?), the grief and rage that follows haunts Preciado's study. In a similar fashion, Hervé Guibert, author of *To the Friend Who Did Not Save My Life* (1990), also appears as one of the influential French writers whose premature AIDS-related death prompts Preciado to ask in the form of apostrophe, "Do I belong more to your world than I do to the world of the living? Isn't my politics yours; my house, my body, yours?" (Preciado 20). The author's perpetual acknowledgment that hir intellectual drives and impulses are foregrounded by a queer dead readership confronts the haunted and unacknowledged practice in our scholarship in which we endeavor to speak of the dead, but seldom do we allow ourselves in our scholarship to speak *to* the dead.

Mourning, however, as Douglas Crimp has suggested, may move a subject powerfully beyond melancholia to militant ends. As Preciado admits in the beginning of *Testo Junkie* to the ghost of GD, "I take [testosterone] to foil what society wanted to make of me . . . I do it to avenge your death"(16). To take testosterone as a gesture of mourning, refusal, and tribute may strike one as genuinely risky business. For example, before applying a 50mg swath of Testogel, Preciado is forewarned in the Testogel's package insert: "Attention: TESTOGEL should not be used by women" (58). Why not? The packaging prompts one to wonder if Testogel is in fact toxic or physically harmful and potentially life threatening when consumed by anyone who might identify as a woman. Although Testogel was originally designed as a low-tech treatment for men who suffer from "illnesses related to a deficiency of testosterone," a combination of skepticism, doubt, and frustration rouses Preciado's desire to know: for whom is it dangerous if women start stealing testosterone? (58). The gender outlaw, inevitably, goes forth and disrupts notions of bodily integrity and mores of social hygiene by layering on the gel; curiously, because testosterone is "one of the rare drugs that is spread by sweat, from skin to skin, body to body," the testo junkie, as a result of hir intoxication, becomes a high-risk harbor for future potential contaminations (65). Queer contact = contact high.

Preciado, however, is careful not to confuse hir desire for testosterone with that of hir trans friends'; s/he distinguishes these friends as "taking hormones as part of a protocol to change sex" while "others are fooling with it, self-medicating without trying to change their gender legally or going through any psychiatric follow-up. They don't identify with the term *gender dysphorics* and declare themselves 'gender pirates,' or 'gender hackers.' I belong to this latter group of testosterone users" (55). Preciado's decision to "self-medicate" is self-marginalizing as s/he groups hirself with "the others." Such a self-naming locates hir desires in a different discourse than that of hir trans friends and colleagues and aligns hir curiosity (and hir subsequent guilt) with that of the drug user; s/he writes: "When I decide to take my first dose of testosterone, I don't talk about it to anyone. As if it were a hard drug, I wait until I'm alone in my home to try it" (56). As Preciado has marked hir interests in and illegal acquisition of testosterone apart from those of hir trans friends rather than relying on a trans discourse in which to justify hir actions, Preciado narrates hir fears and anxieties using the discourse of the junkie. Given Avital Ronell's claim in her book *Crack Wars: Literature Addiction Mania* (2004: 63), "Drugs make us ask what it means to consume," Preciado, a philosopher of gender, wears the guise of the testo junkie in order to speak in new ways of the body as it consumes gender outside medically sanctioned protocols. Perhaps if we consider the user of gender as a junkie, we will no longer feel compelled to go along with the policing and pathologizing of gender as it does and does not belong to the State, to "feminism or to the lesbian community or to queer theory" (Preciado 397).

To speak of the junkie hooked on "political drugs," one begins to grasp some of the risks Preciado faces in hir project (396). The narrator's refusal to recognize hir experiment with T as simply a flirtation with trans politics marks hir within a trans discourse as a transgressive subject. As Foucault has observed in his "Preface to Transgression," transgression "affirms limited being—affirms the limitlessness" into which being leaps (1977: 35). Preciado's self-imposed alienation marks hir as an agent and an experiment more invested in the leap toward possible identifications (and disidentifications) than in theorizing a project whose aims prioritize assimilation and passing. Anticipating judgment and accusations of betrayal from hir own community, s/he admits, "I know they're going to judge me for having taken testosterone . . . because I took testosterone outside of a medical protocol . . . because I used testosterone like a hard drug . . . and gave bad press to testosterone at the very moment when the law is beginning to integrate transsexuals into society" (Preciado 56). However, Preciado also acknowledges that the decision (and privilege) to keep hir "legal identity as a woman and to take testosterone without subscribing to a sex change protocol" need not "enter into conflict with the position of all the transsexuals who've decided to sign a contract with the state" (61). In the eyes of the testo junkie, no matter what our relationship to liberationist goals of integration, "all of us are united by the same carbon chains, by the same invisible gel" (61). We are all uncanny harbingers of gender, and so to that effect, perhaps Preciado is proposing we add to our list of fundamental inalienable rights the right to enact, perform, and consume gender in the fashions and forms we desire without fear of reprisal.

Lara Rossana Rodriguez is a PhD candidate in English at the CUNY Graduate Center. She also performs and publishes often in racial drag under the name Lara Mimosa Montes.

References

Currah, Paisley, Lisa Jean Moore, and Susan Stryker. 2008. "Introduction: Trans-, Trans, or Transgender?" *WSQ: Women's Studies Quarterly* 36, no. 3–4: 11–22.

Despentes, Virginie. 2010. *King Kong Theory*. Translated by Stéphanie Benson. New York: Feminist Press.

Foucault, Michel. 1977. "A Preface to Transgression." In *Language, Counter-Memory, Practice: Selected Essays and Interviews*, ed. and trans. Donald F. Bouchard. Ithaca, NY: Cornell University Press.

Ronell, Avital. 2004. *Crack Wars: Literature Addiction Mania*. Urbana: University of Illinois Press.

Two-Spirit Literature

Decolonizing Race and Gender Binaries

T.J. TALLIE

Sovereign Erotics: A Collection of Two-Spirit Literature
Edited by Qwo-Li Driskill, Daniel Heath Justice, Deborah Miranda,
and Lisa Tatonetti
Tucson: University of Arizona Press, 2011. 248 pp.

Sovereign Erotics is a powerful and provocative collection of writing by two-spirit/ queer indigenous-identified authors that presents an embodied challenge on multiple fronts—an intellectual and literary call to challenge historical, colonial, and reified sexual and social formations. *Sovereign Erotics* traces its intellectual lineage from both *Living the Spirit: A Gay American Indian Anthology* (1988) and *This Bridge Called My Back: Writings by Radical Women of Color* (1981), among other collections. In so doing, the book offers a call born from multiple identifications and subject positions in order to provide a model of queer/two-spirit indigenous existence.

The collection's editors proclaim in the introduction that the book exists for "those who—like so many of us—had no role models, no one to tell us that we were valuable human beings just as we are" (1). To this end, the book utilizes the concept of "sovereign erotics," first articulated by Qwo-Li Driskill but used similarly by other authors, to privilege the productive and profoundly dynamic potential of erotic pleasure. When combined with the idea of indigenous interpretations of sovereignty, the erotic becomes a powerful and communal site of contestation, extending from individual pleasure to encompass collective histories, goals, and events. By reinscribing individual pleasure in the pursuit of larger political and historical aims, the use of such sovereign erotics confronts the hegemonic work of settler societies to regulate indigenous bodies and sexualities

TSQ: Transgender Studies Quarterly ★ Volume 1, Number 3 ★ August 2014
DOI 10.1215/23289252-2685705 © 2014 Duke University Press

as part of a colonial project. The sovereign erotics, then, are most clearly articulated in the collection's retelling of personal stories, which lay out the productive potential of daily, embodied acts of resistance and reorientation.

Despite its claim to offer a collection of two-spirit literature in its subtitle, *Sovereign Erotics* remains somewhat ambiguous on the actual deployment of the category within the larger book. Offering a deserved if somewhat predictable critique of academia's obsession with defining terms, *Sovereign Erotics* describes *two-spirit* as an umbrella term that denotes either historical indigenous constructions of gender that exist outside colonial normative binaries or contemporary indigenous people who reclaim/enact these roles within their local communities. The collection appears to privilege the use of the term *two-spirit* (even though not all of the contributors identity as such) as an indigenous-derived umbrella alternative to the Western-derived *queer*. The stories of the individuals within the collection are organized both in a shared nonheterosexual orientation but also through a pronounced ambivalence toward nonindigenous definitions of gender and, as a result, sexuality. By organizing under the intentionally vague label of two-spiritedness, the contributors remind readers not only that constructions of gender are flexible but that they are negotiated in relation to colonially imposed gender binaries that set themselves up as neutral and universal. A purposeful fluidity, then, lies at the heart of *Sovereign Erotics*' organization; as the editors explain, "what brings us together as movements and individuals, regardless of what our personal choices of identity labels may be, is a commitment to decolonial movements" (6).

Sovereign Erotics is organized into four general sections, each of which speaks to a different although interconnected aspect of two-spirit/queer indigenous life. The first section, "Dreams/Ancestors," is pointedly Janus-faced, evoking the historical roots of two-spirit identities and pasts while also privileging the generative potential of new ways of imagining existence. Rather than simply rely on the idea that two-spirit identities existed before European colonization and therefore are legitimate by means of a static and unchanging indigenous past, the pieces within "Dreams/Ancestors" gesture toward the past existence of what are now nonheteronormative formations but ground these historical traces firmly in present lived experiences. In this way, the doubly viewed perspectives within this first section foreground a precolonial history but underscore its relevance in a colonized present.

The first section contains a selection from Craig Womack's 2001 novel *Drowning in Fire*, whose protagonist, Josh Henneha, evokes the longing, alienation, and insecurity of a native teenager who falls far short of prescribed masculine roles while nursing a constant attraction to his older male friend. The piece touches on a variety of topics surrounding racial tensions within Oklahoma, from white schoolteachers to indigenous children with African ancestry, while anchoring the larger story to family mythologies shared by Josh's grandfather. The nonlinear chronologies and alienation speak to indigenous pasts and presents entangled in potentially aberrant sexualities. In "Santa Claus, Indiana," Michael Koby discusses interracial adoption in rural Indiana, interspersing family tragedies with monster films. In these ways, the first section offers both moments of historical grounding and contemporary instability in recording the multiple voices of the collection.

The second section, "Love/Medicine," offers the power of erotic potential to salve personal and historical wounds. Maurice Kenny's "My First Book" is both a poignant and a playful reorienting of tropes surrounding literacy and civilization. Kenny's first book in this instance was a paperback copy of *Tarzan: Man of the Apes*, itself a reminder of themes of white civilization and native savagery. Yet as Kenny notes, the book was important, for it contained his "first naked man," one important

> to my dreams
> then and now,
> dreams of all
> the naked men
> I've touched. (77)

Chip Livingston's "Ghost Dance" evokes both the pan-indigenous religious movement in the late nineteenth century and the contemporary loneliness of dancing in a club while remembering a deceased partner. Spectral images of past dances echo through the present-day club as Livingston's narrator recalls the steps of his former lover. By turning to the erotic as a form of healing, the authors reject historical Christian and colonial constructions of uncontrolled sexuality as damaging and destructive. In so doing, they subvert notions of respectability and civilization, privileging the idea of personal and sexual freedom in the face of historical and present pain.

The third section, "Long/Walks," delves into darker territory, discussing the loneliness, alienation, and historical violence enacted on two-spirited people who attempt to live honestly and openly in their many contexts. Qwo-Li Driskill's "(Auto)biography of Mad" depicts the shattering violence of the Carlton Indian Insane Asylum from the clinical detachment of a hypothetical book index. Containing listings for "Abuse, Physical," "Trauma, Sexual," and "Memory, Historical," Driskill's piece simultaneously depicts the past brutalities to indigenous peoples and their contemporary removal into neatly contained historical indexes. The Indians of Driskill's piece have become historical footnotes—but ones still made very present through their categories of suffering. In a similar vein, Luna Maia challenges questions of "genuine" Indian status in "authentically ethnic." Responding to claims that fry-bread isn't genuine since it was made from federal rations, Maia discusses historical means of survival practiced by indigenous peoples and loudly declares that daily choices made to live need not fit into preconceived notions of "AUTHENTICALLY ETHNIC TRADITION" (124). This section, perhaps more than the others, brings the *intersectional* nature of indigenous two-spirit/queer to the fore. By situating themselves within a matrix of historical and personal claims, the authors reject the idea that two-spiritedness is just a specific flavor of queerness or trans identity. Rather, the multiple pressures brought by colonialism, indigeneity, and gender/sexuality challenge the neat divisions implied by labels of native, queer, or trans.

The final section, "Wild/Flowers," celebrates thriving and vitality in spite of historical suppression and looks toward continued futures of survival and celebration. M. Carmen Lane's "Remember: She Bought Those Panties for You" focuses on a person who straddles the categories between "being a butch Black lesbian and a Two-Spirit Indian Man." After elaborating the contradictions and tribulations of such an existence, the narrator realizes that others are "jealous that you can walk between worlds and they cannot" (195). The final section of *Sovereign Erotics* ends with acknowledgments of both histories and contemporary realities, but it primarily focuses on the future of imaginative potential, of reclaiming spaces from colonization and religious judgment.

Sovereign Erotics demonstrates that the stakes are ultimately very high in negotiating indigenous two-spirit/queer identities. Indigenous studies–based approaches have placed the issues of land access and settler invasion at the forefront of colonial analysis. As a result, settler colonial histories become unmoored from claims of legitimacy through law or government action. Likewise, queer theory offers a means of understanding how lines of assumed order are skewed by ideas, actions, or formations. If settler colonialism itself is presented as a form of orientation, of making a recognizable and inhabitable home space for European arrivals on indigenous land, then native peoples and their continued resistance can serve to "queer" these attempted forms of order. Such an approach is essential to decolonizing the conditions of modern sexuality that underpin both heteronormative realities in settler societies like the United States *as well as* queer and trans challenges to those colonially created realities. In *Queer Indigenous Studies* (the companion piece to *Sovereign Erotics*), theorist Scott L. Morgensen offers a direct challenge to nonnative queer organizers, arguing that "Two-Spirit organizing does not reduce to the work of a sexual or racial minority, or any form of multicultural diversity, but asserts an Indigenous relationship to ongoing colonization that non-Natives must meet across a national difference" (Morgensen

2011: 144). This, then, is the most provocative and powerful achievement of *Sovereign Erotics*: the experiential demonstration of native nonheteronormative life in its messy multiplicities. These multiplicities, with their challenges to orthodox temporal, gendered, racial, or social formations, provide a profound opportunity of rupture and creation.

By "rupture," I mean that indigenous queer/two-spirit narratives can interrupt conceptions of queer progress by pointing to the fact that the material and discursive conditions for liberation are built upon ideas of indigenous removal and assimilation. In her path-breaking book *Transit of Empire*, Chickasaw scholar Jodi A. Byrd has taken aim at naturalized "American" histories that "continually foreground the arrival of Europeans as the defining event within settler societies, consistently place horizontal histories of oppressions into zero-sum struggles for hegemony, and distract from the complicities of colonialism and the possibilities for anticolonial action that emerge outside and beyond Manichean allegories that define oppression" (Byrd 2011: xxxiv). Queer studies—and more immediately, transgender studies—are not immune from these colonial complicities. As the many voices of *Sovereign Erotics* remind us, gender and sexuality are not neutrally extracted from the spatial and embodied histories of colonialism and occupation. Their very imbrication within these larger processes requires a disruptive challenge.

By "creation," I refer to the ludic and imaginative potential of indigenous two-spirit/queer stories within *Sovereign Erotics*. Such a playful engagement happens directly at the intersection of indigenous and queer theorizing. This "queering" of norms created in the collisions of colonial domination allows for a praxis of joy, mockery, and freedom. The stories of *Sovereign Erotics* foster a form of queerness perhaps most clearly articulated by the late José Esteban Muñoz as "the rejection of a here and now and an insistence on potentiality or concrete possibility for another world" (Muñoz 2011: 1). These moments of potential are clearest when writers like Lane underscore that they can "walk between worlds," not merely implying multiple identities but asserting that a different world, one outside the claims of the colonizer, is possible.

Sovereign Erotics is, by and large, an impressive and multifaceted achievement, presenting multiple voices of indigenous queer/two-spirit–identified people pushing the boundaries of sexuality and identity. By embracing the two-spirit label, *Sovereign Erotics* specifically refutes the easy universalism of Western-derived categories like queer, gay, or transgender. Instead, the contributors imagine a world centered on the powerful potential of erotic pleasure that destabilizes colonially derived conceptions of gender, propriety, and belonging. *Sovereign Erotics* offers a series of personal glimpses into a cacophonous world of resistance, struggle, survival, and joy, one that destabilizes by its stubborn insistence on continuing to defy colonial systems of order and control.

T.J. Tallie is a PhD candidate in the History Department at the University of Illinois at Urbana-Champaign. As a critical historian of the British Empire, he works specifically on the relationships between race, masculinity, indigeneity, and sovereignty in nineteenth-century colonial South Africa. He is completing his dissertation, "Limits of Settlement: Racialized Masculinity, Sovereignty, and the Imperial Project in Colonial Natal, 1850–1897."

References

Byrd, Jodi A. 2011. *The Transit of Empire: Indigenous Critiques of Colonialism*. Minneapolis: University of Minnesota Press.

Morgensen, Scott L. 2011. "Unsettling Queer Politics: What Can Non-Natives Learn from Two-Spirit Organizing?" In *Queer Indigenous Studies: Critical Interventions in Theory, Politics, and Literature*, ed. Qwo-Li Driskill, Chris Finley, Brian Joseph Gilley, and Scott L. Morgensen, 132–52. Tucson: University of Arizona Press.

Muñoz, José Esteban. 2009. *Cruising Utopia: The Then and There of Queer Futurity*. New York: NYU Press.

Wu Tsang's *Wildness* and the Quest for Queer Utopia

FINN JACKSON BALLARD

Wildness
Directed by Wu Tsang
Documentary, 74 min., United States, 2012

Wildness (2012), the first feature film by transgender artist Wu Tsang, follows a group of queer young artists who establish a weekly party and performance event at the Silver Platter, a historic bar in downtown Los Angeles frequented mostly by Latino transwomen and their friends and admirers. After some initial friction, the two groups begin to tessellate well together, but the popularity of the party leads to some negative attention from the press—and also from immigration services—which has devastating consequences for some of the bar regulars and leads the splintered community to question and renegotiate its shared identity. The film is stylistically experimental, blending documentary with magical-realist techniques to create a dreamlike meditation on a small moment in queer history, the ramifications of which tell an important tale about safe space and solidarity.

Wu Tsang describes the making of *Wildness* as a considerable learning process during which he taught himself to write, direct, and edit, and he also appears in the film as a central character, stepping back and forth behind the camera as the documentary progresses. He shares the narration with the bar itself, which, with a magical touch, becomes a protagonist of the film, describing its last half-century of existence during which it has been looked after by generations of the Ramirez family and has shifted from a "normal" gay bar into a particular haven for transwomen. The Silver Platter speaks in a female (perhaps a trans-female) voice suffused with experience, wisdom, and melancholy. She is maternal, "a beacon, guiding [her] young out of the darkness," and within the walls of her womb, thousands of curious gay men, transvestites, and transsexual women have been reborn. Her motherliness is not always benevolent; she is variously excited, apprehensive, weary, and unforgiving. She is the collective Spanish voice of her attendees, and like them she balances a love of community hedonism with an underlying precarious anxiety about the future. "There are not many like me left," she says, "and I wonder, what will become of me?"

The Silver Platter is frequented by younger and older generations of transwomen from Mexico, El Salvador, and Cuba who exude tenacity, pride, and joie de vivre, many of whom have been living for years in the MacArthur Park area, a part of Los Angeles that has gone from initial glamour to deprivation to a recent injection of gentrification, "a layer of new wealth trying to cover up the poverty, violence and failure." In this transitional phase from deprivation to "revitalization," the area remains cheap and an ideal haven for young queer artists such as Tsang and his friends. Tsang finds a "sisterhood" within the bar, enthralled by the glamorous festivity and performances of its patrons, and a mutual attraction begins: the Silver Platter wins them over, she proudly says, and she herself cannot resist the youthful energy of Tsang's group. The new party, "Wildness," begins and quickly attracts huge crowds, but it displaces some of the original patrons of the Silver Platter who are unused to sharing the spotlight. In time, the party becomes a remarkable success, the regulars are reconciled to it, and the two groups inspire each other and become ever more cohesive.

Although the bar tries to remain a safe space, tension outside the Silver Platter grows; an extensive hunt for and deportation of undocumented immigrants causes protests and riots. The gap begins to widen between the ambitions of the Wildness attendees—"university students, American, white . . . a different class of person," as one Silver Platter regular, Betty, describes them—and those of the Latino transwomen, concerned with keeping their homes and with surviving, aware that they have no recourse to assistance from any greater authority than their own community. As Wildness gets wilder, tension grows within the walls of the Silver Platter too; Tsang's fear—that the "wrong people" would start attending the party and displacing the former attendees even more—starts to manifest itself. The success of the party throws a new limelight on the bar, which becomes a target for graffiti and hate mail. The presenter of the "Daily Freak Show" arrives looking for "trannies and tranny fuckers"—exactly the kind of lascivious fetishization from which, says one of the Silver Platter regulars, Morales, the bar operates as a haven. The *LA Weekly*, despite Tsang's demand to the contrary, features Silver Platter as "L.A.'s Best Tranny Bar . . . a crossroads convergence of self-involved, art-damaged twenty-something kids and Third World gender illusionists" staffed by "he-shes" and attended by "she-male" prostitutes, where "tits and dick are always on the menu." The party continues and attempts to synthesize its communities, dramatizing the stories of the Latino transwomen through performance, and the attendees set up a free legal clinic to assist the Los Angeles transgender community. Soon, however, things begin to fall apart; Wildness eventually closes down, and the bar returns to its original equilibrium.

Watching this film in Berlin in 2013, the Wildness experiment seems particularly pertinent. This city is experiencing a process of "revitalization" remarkably similar to that of Los Angeles, in which the Kreuzberg and Neukölln neighborhoods of West Berlin, formerly neglected because of their proximity to the Berlin Wall and with a prevalent population of lower-income Turkish immigrants, are becoming very popular among young queers looking for places of cheap residence and artistic experimentation. However, much tension is caused by suspicion of the ramifications of gentrification supposedly inextricably tied with immigration from other parts of mainland Europe as well as the United Kingdom, the United States, and Australia, much of which is also caused by conflicting ideas about gender and sexuality. The city and the country as a whole continue to struggle with the strains between German, Turkish, and other immigrant identities so severely that Chancellor Angela Merkel maintains that multiculturalism in Germany has "utterly failed." And while Berlin, under gay mayor Klaus Wowereit, rightfully capitalizes on its status as the European queer capital, its rainbow does remain somewhat conspicuously Caucasian. Comparing the Silver Platter to the Silverfuture queer bar in Berlin, for instance, an even rougher aggregation of differing ideologies is apparent than with the establishment of the Wildness party in a Latino bar; Silverfuture opened on a street lined with predominantly Turkish residences and coffee-houses, struggled for a time as the only queer bar in the neighborhood, and eventually became a focal point of a gentrifying community that has seen the gradual retreat of "Little Istanbul" and, unfortunately, little integration of the two together. If anything, in recent months, Silverfuture has come to attract an increasingly affluent, touristic, and voyeuristic crowd. As pub crawls promise the chance to "flirt with transvestites in dive bars" the queer locals keep moving on. (Alternative Berlin Tours 2014). In other parts of town, however, the arrival of a queer population in an old Turkish neighborhood has met with greater success; around the area of Kottbusser Tor, a number of queer meeting spots such as Südblock, Café Anal, Roses, Möbel Olfe, and SO36 (which regularly hosts the Turkish queer party Gayhane) sit fairly comfortably within their surroundings—one of these bars is in fact located within the Kreuzberg Zentrum housing project, and Turkish families sit alongside queer kids at Südblock, at least during the day. A little further west in the city are the headquarters of GLADT, an organization of Turkish and Turkish-German queers and allies. While we aspire that one day our entire cities, not just our bars, will be safe spaces, for the moment these community focal points remain extremely important, for we do remain vulnerable outside them. There is yet another element of friction between the the Kreuzberg and Neukölln areas and the historical gay and rather more racially homogenous neighborhood of Schöneberg, the bars and patrons of which are not always so welcoming to openly transgender people unless they are performing. In the middle of the old gay district sits the headquarters of the organization Maneo, which works to combat homophobia and hate crimes but which has unfortunately tended to lay the blame for these upon "youths of migrational backgrounds," adding an extra layer of racial tension to this already complex situation. As in the case of Wildness, sometimes the attempt to create safe space has the negative consequence of compromising exactly that haven for others. But also as in the case of Wildness, we continue to strive to produce this utopian ideal and we continue to learn from each other along the way.

Perhaps one of the most intriguing and courageous elements of this film is that Tsang, having stepped into the spotlight as central protagonist, also illuminates his own shortcomings and is not shy about self-criticism. As the film progresses, he moves from naïveté to a greater comprehension of a community that is both enriched and endangered by the arrival of Tsang's group on its scene. Tsang makes a valiant effort at uniting two communities; even if their party dissipates, the film's final shots of Tsang and their new "sisterhood" seem to suggest that Wildness will be outlasted by the solidarity it inspired. The film highlights a topic more pertinent for young queer artists than ever: our quest for empowerment, often motivated by feelings of disenfranchisement, must be balanced by a recognition of the tensions already inherent within the space we make our own. And our efforts not to disenfranchise others at the same time must be doubled when we come to occupy a space inhabited by people who have already experienced disenfranchisement. This involves shaking ourselves from complacency and contending with the unwelcome realization that we must examine our own part in the ongoing process of queer gentrification. Ashland, one of the Wildness organizers, insists that he does not represent "money and power . . . that is going to come and clean up everything . . . knock everyone out of the way"; but this is indeed the threat that his party brings to the Silver Platter, unpleasant as it is to acknowledge. As Tsang's group arrives in Los Angeles, he ambiguously acknowledges that their previous efforts to set up queer space in Chicago "got messy and fell apart"; we may well ask: are we destined to repeat this pattern of struggle—failure—resignation—relocation ad infinitum? Maybe, *Wildness* suggests; but we can learn and leave a positive legacy in doing so. Parties, even those generating artistic experimentation, political discourse, and reflections on the destiny of our communities, will not solve all of our problems; they will not eliminate friction, they will not be without failure, and they will not create a queer utopia overnight. But perhaps this very failure produces the opportunity for regeneration and for the continual negotiation of collective identity necessitated by queer community.

Finn Jackson Ballard is currently researching queer history in Berlin. He recently obtained his PhD in film and television studies from the University of Warwick. Publications include "Transmasculinities" (*Nyx*, June 2013) and "Dismantling the Phallocentric Gaze? Pornographic Representations of Transmasculinity" in *Sensational Pleasures in Cinema, Literature, and Visual Culture: The Phallic Eye*, edited by Gilad Padva and Nurit Buchweitz (2014).

Reference

Alternative Berlin Tours. 2014. "Berlin's Alternative Pubcrawl." alternativeberlin.com/berlin
-alternative-pubcrawl (accessed April 18, 2014).

JOURNAL OF THE HISTORY OF SEXUALITY

VOLUME 23 NUMBER 2 MAY 2014

UNIVERSITY OF TEXAS PRESS

Post Office Box 7819, Austin, Texas 78713-7819
P: 512.471.7233 | F: 512.232.7178 | journals@utpress.utexas.edu
UTPRESS.UTEXAS.EDU